HUMOR *in* ADVERTISING

HUMOR *in* ADVERTISING

A COMPREHENSIVE ANALYSIS

CHARLES S. GULAS AND MARC G. WEINBERGER

M.E.Sharpe
Armonk, New York
London, England

Library of Congress Cataloging-in-Publication Data

Gulas, Charles S., 1962–
    Humor in advertising : a comprehensive analysis / by Charles S. Gulas and Marc G. Weinberger.
        p. cm.
Includes bibliographical references and index.
ISBN 0-7656-1613-0 (cloth : alk. paper)
    1. Humor in advertising. I. Weinberger, Marc G. II. Title.

HF5821.G87 2006
659.1'02'07—dc22

2005017678

Printed in the United States of America

The paper used in this publication meets the minimum requirements of
American National Standard for Information Sciences
Permanence of Paper for Printed Library Materials,
ANSI Z 39.48-1984.

BM (c)   10   9   8   7   6   5   4   3   2

We dedicate this book to our wives, Diane Gulas and Sharon Weinberger, who have always provided the love, support, and understanding needed to sustain our writing, and to our loving children, Christine and Joseph Gulas and Michelle and Dan Weinberger, who have provided us with great joy and satisfaction. We also dedicate this book to our mothers, Betty Gulas and Minnette Lewis, and in memory of our fathers, Joseph Gulas and Larry Weinberger. Our parents always encouraged us to study, to learn, and to strive to do our best.

Contents

Tables, Figures, and Exhibits

Tables

Preface and Acknowledgments

This book synthesizes what has been learned about the application of humor in advertising and helps provide a roadmap for future research by way of methodology and topics that need attention. Those seeking a book that is itself humorous will find this one lacking. There is little if any actual humor in any of the studies or theories we discuss. We hope that a serious book about humor is not an oxymoron, but rather a necessity for achieving our goal.

Our collaboration on this book is the result of work that began in 1990 at the University of Massachusetts Amherst. Charles Gulas arrived as a doctoral student with a prior career as a stand-up comedian and owner of a comedy club. Marc Weinberger has had the good fortune of friends and former students working on humor dating back to the mid-1970s. In 1974, while at Arizona State University, he among others was commandeered by fellow doctoral student Paul Solomon to code humorous TV ads for what later became the much cited Kelly and Solomon (1975) study. In the late 1970s a new doctoral student, Tom Madden, arrived at Massachusetts with an interest in humor. Coauthoring two humor projects and serving on Tom's dissertation committee served as a springboard for future studies. Interest in the topic continued with generations of doctoral students over a twenty-year period. This book owes much to this coauthored work with Tom Madden, Harlan Spotts, Lee Campbell, Amy Parsons, and Karen Flaherty. In 1992 we published the widely quoted Weinberger and Gulas review of humor in advertising and now, more than a decade later, we develop here a major update to that work unfettered by the space restrictions of a journal article. We thank all our professional predecessors for the work that we attempt to document in this book. We would also like to thank Jacqueline

Reid, interim director of the John W. Hartman Center for Sales, Advertising, and Marketing History at Duke University for assistance in acquiring some of the examples for the book. Finally, we would like to thank our colleagues at the Raj Soin College of Business at Wright State University and the Isenberg School of Management at the University of Massachusetts Amherst for providing supportive environments for our research.

HUMOR *in* ADVERTISING

─── 1 ───

History of Humor
in Advertising

We find advertisements engraved on walls and tombs, written on parchment and papyrus, and printed by the first printing presses. The eruption of Vesuvius preserved Pompeian advertising. Babylonian barkers shouted the availability of wares, and, as a precursor to the media explosion that was to come, in France twelve town criers organized a company in 1141 (Presbrey 1929). Advertising extends back to the very beginnings of formalized trade.

Although advertising is an ancient form of communications, early ads tended to be very rudimentary. Most innovations in advertising are relatively recent. Posters, painted signs, transit placards, booklets, calendars, almanacs, handbills, and magazine and newspaper advertising have now become so well established that we look upon them as a part of the landscape. Or perhaps they are so common that we fail to notice them at all. Advertising has become so omnipresent that it is surprising to learn that most forms of advertising are relatively modern innovations.

It has been reported that the first ad in English was a printed notice tacked to church doors in 1477 announcing prayer books for sale (Goodrum and Dalrymple 1990). Although qualifying as an ad, this simple posted bulletin was hardly mass communication. The first evidence of advertising in a mass communication, albeit with very limited circulation, has been attributed to a German news pamphlet of 1525 (Presbrey 1929). This "ad" exhorted the reader to purchase a book written by a Dr. Laster. However, it is not known whether this promotion was a paid endorsement. Thus it cannot, with certainty, be determined whether this was an advertisement or an early example of publicity.

The importance of advertising is evidenced by the fact that the first regularly published periodical was an advertising vehicle. This was a regularly published list of want ads first produced in Paris in 1612 (Presbrey 1929). The first definitive instance of mass media advertising in English was an ad printed in the *Weekly Newes* on February 1, 1625 (Presbrey 1929). Advertising caught on quickly in England, so much so that by 1652 readers were complaining about the quantity and character of advertising in "newsbooks" (Presbrey 1929). It was in the mid- to late 1600s that advertising as a distinct phenomenon began to emerge. Although the word "advertisement," meaning a warning or a notice, was in common use by the time of Shakespeare, it was in 1655 that the term gained its modern meaning and replaced "advices" (Presbrey 1929). Although the term had gained its modern meaning, advertising did not yet resemble modern advertising.

As indicated in the following examples from 1692, early print ads were typically blind, with the publisher serving as a broker.

> I have met with a curious gardener that will furnish anybody that sends to me for fruit trees, and floreal shrubs, and garden seeds. I have made him promise with all selemnity that whatever he sends shall be purely good, and I verily believe he may be depended on.
>
> If anyone wants a wet nurse, I can help them, as I am informed, to a very good one.
>
> I know a peruke [wig] maker that pretends to make perukes extraordinary fashionable and will sell good pennyworths; I can direct to him.
>
> (Presbrey 1929, 58)

Blind advertising began to fade away as it became clear that direct advertising was more effective. Correspondingly, advertisers began to take a greater role in the creation of print advertising. By the late 1700s some print advertisers in England had begun to inject creativity into the medium. One of the pioneers of this effort was George Packwood. Packwood sold razor strops, and, more profitably, a paste to be used to condition the strop. He advertised heavily, and while most of his contemporaries were using simple announcements or making exaggerated claims, Packwood was entertaining his audience. Packwood's ads were characterized by the use of "riddles, proverbs, fables, slogans, jokes, jingles, anecdotes, facts, aphorisms, puns, poems, songs, nursery rhymes, parodies, pastiches, stories, dialogs, definitions, conundrums, letters and metaphors" (McKendrick, Brewer, and Plumb 1982, 153). A Packwood ad from 1796 reads:

Why is a dull razor like a famished man?

Because he wants whet.

Why is Packwood's Paste unlike the stocks?

Because it never falls, but always rises in the public opinion.

Why is Packwood's Strop unlike the present lottery?

Because every purchaser draws a prize.

Why is a person that has been shaved with a blunt-edged razor like another on the brink of marriage?

Because each wishes the business over.

And why is the inventor himself like a clergyman?

Because he is never out of orders.

(McKendrick, Brewer, and Plumb 1982, 171)

Packwood's print campaign lasted less than two years, from October 1794 until July 1796. However, in 1800 he published a book, available for one shilling, that contained reproductions of his ads, and, remarkably, stories of adventure featuring the razor strop (McKendrick, Brewer, and Plumb 1982; Presbrey 1929).

Although Packwood was a pioneer in the use of humor in print, his ads employed the all-text format of the era. The first periodical ad featuring a humorous illustration is attributed to Warren's Shoe Blacking in 1820 (Presbrey 1929). Indeed, this ad was not only pioneering in the use of humor, it is considered a milestone of print advertising since it contained the first "idea" illustration, as contrasted with a simple product illustration, to appear in periodical advertising (Presbrey 1929). The ad featured a cartoon of a cat hissing at its reflection on a shiny boot. Humorous verses appeared below the illustration. The ad proved quite successful. As Presbrey (1929) states, "this advertising, because it was a novelty, made Warren's Shoe Blacking known throughout the Kingdom and produced a heavy sale of it" (85).

Early British advertising was a precursor to early American advertising. The colonists brought British notions of advertising with them to the New World, and they brought humor with them as well. Although colonists are often thought of as dour and humorless, evidence of humor is found in some of the earliest English publications in the colonies (Kenney 1976).

Magazines and newspapers appeared in the colonies prior to the founding of the United States. Although the earliest history of print advertising is unclear, it has been reported that the first newspaper advertisements in the United States appeared in May of 1704 in the *Boston News Letter* (Presbrey 1929). These first three ads were very basic, cumulatively occupying four inches of one column. One ad was the offer of a reward for the capture of a thief, one was the offer of a reward for the return of two stolen anvils, and the third offered a piece of property for sale or rent (Presbrey 1929).

Smith (2003) reports that the origin of magazine advertising in the New World has been alternatively traced to either 1719 or 1741. In the earlier case, the first ad was purported to have appeared in a Philadelphia magazine, the *Weekly Mercury,* in 1719 (Smith 2003). Others trace the roots of magazines in America to Ben Franklin and Andrew Bradford, each of whom launched magazines in 1741 (Smith 2003). The confusion stems from incomplete records from this early period, in part due to the short life span of many early publications. Most early magazines, including Franklin's, lasted less than six months (Russell and Lane 1996). Some confusion about this early period may also be due to differing definitions of advertising. Some scholars consider only paid advertising, while others have a broader interpretation of the term and include self-promotion by the publisher as advertising.

The real growth in magazine publishing, and correspondingly magazine advertising, in the United States, did not occur until more than a century later when increasing literacy rates, improved printing technology, and railway mail delivery—with second class postage rates for magazines—gave birth to several magazines that still survive today. By the late 1800s *Town & Country, Cosmopolitan, National Geographic, Atlantic Monthly, Harper's* and other "modern" magazines had been founded. Yet the nature and volume of advertising in these early magazines were very different from magazine advertising today.

> The first advertisement appeared in *Harper's Magazine* in 1864. In this magazine more space has been devoted to advertising during the past year than the sum total of space for the twenty-four years from 1864 to 1887, inclusive. Indeed, advertising may be said to have been in its swaddling clothes until about the year 1887. The most rapid development has taken place during the last fifteen years. The change has been so great that the leading advertisers say that in comparison with today there was in existence fifteen years ago no advertising worthy of the name. (Scott 1904, 29)

Although we can trace the roots of early advertising with some degree of certainty, the origin of humor in advertising is less clear. Packwood's use of humor in the 1790s has been noted. However, humor in advertising certainly predates Packwood and may extend back to the very beginnings of advertising, broadly defined. Indeed, humorous advertising may predate widespread literacy.

When literacy was confined to a narrow sliver of society, it was common for shops and tradesmen to advertise their businesses graphically. Although many modern scholars may not consider simple signage a form of advertising, such signage was a dominant form of commercial communication throughout much of human history. Therefore it seems appropriate to include signage in a discussion of advertising, or more accurately marketing communication. Early versions of this form of communication were very rudimentary. The ironmonger might simply hang a pan outside of his shop while a cobbler might hang a last or clog outside of his (Larwood and Hotten 1866: 1951). Other shops might hang a signboard featuring a painting or a relief showing the nature of the good provided, such as a loaf of bread or a hat. As the medium became more sophisticated, symbolic images were also employed. A painting of scissors might be used to represent a tailor (Larwood and Hotten 1866: 1951). The use of pictorial images to facilitate trade began in ancient times and continues to some extent today in the form of logos. But as literacy spread so did other forms of advertising.

The Romans brought their tradition of tradesmen's pictorial signs to the British Isles along with the concept of the public house. Most ancient people lived their entire lives confined to a relatively small geographic area. However, the widespread nature of the Roman Empire required oversight, and thus travel, by Roman officials. The need to provide lodging for these travelers gave rise to the concept of the public house in Britain. Public houses have continued to exist ever since and have become an important part of British culture. By the Middle Ages the public house was a well-established part of the commercial landscape. Records indicate that by 1393 the law in England required inns to post signs, and by 1419 laws had been passed to regulate the size and placement of these signs.[1]

Initially, in the manner of other trades, these public houses used pictorial signs that were representative. Typically, taverns were indicated by a bunch of grapes or a bush (Larwood and Hotten 1866: 1951). The use of the bush as a symbol of the tavern gave rise to the proverb "good wine needs no bush," in other words, good wine needs no label (Presbrey 1929). However, by the early thirteenth century, pubs had begun to adopt names, and corresponding pictorial signs, that had no literal connection to the goods and services provided. For example, *Ye Olde Trip to Jerusalem* dates back to

1189 and *Ye Olde Man & Scythe* and the *Duke of Wellington* can both trace their roots to the 1200s. By the 1600s an inventory of pubs' names in London reveals all manner of creative names including 20 *Kings Heads*, 4 *Pope's Heads*, 13 *Halfmoons*, and a wide range of animals, both real and mythical (Larwood and Hotten 1866: 1951). Over the years, the names of these pubs and the signs that accompanied them became more cryptic and incongruous. In 1708 a visitor wrote:

> The first amusements we encountered were the variety and contradictory language of the signs, enough to persuade a man there were no rules of concord among the citizens. Here we saw *Joseph's Dream*, the *Bull & Mouth*, the *Whale and Crow*, the *Shovel & Boot*, the *Leg & Star*, the *Bible & Swan*, the *Frying Pan & Drum*, the *Lute & Tun*, the *Hog in Armour*, and a thousand others that the wise men that put them there can give no reason for. (Larwood and Hotten 1866: 1951, 11)

Although many of these names, and others like them, are incongruous, they were not necessarily intended to be humorous.[2] Some incongruous names are likely to have emerged as the result of corruptions. For example, it has been reported that the *Bull & Mouth* may be a corruption of the Boulogne Mouth—the mouth of the Boulogne harbor (Larwood and Hotten 1866: 1951). Absurd combinations also resulted from the lack of street numbering. Without street numbers, people navigated by landmarks. Thus a bun maker occupying a former blacksmith shop might be found at the sign of the anvil, or a bun could be added to the sign thus becoming the "Bun and Anvil" (Presbrey 1929). Other incongruous names are the result of "quartering." Quartering was the practice of merging names together as a form of respect. Thus a young tradesman might add to his own sign that of the master under whom he learned the trade. This is believed to be the origin of the *Three Nuns & Hare* (Larwood and Hotten 1866: 1951). The quartering process might also take place after a merger or similar action. Thus the oddly named *The Fortune of War and Naked Boy* was created when the owner of the *Fortune of War*, a naval veteran who had lost both legs and an arm in sea battle, purchased *The Naked Boy* (Stanley 1957).

However, intended humor does play a role in early pub names. In fact, the original sign on *The Naked Boy* was inscribed with the following: "So fickle is our English nation, I would be clothed if I knew the fashion" (Stanley 1957, 26). Many signs featured humorous illustrations. Often these were anthropomorphic representations of animals, such as the *Goat in Boots* and the *Dog in Doublet*. The *Cat & Fiddle,* which can be traced back to 1589 or earlier, and *The Hog in Armour* are often-cited examples of this form of humor (Larwood and Hotten 1866: 1951). Humor in the *Cat & Fiddle* stems from the incongruity of the anthropomorphic image plus the fact that the cat chooses to demonstrate his musical ability on an instrument that uses strings made of catgut. The *Jackanapes* (i.e., monkey) *on Horseback* is not an anthropomorphic reference as one might suppose, but rather a literal reference to a very disturbing practice that was considered humorous in the 1500s in which apes and monkeys were saddled to horses. Dogs were often let into the ring to frighten the horse and the primate rider, which added to the "entertainment" (Larwood and Hotten 1866: 1951). Some signs were particularly recognized for their comic nature. A famous comic sign featuring a man carrying a drunken woman, an ape, and a bird, was painted in the 1800s by Hogarth for the *Load of Mischief.*

Visual puns were also a common source of pub names. For example, an arrow (a bolt) sticking in a wine vessel (a tun) marked the *Bolt in Tun* pub. This was a visual pun referring to Prior Bolton, head of the Priory of St. Bartholomew, a well-known brewer (Stanley 1957). A similar visual pun was used on the *Hat and Tun,* the inn of Sir Christopher Hatton (Stanley 1957). Less subtle examples also abound. For example, a sign showing a decapitated woman has been used as a representation of the *Good Woman,* the *Quiet Woman,* and the *Silent Woman.* Similarly, the pub *Ass in a Bandbox,* circa 1712, was a "refined" version of *My Arse in a Bandbox,* named as "a satirical reference to Napoleon's proposed invasion of England" (Larwood and Hotten 1866: 1951, 29). The *Dog's Head in the Pot* probably originated as a "mocking sign to indicate a dirty, sluttish, housewife" (Larwood and Hotten 1866: 1951, 259). Humor was used widely in early pub signs. Indeed, some scholars have classified pub signs into four categories; pagan and priestly, historical and commemorative, heraldic and sporting, and punning and miscellaneous (Larwood and Hotten 1866: 1951).

Although the roots of humor in advertising extend back to pub signs in the 1500s, in the main, early advertising took the form of basic announcements. With all manner of goods in relatively scarce supply, a simple statement of availability would generally suffice as advertising copy.

In the United States it was not until the beginning of the twentieth century that mainstream advertising evolved beyond simple declarative statements (McDonough 2003a). This evolution occurred through the efforts of three people at the Lord & Thomas agency (predecessor to Foote, Cone, & Belding). In 1897 Charles Austin Bates coined the term "salesmanship in print" to

9

describe advertising (Spotts 2003). However, the concept did not take hold until John E. Kennedy used this idea to get a copywriting job at Lord & Thomas (Reeves 1961: 1977). This persuasive philosophy of advertising was embraced by Albert Lasker, Kennedy's employer. In 1907, Lasker hired Claude Hopkins to work at Lord & Thomas for a salary of $185,000 per year when such salaries were beyond the comprehension of most workers (*Advertising Age* 2003). Hopkins had been working on a similar persuasive theory of advertising (Applegate and McDonough 2003). Hopkins (1866–1932) went on to become the most influential copywriter of his era. He made extensive use of testing and through his investigations he learned that subtle changes in the message could have dramatic effects on the results. The title of his book, *Scientific Advertising,* suggests the nature of his creative philosophy. Hopkins was a strong advocate of "reason why" copy and his success drew many followers.

Hopkins took a dim view of humor in advertising, stating in 1923, "People do not buy from clowns." Humor had no place at Lord & Thomas. To again quote Hopkins, "Ads are not written to interest, please or amuse the hoi polloi." Yet the fact that Hopkins found it necessary to condemn humor is evidence of its use in that comparatively early period in the development of the U.S. advertising industry. Indeed there is evidence of humorous print advertising in the United States dating back to the 1880s or earlier (Herold 1963). Even the venerable Ivory Soap, manufactured by historically conservative Procter & Gamble, shows evidence of the early use of humor in advertising. In an 1885 cartoon human-like animals in an auditorium watch attentively as another animal in a tuxedo lectures about Ivory Soap 99 44/100 Pure (Jones 1959) (see Exhibit 1.1).

As advertising developed and expanded, the importance of creativity came to be recognized, and in the 1800s advertising, in the modern sense, emerged in the United States. By the late 1800s several national magazines had circulations in the hundreds of thousands, ad agencies had been formed, and the era of great copywriters had begun. By the 1890s Quaker Oats, Prudential Insurance, Kodak, Ivory Soap, Lipton's Teas, American Express Traveler's Cheques, and other brands had emerged as leading national advertisers (Russell and Lane 1996). As the twentieth century began there were already established a National Association of Advertising Teachers and psychological labs at universities such as Northwestern studying the psychology of advertising. A pioneer of this era was Walter Dill Scott, who in 1908 published one of his many books dealing with psychology applied to advertising and salesmanship (Scott 1908). In 1916, Scott called for research to answer among

Exhibit 1.1   Ivory Soap Ad

Procter and Gamble, 1885.

11

other questions, "What is the relative attention value of representations of the pathetic, humorous, pleasing and displeasing?" (33). Hopkins, who believed he knew the answer to this question, published his book, *Scientific Advertising,* in 1923.

In 1938 Burtt noted that advertisers had been somewhat loath to make widespread use of the comic as an attention-getting device. He made special note that one large advertising agency was so adamant about the uncertainty of using the comic that it had a standing rule to the effect that humor would not be employed in copy for its clients unless approved by the president of the agency. Burtt (1938) was likely referring to Lord & Thomas. With a contrary note, Burtt (1938) remarked that at another agency there was not an account for which the comic had not been considered at some time. In fact, by the 1930s humor had literally become a part of the advertising landscape. Following to some extent in Packwood's footsteps, on roadsides across America Burma Shave signs entertained motorists. These signs doled out ad copy one line at a time, often with humorous intent, such as:

> YOU KNOW
> YOUR ONIONS
> LETTUCE SUPPOSE
> THIS BEETS 'EM ALL
> DON'T TURNIP YOUR NOSE
> BURMA-SHAVE
>   (1935)

It has been reported that at one time over 7,000 sets of Burma Shave signs dotted the U.S. landscape and poets from all over the country submitted jingles for consideration.

Examples of successful and unsuccessful use of humor for breakfast cereal, cigars, brass pipes, and candy bars are testament to the varied use of humor. Yet, despite common usage, there was strong conventional wisdom by many in advertising that good copywriters should resist the temptation to entertain. Indeed, the perspective described by Hopkins in 1923 was echoed by influential ad executive David Ogilvy forty years later (Ogilvy 1963).

Humor Pioneers

Although humor has long played a role in advertising, it was with the advent of broadcasting that humor became a major executional tactic. With the emergence of radio, a new creative channel was opened to advertisers. Ironically,

12

the agency best known to have a stated opposition to humor, Lord & Thomas, was instrumental in ushering in the era of humorous radio advertising. This was not an easy time to advocate using humor. The late 1920s and most of the 1930s was a time of economic depression and a period that saw advertising spending drop from $3.4 billion in 1929 to $1.3 billion by 1934. During this same period unemployment tripled to 12 million. A motto at many agencies was "hard sell for hard times."

Radio advertising began in 1922, but it was not until the late 1920s and early 1930s that radio hit its stride. In its earliest form, radio advertising comprised formal sponsorships—for example, the *Maxwell House Showboat*—rather than actual sales messages. Lord & Thomas was a pioneering agency in radio, with its client American Tobacco sponsoring *Lucky Strike Dance Orchestra* and Bing Crosby as the "Creamo Singer" for Creamo cigars. Between 1927 and 1931 the agency is reported to have controlled 30 percent of all radio ad dollars (McDonough 2003a). A substantial portion of those dollars went to support humor. Humor was a central component of early radio and in 1928 Lord & Thomas and their client Pepsodent created the first radio comedy hit, *Amos 'n' Andy.*

The success of *Amos 'n' Andy* spawned other comedy programs. The first program to integrate a humorous commercial into the fabric of the show was the *Fibber McGee and Molly Show,* produced by the Needham, Louis, & Brorby agency for their client Johnson Wax. The show premiered April 16, 1935, and stayed on the air until September 6, 1959; Johnson Wax was the sponsor throughout most of this run. Rather than commercial spots, the announcer, Harlow Wilcox, would drop by the McGee home in the middle of the program and inject a plug for Johnson's Self-polishing Glo-Coat, often with Fibber and Molly groaning in the background.

In 1938 Pepsodent dropped its backing of the *Amos 'n' Andy* show and, working with Lord & Thomas, created the *Pepsodent Show,* a comedy variety show starring Bob Hope. Pepsodent was the sole sponsor of Bob Hope's radio program from 1938 until 1948. The shows included ads for Pepsodent, and each episode also contained comic references to Pepsodent in the script (Library of Congress 2002). Indeed, Bob Hope kidded his radio sponsor to the point where he would drop references to Pepsodent into his motion pictures. However, despite evidence that audiences liked this form of good-natured kidding of sponsors, and therefore paid attention to the plugs, many sponsors took offense. Canada Dry did not renew its contract with the Jack Benny show because they did not like being the butt of Benny's jokes (Oakner 2002). Later, sponsor Chevrolet dropped Benny for the same reason (Oakner 2002).

Even as advertising shifted from the subtle tactic of sponsorships to the use of distinct "plugs," the association between program content and advertising remained strong because the programs were owned by the advertisers rather than the networks. Consequently, radio talent was employed directly by advertisers, and commercial spots were performed live within the program, often by the stars of the programs themselves. Humor was an important part of programming during the glory days of radio. Thus Bob Hope was joined by Fred Allen, Jack Benny, and Burns and Allen as early product endorsers. This gave humor an early foothold in radio advertising. Though there are few statistics available, Burtt (1938) noted that only 3 to 7 percent of advertising used humor. He comments, "The comic as an attention feature is used sparingly. . . . The fact that the incidence of humor in advertising has decreased through the years suggests, that, on the whole, it has not been a successful technique. In certain cases, however, it may be profitable, as indicated by the survival of a few familiar comic features" (235).

Lord & Thomas participated in humorous campaigns in their radio work, despite the agency's generally negative view of humor. Other agencies, however, embraced the idea of humorous advertising. From its inception, Doyle Dane Bernbach (DDB), which was created in 1949, embraced creativity and wit. By the mid-1960s classic campaigns conducted for clients such as Volkswagen (see Exhibit 1.2), Avis, Ohrbach's, and Levy's rye bread (see Exhibit 1.3) all exhibited the warm, funny style that came to be associated with DDB and with Bill Bernbach in particular (Morrison 2003; Otnes and McDonough 2003). A one-time DDB employee, Mary Wells Lawrence, went on to form Wells, Rich, and Greene, and to become one of the most famous people in advertising. Wells, Rich, and Greene became known for brash ironic humor with accounts such as Alka-Seltzer, Benson & Hedges, and Braniff (McDonough 2003b).

In addition to agencies, others in the advertising industry have developed a strong association with humor. Joe Sedelmaier is perhaps the most widely known director/producer of humorous television commercials. Sedelmaier's 1984 campaign for Wendy's made the slogan "Where's the beef?" a part of American popular culture. Before his work on the Wendy's account, Sedelmaier's reputation for humor already had been well established. His humorous ads for Federal Express ("The Fast-Paced World") featuring the fast-talking actor John Moschitta Jr. in 1982, won Effies, Clios, and One Show awards and were chosen by *Advertising Age* as number 11 in its list of the 100 greatest ad campaigns of the twentieth century (Smoot 2003). As in the case of agencies, and commercial directors, some advertisers have become

Exhibit 1.2   **Volkswagen Theory of Evolution Ad**

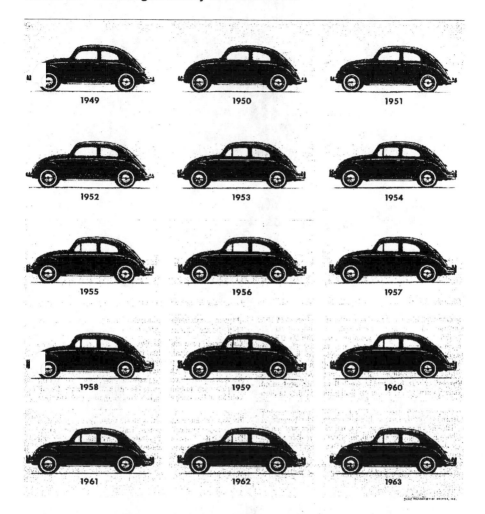

The Volkswagen Theory of Evolution.

Can you spot the Volkswagen with the fins? Or the one that's bigger? Or smaller? Or the one with the fancy chrome work? You can't?

The reason you can't see any revolutionary design changes on our car is simple: there aren't any.

Now, can you spot the Volkswagen with the synchromesh first gear? Or the one with the more efficient heater? How about the one with the anti-sway bar? Or the more powerful engine?

You can't?

The reason you can't see most of our evolutionary changes is because we've made them deep down inside the car.

And that's our theory: never change the VW for the sake of change, only to make it better.

That's what keeps our car ahead of its time. And never out of style.

Even if you aren't driving the most evolved VW of all.

Our '63.

Volkswagen of America, 1962.

Exhibit 1.3 **Levy's Rye Bread Ad**

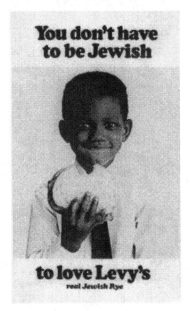

Bestfoods, 1963.

strongly associated with humor over the years. While Federal Express has changed agencies several times over its thirty-year history, and changed its name to FedEx, humor has remained a consistent theme in its advertising (Smoot 2003).

Growth of Humor in Advertising

The growth of humor in advertising was fueled by many factors. First, after nearly twenty years of depression overall advertising expenditures tripled from $1.9 billion in 1945 to $5.7 billion in 1950. Second, television fueled a spending and creative advertising revolution that gave the advertising agencies a new platform and set of tools to express humor. Broadcast media are well suited to the use of humor (reasons for this are discussed in Chapter 4). As broadcasting grew, the use of humor grew along with it. The growth of broadcasting, however, added considerably to an already cluttered media landscape. As media outlets continue to expand, many advertisers have turned toward humor as a way to break through that clutter and to reach increasingly jaded consumers. The entertainment value of advertising has become more important as technology, remote control (zapping), and fast forward (zipping) have allowed consumers to more easily escape from broadcast advertising.

The Super Bowl is emblematic of these trends. Before 1984, Super Bowl ads were not unlike those on any other football broadcast. In the 1984 Super Bowl broadcast, an Orwellian themed "1984" ad for the Apple Macintosh changed all of this. The ad, created by Chiat-Day, revolutionized Super Bowl advertising. This ad, directed by Ridley Scott, has been called the "greatest commercial ever" (Fawcett 1995). The Macintosh ad was not humorous, but it laid the foundation for many humorous ads in two ways. First, it demonstrated the importance of the Super Bowl as an advertising vehicle. Second, it showed the importance of breaking through the clutter, and that entertainment value could do this. The ad ran only once, yet it generated the equivalent of $10 million dollars worth of free media time after the game (McAllister 1999). It also generated countless conversations among consumers and significant early sales for the Macintosh. Since "1984" advertisers have bet hundreds of millions of dollars on Super Bowl advertising and the tactic that many of these advertisers have used has been humor. As Super Bowl advertising has become more entertaining the ads have become an important draw to the broadcast. In 1996, 2 percent of viewers reported watching the game exclusively for the advertising. By 1998 the percentage had grown to 7 percent (McAllister 1999). Seven percent is obviously a distinct minority of viewers, yet given the fact that the 2000 Super Bowl was watched by 134 million viewers in the United States and 800 million worldwide (Tomkovick, Yelkur, Christians 2001), 7 percent represents nearly 10 million viewers in the United States.

Every year since 1989 the *USA Today* has used the "ad meter" as a way of evaluating Super Bowl advertising. Although the methodology used in the *USA Today* ad meter can certainly be called into question, it has become a popular feature of the newspaper as evidenced by its longevity. Other media organizations also critique Super Bowl advertising in one way or another. The most common yardstick used to evaluate these ads is entertainment value (McAllister 1999). Although entertainment value may not necessarily be the best communication strategy, advertisers understand that this is the avenue to good post-game publicity. Hence, humor has become common in Super Bowl advertising. As clear evidence of this, the top ten ads based on ad meter results all used humor in 2003, 2004, and 2005 (*USA Today* 2003; 2004; 2005a). In an analysis of ad meter results over the years, Tomkovick, Yelkur, and Christians (2001) found that humor was the most important variable in influencing liking. Each of the ads to win the ad meter poll since 2001 has been humorous (*USA Today* 2005b). This fact has clearly been recognized by advertisers. Perennial Super Bowl sponsor Anheuser-Busch commonly uses humor in its Super Bowl ads and Bob Dole has developed a post-political career as a humorous pitchman in Super Bowl ads for Visa and Pepsi.

Another indication of the rise of humor in advertising is its prevalence in award-winning Clio competitions. Murphy, Morrison, and Zahn (1993) found that the use of humor in Clio-winning radio ads went from an average of 47 percent during the period from 1974 to 1978 to an astonishing 76 percent during the period from 1984 until 1988. Research on humor in advertising has paralleled the growth of humor in advertising.

History of Research on Humor in Advertising

Humor has been widely studied. It is a topic of interest in linguistics, mass communications, popular culture, psychology, and many other fields, including marketing. Although the use of humor as an executional tactic grew with the early days of radio, scholarly research on the topic did not begin in earnest until the 1970s. Two doctoral dissertations, prepared at rival Big Ten universities in 1972, paved the way for serious academic research on humor in advertising (Kennedy 1972; Markiewicz 1972). Both of these dissertations dealt with humor and persuasion and not humor in advertising per se. Citing work going back to Lull in 1940, and drawing on numerous studies by Gruner in the 1960s and 1970s (see, e.g., Gruner 1967: 1970), Markiewicz highlights the point that humor is not a sure choice to enhance persuasion. Shortly after these two dissertations, work on humor in advertising entered the mainstream of academic literature with Sternthal and Craig's (1973) work published in the *Journal of Marketing* and Kelly and Solomon's (1975) work published in the *Journal of Advertising.* As the body of humor research grew, the credibility of humor as an executional tactic grew as well. David Ogilvy's 1982 paper in the *Harvard Business Review* (Ogilvy and Raphaelson 1982), in which he reversed his earlier position and indicated that humor could change brand preference, may have been the watershed signaling the broader acceptance of humor as a legitimate executional tactic among mainstream advertising executives.

The study of humor in advertising has continued to gain credibility and attract scholarly attention. Madden (1982) published the first dissertation devoted to humor applied to advertising a full decade after the earlier persuasion studies in psychology. In the 1980s and 1990s five more doctoral dissertations were devoted to studying humor in advertising with message type (Speck 1987), product type, target, and program context (Bauerly 1989), audience involvement (Zhang 1992), gender (Bender 1993), and cognitive and affective responses (Michaels 1997). By 2004 over forty journal articles had been devoted to studying humor in advertising.

Analysis of Research on Humor in Advertising

We believe this book is a comprehensive, integrative review of the research regarding humor in advertising. Much of the research we review was conducted specifically to explore humor in advertising. Some was conducted in related areas, such as psychology, education, or communications. We have also drawn from the relatively nascent field of humor research. This interdisciplinary field draws researchers from many fields and includes scholarly conferences and peer-reviewed journals dedicated to the topic of humor. We have also integrated information from trade publications and general audience publications where appropriate. What emerges from all of this research is that humor in advertising and marketing communications is a very rich and complex area.

As noted earlier, the growth of broadcasting stimulated the growth of humor in advertising. As a technique, humor is closely tied to the advertising media. A humorous ad that is effective on radio may not necessarily be translatable into an effective print ad. In fact, humor is a relatively fragile tactic. Whether a humorous ad succeeds or fails is a function of many variables including media. Given the complexities of these variables and their interactions, we will not endeavor to fully discuss them here; rather we will introduce the topics that will be explored in greater depth later in the book.

There are many types of humor. For example, the difference between complex satire and slapstick comedy is one not of degree but of substance. Certain types of humor are more suited to use in advertising than others. The theoretical foundation of humor in advertising will be explored in Chapter 2.

Chapter 3 will examine the audience differences that impact the use of humor. Humor is dependent on a shared experience. As such, it is affected by demographic, psychographic, cultural, and subcultural factors. These audience factors also interact with humor type and with media placement, adding to the complexity of humor usage. Additionally, something that is humorous to one individual may be offensive to another. The potentially offensive nature of humor in advertising will be explored in Chapter 9.

The media factors alluded to earlier will be explored in detail in Chapter 4 as will humor usage in various media. A related factor, the context of the ad, will be explored in Chapter 7.

Some products are better suited to humorous strategies than others. The product factors that affect humor are examined in Chapter 5. Similarly, communications goals often differ by product or by company. These differing communications goals can also influence the success or failure of a humorous advertising approach. Chapter 6 will explore communications goals and execution factors as they relate to humor in advertising.

As evidenced by the preceding paragraphs, humor in advertising is a complex issue. As such, it presents some unique research challenges. We explore the research methodology issues related to humor studies in Chapter 8.

Finally, in Chapter 10 we draw conclusions. What can humor do for an advertiser? When is it likely to succeed? We will draw from the sizable body of research available to answer these and related questions.

Notes

1. Under Edward VI (1547–53) a legal distinction was drawn between taverns and inns. However, Stanley (1957) notes that the term "public house" is used broadly to include both taverns and inns.
2. The issue of intended humor versus perceived humor is addressed in chapters 3, 8, and 9.

——— 2 ———

What Is Humor? And How Does It Work?

What is humor? Should we call it humor? Is there a theory of humor? For a phenomenon that is so universal to humans, it is a paradox that there is so little agreement among scholars about how it operates, what it is, or what to label it.

Stern (1996) suggests that "the term *humo(u)r* itself breeds confusion by confounding the formal aspects of the stimulus advertisement with the response aspects of effects on consumers." She does away with the term *humo(u)r* completely, substituting the term *comedy* when referring to advertisements or stimulus-side phenomena, and the term *laughter* when referring to response-side effects. Citing historical references from Elizabethan works, Stern argues that comedy of humours is a subcategory of the broader term comedy.

Freud's (1905: 1960) path-breaking work divides his discussions between wit and the comic. He defines wit with twelve techniques, but argues that it is fundamentally different from the comic. The comic requires just two persons while wit requires three. One makes a witticism but finds something comical. The comical he argues is found primarily as an unintentional discovery in the social relations of human beings, often exemplified as aggressive or hostile tendencies. In Freud's 1928 work titled "Humor," the term refers to a series of painful emotions transformed in a manner that produces pleasure. He argues that humor is the "most self-sufficient of the comic forms"; all its processes can be exercised in a single person. In making this distinction, it is clear that Freud is not using humor in a broad sense. On this point there is agreement with Stern, but any similarity in definition of humor ends abruptly there.

The more modern and general use of humor has been adopted to include what Freud used as wit, the comic and humor in all their variant forms of delivery. Despite Stern's use of the word *comedy* to describe drama that evokes laughter, humor is the rubric most accepted as the stimulus evoking an intended or unintended pleasurable effect often resulting in a form of subdued or exuberant laughter. A dictionary definition may help here. "(1) The quality of being laughable, or comical; funniness. (2) Something designed to induce laughter or amusement" (*American Heritage Dictionary* 1978). The truth is that as we pointed out in a previous work, "an all-encompassing, generally accepted definition of humor does not exist" (Weinberger and Gulas 1992, 49). Rather, what exists is a series of possible general behavioral explanations that may help describe how humor works. Duncan (1979) provided a list that includes (1) humor as a distraction (from counterargumentation), (2) humor as a reward (operant conditioning), (3) humor as a positive stimulus paired with sales proposition (classical conditioning), (4) humor as a creator of a positive/arousing reception environment (environmental psychology), and (5) humor as a creator of source credibility or likeability (source effects). In addition, affect transfer, elaboration likelihood models, and dual mediation models have been suggested as frameworks to explain the workings of humor. Unfortunately, though all these perspectives may have a role in explaining humor, the literature has not focused on testing these explanations. There are of course exceptions here and there. For example, Nelson, Duncan, and Frontczak (1985) examined the distraction hypothesis with results that did not support the theory. In his dissertation, Speck (1987) broadly utilized an Elaboration Likelihood Model (ELM) framework, but did not specifically test that model. More generally, the humor literature has been mostly effects-based, with only modest connections to conceptual perspectives.

Taking a broader perspective, Speck (1987) suggests that humor is multidimensional and is "a family of related phenomena made up of several distinct humor species" (61). We discuss these humor species in the remainder of this chapter.

What Mechanism Explains How Humor Works?

The difficulty of defining humor is that the domain is made up of several distinct types, all of which result in some form of satisfaction or pleasure to the teller, the object, and/or the hearer. Dozens of writers have contributed to the discourse about humor with a seemingly irreconcilable jumble of incomplete explanations for humor. Our goal is not to recount the voluminous literature on the topic, which can be traced back to Plato and Aristotle over twenty-four hundred years ago, but rather to summarize the main threads of the theories that have emerged, and then attempt to outline the conditions and elements that are necessary and sufficient for humor.

Theories of humor fall broadly into three wide categories, each of which is composed of dozens of variations, which devotees often doggedly defend as the key to understanding the topic. The three categories are:

Cognitive-perceptual (including the incongruity theories);
Superiority (affective-evaluative theories);
Relief (including psychodynamic theories).

Cognitive Theories

Cognitive theories of humor date to the 1700s and early 1800s in work by Kant (1790) and Schopenhauer (1819). Surveys of television and magazine advertising have shown that the cognitive mechanism revealed in incongruity is the most prevalent form of the trio of cognitive, superiority, and relief theories (Speck 1987; Spotts, Weinberger, and Parsons 1997). An essential aspect of the cognitive theorists focuses on incongruity, though they differ about whether incongruity is a necessary and sufficient condition for humor. According to Schopenhauer, humor requires that some expectation be negated by what the listener perceives. The debate among the incongruity theorists has been whether incongruity is sufficient to trigger humor, whether resolution of the incongruity is needed, and whether incongruity combined with relief is needed.

The group of incongruity-only theories has had many proponents (Maier 1932; Bateson 1953; Koestler 1964; Nerhardt 1977). The pleasure derived from incongruity is the divergence from expectation, and the greater the divergence the funnier the material. The pleasure is in the playful confusion and contrasts.

The more dominant view among cognitive theorists is that incongruity alone can, at best, account for some humor but that most humor requires resolution. Schultz (1976) goes so far as to develop a definition of humor that rules out pure incongruity. Without resolution, incongruity is simply nonsense, but when resolution is added we have humor. In an analysis of Chinese jokes Suls (1983) found that over 85 percent contained incongruity and resolution. A sub-debate among contemporary Incongruity Resolution (IR) theorists, who include Jones (1970), Schultz (1976), Suls (1983) and McGhee

(1979), revolves around whether incomplete resolution can also be humorous (Rothbart and Pien 1977). Advocates argue that in both IR and partial IR there is a need for a real cognitive integration to occur in order to process the meaning of the resolution. Based on brain wave research, McGhee (1983) suggests that the feeling side of the brain (left side) is responsible for recognizing incongruity and the right-hand thinking side is related to the resolution of the humor. IR humor depends on: "(1) rapid resolution of the incongruity; a (2) 'playful' context, that is, with cues signifying that the information is not to be taken seriously; and (3) an appropriate mood for the listener" (Suls 1983). The literature suggests that whereas incongruity (I) alone may be sufficient to generate humor, incongruity-resolution is a "stronger" humor type (Suls 1977). There is some evidence for the greater effect of IR compared to I-based humor in an advertising context (Flaherty, Weinberger, and Gulas 2004). The Nynex ad in Exhibit 2.1 illustrates both an incongruity and an incongruity resolution in the same ad. On the left is an odd image of a cat balancing packages from a shopping spree. The right panel has the same image, but with the words "Pet Shops" at the top with the Nynex tag line at the bottom. The resolving words give meaning to the nonsensical cat image. Though the cat image is itself whimsical, the words help make it more humorous.

In a series of articles Alden and Hoyer and their colleagues (e.g., Alden and Hoyer 1993; Alden, Mukherjee, and Hoyer 2000) utilize an incongruity-based analysis to identify the features that make one incongruity more effective than another. Citing the cognitive structure perspective outlined by Meyers-Levy and Tybout (1989) to explain the positive evaluative effects of moderate differences or incongruities between new product information and cued product category information stored in memory, Alden and Hoyer (1993) argue that resolving incongruities in an advertising context may result in more positive affect. This line of thinking is consistent with the cognitive theories of humor. They proceed to examine aspects of Raskin's (1985) semantic theory that jokes produce a mirthful response by including incongruities (structural contrasts) between expected and unexpected situations. Contrasts can arise from (1) actual/existing and non-actual/non-existing; (2) normal/expected and abnormal/unexpected; and (3) possible/plausible and fully/partially impossible or much less plausible. Though Raskin's script-based theory is not strictly IR, Alden and Hoyer blend it with IR to predict the types of incongruent contrasts in advertising and which are likely to produce a stronger positive reaction. Alden, Hoyer, and Lee (1993) found that the types of contrasts suggested by Raskin are present in most of the advertising that

Exhibit 2.1   Incongruity Humor: NYNEX Pet Shops Ad

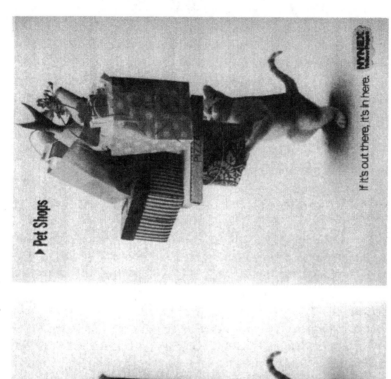

Compliments of NYNEX, a subsidiary of Verizon Communications, Inc.

attempts to be humorous. Alden and Hoyer (1993) examined fifty-two television ads judged as making an attempt at humor. Their results suggest that "reality-based contrasts may on average deviate less from well-formed expectations than those involving the impossible. This in turn may lead to faster resolution of reality-based contrasts, easier assimilation within cued schemas and hence, stronger positive affect" (Alden, Mukherjee, and Hoyer 2000). In this analysis, Alden and his colleagues examined surprise and found that 80 to 90 percent of the observed variance in humor could be accounted for by this single antecedent.

Speck (1991) asserts that in the widespread use of incongruity in advertising superiority (disparagement) and relief (arousal-safety including psychodynamic) theories are special cases of incongruity processes.

Superiority Theories

Superiority in humor, often labeled disparagement, has a long history of proponents dating to Plato, Aristotle, and Hobbes, and is among the subjects of a broader class of research that examines the social function of humor. Morreall (1983) believes that this is probably the oldest and most widespread theory of laughter. Aristotle viewed laughter as a form of derision and even wit as a form of educated insolence. Rapp (1951) in the *Origins of Wit and Humor* traced the evolution of laughter from primitive physical battles of triumph. In more modern versions, he argues, the physical derision is substituted by ridicule. In genial humor the laughter is ridicule tempered by love. Despite work by many proponents (La Fave, Haddad, and Maesen 1976; Zillmann and Cantor 1976; Zillmann 1983; Morreall 1983), they conclude that disparagement does not provide a complete explanation of humor response because there are cases of both humorous and non-humorous laughter that do not involve feelings of superiority. Zillmann (1983) asserts that other essential humor cues must be part of any disparagement for humor to be present.

Gruner (1997), a contemporary of many of the other superiority researchers, leaves no doubt that in his view "superiority theory" is the dominant and only universal thread that is present in all humor. He argues that there is a social inhibition that most of us and probably his colleagues have against believing that humor can be explained in the negative terms of superiority, aggression, hostility, ridicule, or degradation. Nonetheless, Gruner, quoting Jay Leno, believes "jokes have to be demeaning to be funny" (2). He argues that:

1. For every humorous situation there is a winner.
2. For every humorous situation there is a loser.
3. Finding the "winner" in every situation and what the "winner" wins, is often not easy.
4. Finding the "loser" in every humorous situation and what the "loser" loses, is often even less easy.

But, that having been said:

5. Humorous situations can be best understood by knowing who wins what, and who loses what.
6. Removing from a humorous situation (joke, etc.) what is won or lost, or the suddenness with which it is won or lost, removes the essential elements of the situation and renders it humorless (9).

Gruner asserts that superiority explains all humor and not understanding this is a deficiency in those who misunderstand the theory. Since parsimony is essential to any good theory, the fact that he believes that *a* superiority theory explains all humor is strong support to accept it as *the* theory of humor. "Must we laugh only at our own sudden sense of superiority over someone else (including ourselves)? Well yes, basically" (14).

Though superiority has long been recognized as an important component of humor (Zillmann, Bryant, and Cantor 1974), its presence as a necessary condition is what distinguishes Gruner's (1997) work. Even in humor that appears to be harmless Gruner argues that there is superiority. He uses punning riddles as an example:

Why is Sampson like a comedian? Because he brought down the house.
Who was the first man to bear arms? Adam. He had two.

Here the superiority is the joke teller on the joke listener, who is defeated by not knowing the answer to the puns. Such situations depart from the more blatant Rodney Dangerfield disparagement of himself, the audience, or another target of the humor. Gruner even offers the following analysis of a cartoon used by Morreall (1989) to demonstrate an incongruity that is sufficient to cause humor. The classic cartoon, which appeared in the *New Yorker* and elsewhere, shows a ski slope with a large tree with ski tracks left by a recent downhill skier, his tracks going completely around both sides of the tree. Further up the slope looking backward is a puzzled skier who witnessed the event. Gruner argues that Morreall failed to see that "the amazed/baffled/ mystified poor devil of a witness" is the loser. In this vein, Gruner dismisses most theories that do not include some form of aggression against someone. Innocent humor is a mirage. Even the joke "When asked how birds know when they should fly south, one third-grader replied: 'It's a family tradition,'" Gruner argues contains humor because of the naiveté (could we say, "ignorance," or even "stupidity"?) of the young speaker (148).

We do not have to parse superiority as deeply as Gruner to find examples in advertising. Though it is less common than incongruity, disparagement is found with some frequency. Spotts, Weinberger, and Parsons (1997) found that 8 percent of magazine ads attempting humor used some disparagement while Speck found 30 percent in humorous television ads. In TV Budweiser used the lizards to disparage the frogs and even plot their demise. Exhibit 2.2 shows a magazine ad with a heavyset female model dressed somewhat comically in shorts too tight and accessories that do not quite make sense for her. The words "It's in, but maybe you shouldn't be in it" are an obvious put down of the model. In Exhibit 2.3 we have the Episcopal Church playfully disparaging its own origins to promote its compassion. These are examples of disparagement, but it should be noted that to be humorous, disparagement humor per se does not exist but is only present with incongruity and perhaps relief (arousal-safety) as well.

Arousal and Relief

Different sub-theories of arousal safety have in common a view that there is a physiological release in which humor helps to vent tension. Spencer (1860) advocated this "safety valve" view of humor. Morreall (1983) summarizes the relationship between arousal-safety and the other theories: "While superiority theory focuses on emotions involved in laughter, and the incongruity theory on objects or ideas causing laughter, relief theory addresses a question little discussed in the other two theories, namely: Why does laughter take the physical form it does, and what is its biological function?" (20). Relief theory, Morreall argues, may coexist with an incongruity (relief through resolution) or superiority (relief as triumph) situation. The arousal may be triggered by circumstances outside the humor stimulus or may be created within it. Pent-up repression is at the core of the psychoanalytic theories that have long supported the relief theory of wit, comedy, and humor and the release of psychic energy (Freud 1905: 1960). Berlyne (1972) tempered the pent-up tension view and argued that humor plays a cathartic role. Humor causes arousal through the stimulus properties of novelty, complexity, in-

Exhibit 2.2 **Disparagement Humor: Ohrbach's Ad**

Ohrbach's department store, circa 1960s.

Exhibit 2.3 **Self-Deprecating Humor: Episcopal Church**

Domestic and Foreign Ministry Society.

congruity, and perhaps redundancy (52). Berlyne argues that up to a point greater arousal results in greater pleasure when released. Thus, an inverted-U of arousal to humor appreciation would be expected. This inverted-U is not universally held. McGhee concludes that "greater amounts of induced arousal are associated with increased enjoyment" (1983, 19). Thus, a linear relationship rather than a U-shape is expected between arousal and pleasure. Godkewitsch (1976), also a proponent of arousal as necessary for humor and the linear connection to pleasure, argues that other humor cues that signal play are important for humor and that this may explain why his work found a linear relationship between arousal and humor response while Berlyne found that higher levels of arousal may be dysfunctional. It is not clear after all the research whether the increased enjoyment results from arousal or an arousal-relief mechanism. Much like the incongruity versus incongruity-resolution debate, each group has its proponents and the matter remains unresolved.

Speck (1987) found that 36 percent of humorous TV ads employed arousal-safety while Spotts, Weinberger, and Parsons (1997) as with disparagement, found a much lower incidence in consumer magazines, with just 9 percent. Perhaps the ability to play out drama and build the arousal and safety sequence lends itself better to the mechanism. In effect arousal safety is a variation of the time-tested problem solution format. Make them hurt and then heal them was the old saying. Award-winning Federal Express ads on TV starting in the 1980s humorously showed the problem of unreliable overnight delivery service with Federal Express as the hero "when it absolutely positively has to be there overnight." Personal care products use this same format. Scope mouthwash commercials engendered anxiety in the viewer with the "dreaded morning breath." In a playful context the Scope solution provides relief with an approving kiss from the spouse. The same sequence described in the FedEx and Scope ads is more difficult to execute in print but it is used, albeit infrequently, as can be seen in Exhibit 2.4.

What Makes Humor Work? Enabling Factors

There does seem to be unity among the proponents of all the theories that contextual cues play a vital role in turning an ordinary incongruity, disparagement, or arousal situation from being fearful, strange, or simply tension filled. These cues may be embedded in the surrounding situation and social context (Rothbart 1976; Foot and Chapman 1976), other observers of the humor (i.e., audiences) (Chapman and Foot 1976), the deliverer of the humor (McGhee 1979), the stimulus itself (Berlyne 1972; Freud 1905: 1960;

31

Exhibit 2.4 **Arousal Safety Humor: Clorox Wipes**

CLOROX®WIPES, The Clorox Company, DDB, SF, Photographer Leigh Beisch.

Zillmann 1983), or internal cues related to the subjects' own mood or predisposition and affective and behavioral response (Leventhal and Cupchik 1976).

For McGhee, the play signals "communicate to the person pondering over the incongruity that, 'this is not a situation to be taken seriously.'" Again such signals are necessary, but not sufficient conditions for humor. In the absence of a play signal, an attempt will be made to make sense out of the incongruity in a realistic or adaptive fashion—a condition incompatible with humor (McGhee 1979, 47).

In addition to play signals, there is some agreement, though it is not universal, that there are other humor stimulus properties (such as surprise) related to the amount of mirth that a humor situation evokes. In this regard Berlyne (1969; 1972) discusses a set of collative variables such as novelty, surprise, incongruity, strangeness, and ambiguity. Some of these may be play signals while others such as surprise, ambiguity, and novelty may not be. In an advertising context, Alden and Hoyer (1993) found surprise to be the dominant factor in determining the effect of incongruity humor. Alden, Mukherjee, and Hoyer (2000) argue that schema familiarity by an audience is necessary for an incongruity to lead to surprise. It is not clear whether greater mirth results because these factors cause greater arousal that can be released or, as Zillmann (1983) argues, these cues reduce any possible social reproach for laughing at a situation or an object of humor. Alden and colleagues suggest that a combination of warmth, playfulness, and ease of resolution help convert a surprise generated by incongruity into a perception of humor. Whatever the psychological mechanism, the research points to these factors as enabling a humor response. They are necessary but not sufficient conditions for most conceptions of humor.

In his proposal for a new theory of laughter, Morreall (1983) suggests that in examining the incongruity, superiority, and relief theories three general factors emerge that can form the basis of a comprehensive theory. The first is change of psychological state that involves either a shift in cognition (serious to non-serious state) and/or affect (boost in positive feelings or release of suppressed feelings). Second, the change of psychological state must be sudden. To laugh, Morreall argues, we need to be caught off guard. Finally, the psychological shift must be pleasant. The result is a feeling of amusement or mirth, which may or may not result in laughter.

Integrating Humor: A Challenge Framework

We agree with Speck (1987) that humor is made up of distinct species. However, as we examine the three major theories of humor, it appears that there may be an embedded thread that unites them all but favors none. Figure 2.1 illustrates the simple idea that incongruity, arousal, and disparagement have a common impact, that of a "challenge." The prevailing order is upset through this challenge. Each of the major humor mechanisms that we have reviewed in this chapter presents variations of a challenge either to the audience or to a target of the humor. In incongruity there is a departure from normality or expectation that presents a challenge for the audience to resolve. In aggressive humor there is a social, physical, or psychological challenge faced by the target of the humor in the situation. This may be self-deprecating or aimed at others. In arousal-safety there is some tension or challenge to the order of the psyche. All of these humor mechanisms are valid explanations and are often used in combination with one another. Our contention is that the common element in each theory is challenge, with each one being a special case, but a challenge nonetheless. Superiority or aggressive humor is one way to generate the challenge, but it is not in itself the unifying theory as Gruner suggests, since it interprets even the most whimsical playful humor as aggression. The examples of the skier and children's jokes are challenges to expectation in each case but calling them superiority or aggressive humor stretches the credibility of the theory. Mirth may or may not result depending upon a set of many of the preconditions highlighted in the previous section.

We show the set of enabling conditions in a circular rather than sequential order because the variety of humor forms require that we allow for maximum flexibility in order to anticipate the conditions that can foster humor. There is considerable agreement that arousal, surprise, and play signals are important to establishing a humor situation and that there needs to be a common understanding of the situation (schema familiarity) to decipher the challenge triggered by the message. Schema familiarity explains why some humor developed in one culture falls flat in another where the audience may have no idea of the schema that may be the basis for the challenge. Executional receptivity refers to a predisposition toward the humor in the given situation. For example, over the past fifty years audiences have become more receptive to sexual humor in advertising and less receptive to racial humor in advertising.

The Wonderbra ad in Exhibit 2.5 helps illustrate several of the enabling features. First, there must be schema familiarity to know that the cardboard eyeglasses are used for 3-D viewing, thus helping make meaning out of a simple incongruity of a voluptuous torso and cardboard glasses. Second, the glasses also act as a play signal. Third, there must be audience receptivity to a racy and sexist image. Finally, there is surprise through the resolution of the connection between 3-D glasses and the Wonderbra enhanced breasts.

Figure 2.1 **The Challenge Model of Humor**

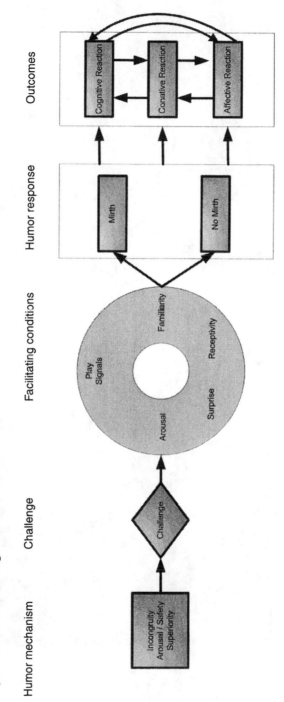

Humor mechanism   Challenge   Facilitating conditions   Humor response   Outcomes

35

Exhibit 2.5 **Facilitating Conditions for Humor: Wonderbra 3-D**

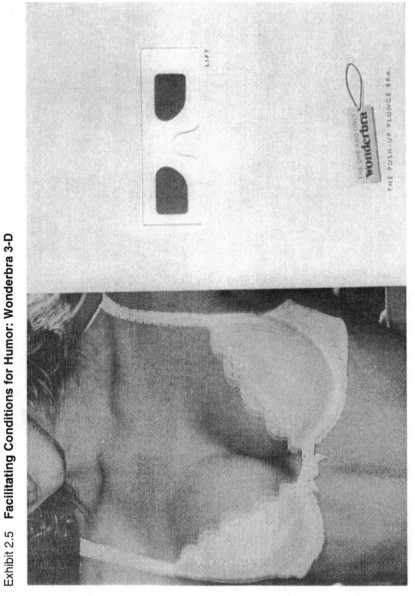

Wonderbra, TBWA Hunt Lascaris, 1996.

We label the immediate product of this or any attempt at humor as mirth (or no mirth), a generic positive (or negative) affective response that can be gladness, gayety, merriment, laughter, amusement, cheer, grins, happiness, fun, pleasure, lightheartedness, and so on, or their negative polar opposites. In short, the word mirth encompasses the many different humor responses that can be triggered without restriction to a particular type. This is important because a specific term such as laughter used by some authors refers to a specific physical reaction that may not be associated with more subtle forms of humor such as puns or word play.

The outcome of the humor response may be a complex impact on feelings, thoughts, or actions that can result in positive, neutral, or negative outcomes. We can easily imagine a wide range of both positive and negative humor responses and higher order outcomes from exposure of different audiences to the Wonderbra ad.

The challenge model is simply a descriptive integration of the three main strands of humor theory that often are codependent on one another. They share a simple idea that in the presence of the facilitating conditions provides for a humor response we label mirth. We will refer back to the model in many of the chapters that follow as we attempt to both dissect the current advertising humor literature and link it to the basic challenge model.

——— 3 ———

Audience Factors

Humor is very complex. Whether or not something is humorous depends on numerous factors, not the least of which is the nature of the audience. Contemporary audiences may, or may not, be entertained by the humor of an earlier era. Similarly, what is funny to people of one culture may not be funny to people of another. The perception of humor may also vary by gender, educational level, ethnic or age group, and by many psychological factors. Additionally, audience factors interact with executional tactics and message factors. Of particular importance is the object of the humor. In other words, who is the butt of the joke? Thus, although a given humorous approach may be funny to one individual or group, it may be offensive to another. The issue of the potentially offensive nature of humor is discussed in Chapter 9.

Even if the attempted humor is innocuous and humorous to some, it may not have broad appeal. Certain individuals or groups may simply not be able to relate to the humor due to different points of reference, different cognitive abilities, or other differences. This is very important since recent research suggests that if an ad intended as humorous is not perceived as humorous, its effectiveness at influencing attitudes and purchases can be seriously harmed (Flaherty, Weinberger, and Gulas 2004).

Components of Humor

The humor process typically includes an agent, an object, and an audience. The agent is the source of the humor, the joke teller. The object is the butt of the joke. The audience is the recipient of the humor. These components can sometimes be collapsed (see Figure 3.1). For example, in self-deprecating humor, the agent is also the object of the humor. In other situations, the audience may be the object of the humor.

Figure 3.1 **Humor Target**

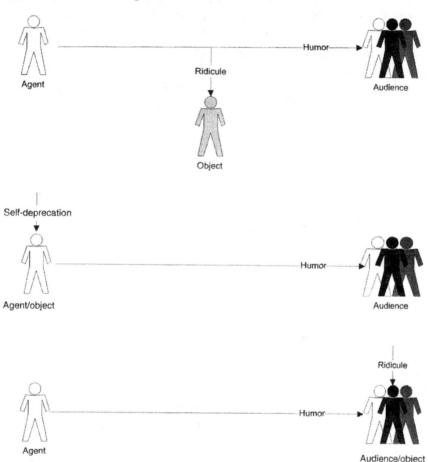

Agent or Source

Unlike in other humorous applications, in advertising there are often two levels of agency. A given execution may have a humor agent that is internal to the ad. For example, a character who delivers a punch line would be an internal humor agent. However, one of the primary rationales behind the use of humor in advertising is that there is an affect transfer. Thus the secondary humor agent would be the advertiser. Depending on the nature of the ad execution, the internal agent may or may not be present. However, the advertiser is always the ultimate humor agent.[1]

The advertiser may, or may not, get benefits from a successful use of humor. This is largely dependent on the success of the affect transfer. On the other hand, in the case of a failed attempt at humor, the advertiser will pay a price. At a minimum, the advertiser will have the opportunity costs associated with an ineffectual ad. However, in a very bad humor execution, the advertiser may pay a significantly higher price. This will be illustrated in detail in the Just for Feet case discussed in Chapter 9.

Object or Target

The object of the humor is the butt of the joke. As noted earlier, in self-deprecating humor the object is the agent. Generally, however, the butt of the joke is a third party.

The third-party target may be a specific, known individual such as a politician or a celebrity. The humor might also be directed at a more general target; for example, an animal or an anonymous, hapless blunderer. However, even an anonymous individual will be associated with some group—blondes, men, children, and so on—either by design or by default. Often the humorous execution is dependent upon some attribute of the target. Humor targets are often associated with an ethnic group, and ethnic humor is a universal phenomenon found across cultures. Indeed, Davies (1982) notes that most nations have two ethnic targets for humor: one "stupid group" and one "canny group."

Although ethnic humor was once common in advertising, it is rare today. However, in modern advertising other group-based targets are common. These target groups may be defined by age, gender, physical characteristics, political affiliation, or numerous other grouping attributes. Targeting any group of people is likely to offend some. The Advertising Standards Authority in the United Kingdom recently ruled that a Carling ad that included a photo of plastic wedding cake figurines featuring a red-haired overweight bride is "not offensive," in spite of complaints from consumers that "argued that the image of the figures on the cake 'mocked overweight people, especially those with red hair'" (Ananova 2003). The propensity of humorous advertising to offend is discussed in Chapter 9.

Audience

The audience is the recipient of the humor and, since the humor is designed to entertain it, in a sense, the audience is the true "target" of the humor and in the parlance of marketing it is the target of the ad. The audience is critical in humorous communication because the audience is, in fact, the arbiter of what constitutes humor. The difficulty of defining humor, discussed in Chapter 2, in part comes from the perception of humor. If a sender intends for something to be humorous, but it is not perceived as humorous, is it humor? While this question has the flavor of a Zen koan, it has practical implications for the use of humor in advertising. And it has been a limitation of some academic studies of humor that used "attempted humor" as a proxy for "humor." Although clearly related, the two are separate phenomena and the distinction between them is important. Flaherty, Weinberger, and Gulas (2004) found that attempts at humor in advertising that are not perceived by the audience as funny are not likely to succeed in achieving marketing objectives.

Many things may affect whether an attempt at humor is perceived as humorous. Of particular importance is the nature of the audience and the relationships between the agent, audience, and object of the humor. Not surprisingly, these interactions can be quite complex. In a study of children aged three years to six years from different ethnic and income backgrounds, McGhee and Duffey (1983) found that, in general, humor victimizing parents was perceived as funnier than humor victimizing children, and humor victimizing the opposite sex was perceived as funnier than humor victimizing one's own sex. These findings are consistent with disposition theory (Zillmann and Cantor 1976: 1996), which posits that perception of humor is negatively correlated with the favorableness of the disposition toward the disparaged target and positively correlated with the favorableness of the disposition toward the source of the disparagement. More specifically, Zillmann and Cantor (1976: 1996) propose:

1. The more intense the negative disposition toward the disparaged agent or entity, the greater the magnitude of the humor response.
2. The more intense the positive disposition toward the disparaged agent or entity, the smaller the magnitude of the humor response.
3. The more intense the negative disposition toward the disparaging agent or entity, the smaller the magnitude of the humor response.
4. The more intense the positive disposition toward the disparaging agent or entity, the greater the magnitude of the humor response. (Zillmann and Cantor 1976: 1996, 100)

The authors summarize, "appreciation should be maximal when our friends humiliate our enemies, and minimal when our enemies manage to get the upper hand over our friends" (101).

Although McGhee and Duffey's (1983) study generally supports disposition theory, one of their findings is contrary to it. They found that low-income girls, regardless of ethnic group, perceived humor victimizing girls as funnier than humor victimizing boys. The authors note that this finding is consistent with other studies that report "preference for humor disparaging one's own sex over humor disparaging the opposite sex occurs only among women with strong traditional sex-role orientations" (McGhee and Duffey 1983, 268). The author's suggest that these traditional sex-role orientations are already present among low-income young girls. The apparent implication of this is that women with traditional sex-role orientations have lower self-perceptions than women with less traditional sex-role orientations. However, this phenomenon may be driven by a very different mechanism.

Ethnic humor is universal; it is found to some extent in every culture. In an empirical study of ethnic humor, Gallois and Callan (1985) found that the mere presence of an ethnic label in a joke could affect humor ratings. High ethnocentric audience members "rated the jokes with ethnic victims as funnier, but low ethnocentrics found them slightly less funny, than the same jokes without ethnic labels" (Gallois and Callan 1985, 73). Although the study was not designed as a test for disposition theory, the findings are supportive of the theory. But this is only part of the picture.

McGhee and Duffey (1983) and Gallois and Callan (1985) provide interesting insights into the interaction between audience and humor target. However, there may be a mechanism operating beyond positive and negative disposition to the agent and audience. For example, if an overweight person tells a "fat joke" to an audience of overweight people, how would it be perceived relative to a thin person telling the same joke to the same audience? Even if the audience was previously disposed favorably toward the joke teller, it is likely that the humor would not be perceived as humorous, and the disposition toward the joke teller may change. Humor is dependent not only on the joke itself, but also on the complex interaction between the joke, the joke teller, and the audience. Indeed, a given joke may be humorous from one source and highly offensive from another. As Kruger (1996) notes, Jewish humor may be seen as a form of aggression against a minority group if told by a non-Jewish person, but may actually serve "mastery purposes" when the joke teller is Jewish. Juni and Katz (2001) "reject the analytic notion that self-effacing humor is masochistic" (120). Rather, they argue that, "self-directed humor adopted by an oppressed group is adaptive and beneficial to the group's integrity and emotional well-being" (120). Thus the commonality between agent, object, and audience plays an important role in determining the success of a humor attempt (see Figure 3.2).

Figure 3.2 **Commonality Between Humor Components**

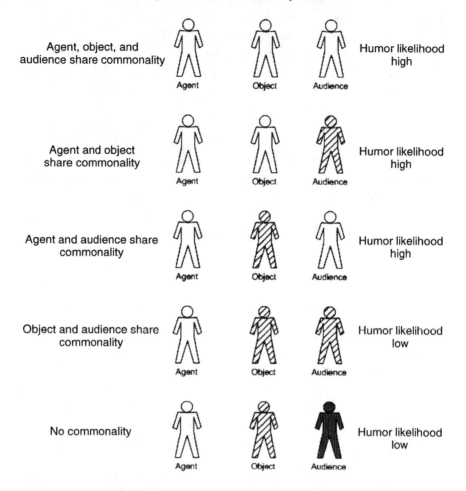

While much of the difference in perception of humor may be related to the commonality issue discussed above, other audience characteristics such as demographics, psychographics, and culture, appear to have independent effects as well.

Demographic Factors

Gender Differences

The interaction between gender and humor has been widely studied and is a topic of general conversation. In fact, some have quipped that the difference between men and women is that men enjoy the Three Stooges. This statement appears to have some empirical support. Men show a greater general appreciation for aggressive humor (Prerost 1995; Whipple and Courtney 1981), and use humor negatively more often than women (Meyers, Ropong, and Rodgers 1997). Men and women also differ in the perceived offensiveness of jokes (Duchaj 1999). Additionally, men have been found to attempt humor more often than women (Meyers, Ropong, and Rodgers 1997; Provine 2000), and women have been found to laugh more frequently than men (Provine 2000). These differences have also been demonstrated in dating behavior. In personal ads, women are much more likely than men to seek a sense of humor in mates, while men are more likely to offer humor (Provine 2000). Very subtle gender differences have also been found. An empirical study found use of humor to more positively affect evaluations of a head soccer coach among female players than among male players, yet this gender difference did not hold for assistant coaches (Grisaffe, Blom, and Burke 2003). Similarly, in a study of cartoon humor, significant gender differences were found for work-related humor but not for the other cartoons in the study (Lowis 2003). In a study comparing recall of humorous advertising material, Bender (1993) found no gender differences in print advertising, but significant gender differences with regard to humor in broadcast advertising. This suggests an interesting yet little explored interaction between gender, humor, and media.

It is clear that humor differences exist between men and women. The implications of these differences are less clear. For example, research in education generally has not found significant gender effects on humor response. In experimental studies, the positive effect of humor on learning has not been found to differ by gender (Davies and Apter 1980; Weaver, Zillmann, and Bryant 1988; Zillmann et al. 1980; Ziv 1988). On the other hand, some research in advertising has found significant and strategically important gender differences.

Lammers and his colleagues found that humor significantly increased liking of an advertising message for male respondents while the same humorous execution decreased liking of the ad for female respondents (Lammers et al. 1983). Similarly, Stewart-Hunter (1985) found that a humorous ad that produced below-average brand registration scores overall produced a very high brand registration score among men in a regional subsample. In an analysis of Starch scores, Madden and Weinberger (1982) found significant differences between men and women with regard to humorous ads.

It is likely that the findings in these and similar studies have informed the opinions of advertising practitioners. The majority of these practitioners were found to believe that humorous ads are best suited to a target audience consisting of better educated younger males (Madden and Weinberger 1984). Madden and Weinberger's study occurred more than twenty years ago. Therefore, we cannot be certain that these attitudes still prevail. However, to the degree that this perception is still held, it is likely that it is incorrect. Although many studies have found gender differences of one sort or another, it cannot be inferred that there is a generalizable male preference for humor. Rather, it is likely that the differences seen are due to more narrow executional factors. This, however, should not to be taken as a criticism of extant research. Humor research raises many unique methodological challenges, which are discussed in detail in Chapter 8. These challenges make humor research akin to quantum physics in some regard. It is simply not possible to simultaneously "know everything" in a humor study. There are too many variables and too many possible interactions to address everything in a given study. Thus researchers must focus on a few variables of interest. Therefore, what is seen as a gender difference in a particular study may reflect a particular humor execution, a class of executions, or an underlying audience characteristic rather than a generalizable effect. For example, Greenwood and Isbell (2002) reported that ratings of "dumb blonde" jokes differed not only by gender but also by the nature of the attitudes held regarding women. Levels of sexism moderated the ratings of humor and offensiveness for both male and female respondents.

In addition, the perspective of the creator of the humor may be an important, yet generally overlooked, moderator, as will be discussed. It is also important to note that humor preferences may be changing as society changes. During the forty years of concentrated research on humor in advertising, many changes have occurred in society. This is particularly true of issues related to gender.

The findings regarding gender effects on response to humor raises some interesting issues. Humor is very closely tied into the culture, experiences, and points of reference that are shared between the humor originator and the humor receiver. For example, research has suggested that the gender response to sexual humor is reversed when the creator of the humor is female (Gallivan 1991), and as noted earlier, the characteristics of the butt of the joke may influence which audiences find the joke funny (Gallois and Callan 1985; Gruner 1991; McGhee and Duffey 1983). If this is indeed the case, then much of the variation based on gender, and perhaps race, age, and other demographic factors as well, may be explained by differing perspectives of the creator of the humorous manipulation and the receiver of that manipulation. Thus the "shared point of view" between the creator of a humorous ad and the target of the ad is a potentially important intervening variable in humor effectiveness. Yet, this issue has been largely overlooked by advertising researchers.

Age Differences

To some extent humor is age dependent. Children develop an appreciation and understanding of humor as they mature. Very young children may understand incongruity. However, comprehension of irony does not emerge until five or six years of age (Dews et al. 1996). Recent research also suggests that older adults may have difficulty in understanding some forms of humor. In a recent study, Shammi and Stuss (2003) found that older adults (average age seventy-three) had some difficulty in understanding complex jokes. They posit that this may be due to deterioration in function in the right frontal lobe, a region of the brain that appears to play an important role in understanding humor (Shammi and Stuss 1999). The Shammi and Stuss (2003) study does not suggest an overall diminished ability to understand humor, only differences in perception of certain types of complex humor. The study also did not find any decrease in affective response to humor when it was perceived.

This slight decrease in the appreciation of certain types of humor due to age is minimal. Yet, as noted earlier, a widespread belief was found among advertising practitioners that humorous ads are most appropriate for younger target audiences (Madden and Weinberger 1984). While age differences exist with regard to the perception of humor, it is likely that these differences are largely an artifact of another variable, and not a fundamental difference in whether or not humorous advertising can work well with an older audience. For example, frames of reference differ by age. Cultural references familiar to a sixty-year-old individual may be completely alien to a twenty-year-old individual, and the reverse is also true. Similarly, slang used by teenagers is likely to be significantly different from that used by their parents. Since humor is often dependent on the subtleties of language, small differences in slang can have major differences in humor perception.

Research regarding nostalgia has found that youthful experiences can have widespread lifelong effects (Schindler and Holbrook 2003). Thus, since the lived experiences of individuals are likely to differ systematically by age, it is likely that the perception of humor differs similarly. However, it should be noted that chronological age is only one component of "age" in the psychological sense. Not all consumers "act their age" with regard to behavior and attitude. Nonetheless, a given humorous execution may work better for one age group or another, but this does not imply that one group has a "better" sense of humor.

Yet, the perception among advertising professionals that the best audience for humor is better educated younger males may have some validity. Weinberger and Gulas (1992) posit that the creators of humorous advertising messages have historically also tended to be better educated younger males, who often use women and older people as the butt of a joke. It is likely that humor created by this demographic group would be most likely to appeal to a similar demographic group.

Educational Level

Joke comprehension is correlated with intelligence (Wierzbicki and Young 1978). Indeed, humor has been used as an indicator of mental function in the development of children and as a tool for assessing the cognitive capacity of apes (Gamble 2001). The understanding and appreciation of subtle satire generally requires a well-educated, or at least a well-informed audience. Similarly, relatively esoteric references used in some humor are not likely to be appreciated by an uneducated audience. Indeed, Dennis Miller's obscure cultural references as a commentator on ABC's Monday Night Football inspired entrepreneurs. Wireless service provider Shadowpack offered a service to its subscribers called "Dennis Miller Dymistified" (sic), which provided real-time explanations of Miller references sent to the subscriber's PDA, while Britannica.com offered a Tuesday recap of Miller references on its Web site (Heltzel 2000). Some humor requires not only an educated audience but also one with specific expertise, such as a cartoon on a NASA Web site (NASA 2003) that shows a cowboy holding a smoking gun standing over a body stating, "You guys are both my witnesses. . . . He insinuated that ZFC set theory is superior to Type Theory!"

On the other hand, humor is universal. While certain jokes may not be appreciated by certain audiences, this does not imply that these individuals are necessarily lacking in a sense of humor. As noted earlier, the commonality between humor creator and humor recipient may be the critical factor. Thus, it may be difficult for a highly educated person to create humor that appeals to a less-educated person and it is likely that the reverse holds true as well.

Culture, Subculture, and Ethnicity

In addition to gender, race, and age, other audience factors may also influence the effectiveness of humor and are worthy of consideration. Of particular interest is the crossing of national boundaries on humor appreciation and effectiveness. Humor is a universal human process exhibited by people of all cultures and throughout all of recorded history (Alden, Hoyer, and Lee 1993). However, the research that has examined humor in advertising cross-culturally indicates differential usage of humor among countries, both in humor types employed and in absolute levels of humor used (e.g., Alden, Hoyer, and Lee 1993; Weinberger and Spotts 1989). As one of the jurors at the Cannes advertising festival stated, "Humour travels, but it sometimes gets a bit car sick" (Archer 1994).

Humor Versus Humour

It has been said that the United States and the United Kingdom are two nations separated by a common language. Indeed, even though English is the dominant language of both nations, and the two countries have strong cultural ties, differences regarding humor are notable. According to a recent Web-based study that attracted more than 40,000 jokes and nearly 2 million ratings, people from the United Kingdom, along with those from Australia, New Zealand, and the Republic of Ireland prefer jokes involving word play. On the other hand, people from the United States and Canada prefer superiority-oriented jokes (CNN 2002). This may be a superficial difference however, since word play may be seen as a form of intellectual superiority (Gruner 2000).

Weinberger and Spotts (1989) also found differences in perceptions of humor among U.S. and UK advertising executives. British advertising practitioners were more favorable to the use of humor and, not surprisingly, humor usage levels in the UK were found to be higher than those in the United States. A more recent study found no significant difference in overall humor usage levels between the United States and the UK (28 percent and 33 percent respectively) (Toncar 2001). However, Toncar (2001) found significant differences in the nature of humor use. Ads in the UK were far more likely to make use of understatement while U.S. ads were significantly more likely to use jokes. In the UK, humor played a central role in the ad significantly more often than in the United States and was integrated with the product more often (Toncar 2001).

Global Humor in Advertising

The complexity of humor has intrigued many researchers. As noted earlier, humor is a universal human activity found among all cultures, and throughout all of recorded history (Alden, Hoyer, and Lee 1993). No cultural group has ever been discovered that was devoid of a sense of humor (Kruger 1996). In fact, as mentioned earlier, evidence of humor can even be found in apes (Gamble 2001). Yet, humor is culturally specific as well.

A study of Finnish and American college students' responses to humorous advertisements found no significant differences (Unger 1995). Alternatively, a study comparing Singaporean students with counterparts in Israel and the United States found that although levels of laughter, smiles, and joke telling were similar, Singaporean students demonstrated less usage of humor as a coping mechanism and were less likely to use sexual and aggressive humor (Nevo, Nevo, and Yin 2001). Numerous studies have examined humor in a given country, or compared one culture with another with regard to use of humor (see e.g., Alden, Hoyer, and Lee 1993; Alden and Martin 1995; De Pelsmacker and Geuens 1998; Pornpitakpan and Tan 2000; Taylor, Bonner, and Dolezal 2002).

Perhaps the most informative of the cross-cultural studies is the multicountry investigation conducted by Alden, Hoyer, and Lee (1993). Although the study found use of incongruity in the television advertising in each of the four countries examined, it also found the use of humor in advertising differed across cultures systematically and varied along major cultural dimensions. For example, Thailand and South Korea rate high on Hofstede's power distance dimension (a measure of the degree to which power is distributed unequally) and tend to be hierarchical. Alden, Hoyer, and Lee (1993) found that this hierarchical cultural dimension was reflected in the nature of humorous advertising employed: 63 percent of the humorous ads in these two countries portrayed characters of unequal status. On the other hand, ads in the United States and Germany, cultures that rate low on the power distance dimension, were significantly less likely to portray characters of unequal status. Indeed, 71 percent of the ads in the sample featured equal-status characters. Additionally, 75 percent of the sampled ads in Thailand and South Korea, both collectivist cultures, featured three or more characters, while only 26 percent of the ads in the sample from the Germany and United States, both individualized cultures, featured three or more characters. These findings suggest that use of humor in advertising follows broad cultural characteristics and is another illustration of both the universal yet parochial nature of humor.

Subculture and Ethnicity

Cultural differences with regard to humor do not just occur across national boundaries. Empirical evidence indicates that people of different cultural backgrounds within the same country respond to humor differently. In an experiment that compared Israeli Jews of Eastern and Western descent, Weller and his colleagues found significant differences between the two groups in the appreciation of absurd jokes (Weller, Amitsour, and Pazzi 1976). They posit that these differences are due to "habits of thought and mental attitudes rooted in cultural backgrounds" (163). Similarly, Nevo (1986) found that Israeli Jews and Arabs differed in their perception of humorous events in a manner consistent with other studies. The traditional majority-minority difference was found in which the majority group (Jews) expressed more aggression in humor (Nevo 1986). These findings imply that jokes may not be easily "translatable" between cultures even in a given country. Religion, patois, levels of urbanization, and any number of other barriers exist to cross-cultural humor perception even within the borders of a given nation. In a very diverse multiethnic marketplace like the United States these differences are likely to be manifest strongly with regard to humor. Humor that works in one cultural group may not be appreciated outside of that group. However, humor can, on occasion, cross these boundaries. The award-winning Whassup campaign used by Budweiser in 2000 was based on a short film called *True*. The film, and the first ad of the series, featured a black cast and introduced the catch phrase "whassup." According to Elijah Anderson, expert on urban culture, this informality and unity captures something unique to black people (Fahri 2000). Yet, the ad proved to have broad appeal and became a cultural phenomenon akin to "Where's the beef?" a generation ago.

Summary of Demographic Issues

The perception of humor differs by age, gender, educational level, culture, and subculture. Additionally, these factors influence the perception of humor through the commonality principle (see Figure 3.2). An ethnic joke told by a member of a given ethnic group to an audience consisting of members of the same ethnic group is a high commonality situation. Thus the joke is likely to be perceived as humorous. However, the same joke told by an outsider, one with low perceived commonality, would likely be interpreted as offensive. Therefore much of what is seen as a demographic difference may be an artifact of execution.

Disposition theory posits that the audience's disposition toward the target of the humor and toward the originator of the humor is critical. The commonality principle posited here extends disposition theory in suggesting that the degree of perceived commonality between agent, object, and audience is critical. Thus a humorous ad created by a young white male that used an older black woman as the object of the humor will likely have widely varying effects depending on audience composition. An audience of young white males may find the ad humorous. On the other hand, women, blacks, and older people are not likely to be positively inclined toward the ad. Thus, finding age, gender, or ethnic differences in response to such an ad is almost certain and cannot be interpreted as generalizable humor effects. Although this is an extreme example, all humor research is confounded to some extent by the complex interactions described in this chapter. This is exacerbated by the fact that historically humorous ads were written by young white males in ad agency creative departments. As creative departments in advertising agencies become more diverse it is likely that humorous ads will be created that appeal to a broader audience spectrum.

Psychographic Factors

Need for Cognition

Cacioppo and Petty (1982) identified need for cognition (NFC) as an important personality variable for the understanding of consumer behavior. Cacioppo and his colleagues defined NFC as "an individual's tendency to engage in and enjoy cognitive endeavors" (Cacioppo, Petty, and Kao 1984, 306). Individuals high in NFC follow the central rather than the peripheral route to persuasion (Geuens and De Pelsmacker 2002). High NFC individuals collect more information and process it more thoroughly than individuals low in NFC (Haugtvedt, Petty, and Cacioppo 1992). NFC affects a wide range of human behavior and it has been examined in the context of advertising in general (Haugtvedt, Petty, and Cacioppo 1992) and with specific regard to humor in advertising (Geuens and De Pelsmacker 2002; Zhang 1996). Since high NFC individuals tend to follow the central route of the Elaboration Likelihood Model (ELM) (Cacioppo and Petty 1984), it would seem likely that they would be less influenced by a humorous appeal. Indeed, this is what was found by Zhang (1996). However, in a more recent study Geuens and De Pelsmacker (2002) found no significant interaction between humor and NFC. Given the mixed findings, this appears to be an area where additional research is required.

Self-monitoring

Individuals high in self-monitoring exhibit considerable variation in their behavior based on situational factors (Snyder and Tanke 1976). High self-monitoring individuals take cues from those around them and use these cues to shape their behavior. Lammers (1991) hypothesized that humorous ads would be relatively more successful for individuals high in self-monitoring than for those low in self-monitoring. "High self-monitors, being more concerned about positive images in social situations, may have learned that humor appreciation is adaptive for their social lifestyle" (Lammers 1991, 59). Lammers (1991) found high self-monitoring men, compared to low self-monitoring men, tended to respond favorably to a humorous ad. However, this pattern was reversed in the case of female respondents. Lammers (1991) suggests this result may be partly due to the nature of the humor treatment. The treatment in this study was a humorous recording by the comedy team Dick and Bert Lammers (1991) argues that high self-monitoring women may have been fighting stereotypic views of women being easily persuaded by men. Whether or not this is indeed the reason behind the finding it does reiterate the complex nature of humor research.

Political Ideology

Other audience factors may also affect humor appreciation. For example, conservatism has been shown to be a predictor of response to humor. Subjects rated high on measures of conservatism have been demonstrated to judge incongruity-resolution humor to be funnier than do liberals (Hehl and Ruch 1990; Ruch and Hehl 1986).

Other Individual-Level Factors

Prior Brand or Product Experience

Consumers have a wide range of relationships with existing products: loyal customers, new users, former users, and a myriad of other relationships (see Fournier 1998). The nature of these relationships is likely to affect the perception of a humorous message. For example, Chattopadhyay and Basu (1990) found that humor has greater positive effect, with regard to persuasion, for those audience members with a prior positive brand attitude. Since the advertiser is the ultimate humor agent, these findings are consistent with dispositional theory (see Figure 3.3). In other words, since consumers are positively

Figure 3.3 **Factors Influencing the Perception of Humor**

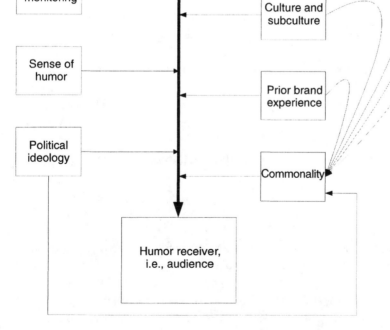

disposed to the source, in this case the product as a proxy for the advertiser, they are positively disposed to the humor. Other product-related issues can also affect the success of humorous advertising. These issues are discussed in Chapter 4.

Individual Sense of Humor

Response to a humorous ad is likely to differ based on humor-specific audience variables. Individuals differ in their senses of humor. There are numerous scales designed to measure sense of humor. However, these scales are typically plagued by self-report bias since people typically rate their own sense of humor as above average (Moran and Massam 1999). Valid measurement of sense of humor in an advertising context is fraught with problems. Costley and her colleagues posit that measuring sense of humor may be similar to measuring past equity returns: Both can describe what happened in the past, but provide little insight as to what will be funny or profitable in the future (Costley, Koslow, and Galloway 2002).

A different approach to examining individual-level difference with regard to humor was introduced by Cline (1997). Cline (1997) developed the "need for levity" scale (NFL). NFL represents an individual's craving for humor (amusement, wit, nonsense) and whimsy (caprice, spontaneity, free-spiritedness) (Cline, Altsech, and Kellaris 2003). The NFL has four dimensions: internal humor, external humor, internal whimsy, and external whimsy (Cline, Altsech, and Kellaris 2003). The humor portion of the measure, NFH, consists of the internal and external humor measures. Internal humor is the need to generate humor, while external humor is the need to experience humor from external sources (Cline, Altsech, and Kellaris 2003). Cline and his colleagues found that NFH moderated responses to humorous advertising (Cline, Altsech, and Kellaris 2003). NFL and the NFH subscales may prove to be important individual-level variables with regard to understanding humor effects.

Paradox of Humor

Humor is a paradox. It is universal and it is individualized. It is found in every culture throughout history, and yet it is specific to time and place. Laughter is social, yet humor is personal. While humor is a natural human trait, response to specific humor executions is a learned behavior. In fact, a study of twins found that differences in perception of humor were due entirely

Figure 3.4 **Audience Factors and the Challenge Model**

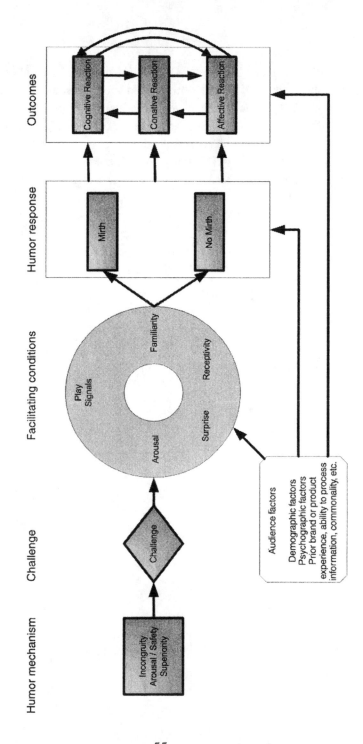

Humor mechanism   Challenge   Facilitating conditions   Humor response   Outcomes

to environmental factors—genetic factors did not appear to play any role (Viegas 2000). Sense of humor differs from most personality traits in this regard (Muir 2000). Thus, humor cannot be examined in isolation from an audience. Indeed, as noted earlier, the audience is the final arbiter of humor. Although an advertiser can decide all the details of a given ad execution, s/he cannot "decide" that an ad will be funny. Only the audience can decide whether an attempt at humor will result in the perception of humor. The transition from an attempt to a success in humor is affected by a wide range of executional as well as audience factors (see Figure 3.3).

Finally, there is a link between the audience factors and the challenge model (see Figure 3.4) introduced in Chapter 2 that serves as a reminder in this and subsequent chapters about the variables under consideration and their relationship to the model as a whole.

Note

1. The use of the term *agency* in this sense should not be confused with an advertising agency. To the viewer of an ad, the source is the advertiser. The extent to which an advertising agency is involved is not relevant.

—— 4 ——

Media and Humor

We know that context surrounding an ad may have an impact on how it is processed and on its effectiveness. We devote an entire chapter later in this book to this topic of context (Chapter 7), but one key aspect broadly related to context is the medium that delivers the message. It should not at all be surprising that the use and impact of humor in advertising may vary in different media because the media themselves bring features that cause us to process information differently. Herbert Krugman notes that broadcast media tend to be processed more passively where we tend to listen or watch passively and with relatively low defensive radar (Krugman 1966; Krugman and Hartley 1970). Additionally, in broadcast media the pacing of the message is governed by the radio or TV programming, with the audience's ability and/ or motivation to process the message limited by this imposed pacing. Also, in contrast to print advertisements, commercials on radio and TV are quite intrusive and there is greater opportunity for forcing exposure on the audience. To Krugman involvement with advertising in broadcast ads is lower involvement, and with "the pace of the experience or rate of stimulation out of the individual's control, there is relatively low opportunity for connections, for dwelling on a point of advertising" (584). Krugman argues that in print media we are more actively involved based upon the need to engage our brains to read and turn pages. Perhaps this leads to a higher level of motivation to process, but by its nature, print is a medium with greater audience choice in advertising exposure. From the standpoint of an advertiser, because of this greater self-selection by the audience, there is less opportunity in print for broad intrusive exposure to a message.

The remainder of this chapter blends expert opinion, analysis, and research about the use and impact of humor in different media. We first look at media strengths and weaknesses in relation to where humor has the best chance to work. This approach (see Table 4.1) considers broad qualities such as Krugman's view of media pacing and attentiveness to subjectively assess each medium. Along the top of the table are media qualities signified by pace, clutter/distraction, and intrusiveness; audience qualities of motivation to process and active audience involvement; and finally tools to develop humor. A summary humor favorability rating, on the far right of the table, is a qualitative result of all the other features along the top of the table. Here TV and radio receive the highest overall scores. With these two media we have the ideal conditions with low-audience motivation to process messages, passive audience involvement, fast media pacing (leading to less ability to process messages), high clutter, and distraction. These are the classic low involvement situations where a peripheral cue like humor should have its best chance at success. At the same time, TV and radio provide an extensive arsenal of dynamic creative tools to develop and execute humor and allow nuances to play out. The result for TV and radio are ✓✓ + and ✓✓ scores respectively, indicating positive preconditions for humor.

Slightly less favorable are conditions in consumer magazines, outdoor, and Internet pop-ups, all of which receive scores of ✓–. Media such as business and trade publications, catalogs, direct mail, and Internet Web sites by contrast receive scores of 0. Here the audience either has a prior motivation to seek the message, in which case humor for attention-getting purposes is less important, or the nature of the products advertised is generally not as likely to fit with a humor appeal. The implication is that the contextual conditions and characteristics of the medium provide only a neutral environment for humor to work. It can work, but will be used much less often and more selectively.

Using Humor in Different Media

Unfortunately, there is only sparse research comparing the actual use and effectiveness of humor in advertising between different media. In comparison to the range of media listed in Table 4.1, published and publicly available studies of humor and media are rare and have only examined a few media.

Madden and Weinberger (1984) and Weinberger and Spotts (1989) surveyed advertising research and creative executives in the top 150 agencies in the United States and the UK about their views on the use of humor. A particular result of that study has a bearing on humor and media. The executives overwhelmingly felt that TV (84 percent) and radio (88 percent) were best suited to the use of humor, while they gave other advertising media much

Table 4.1

Media Factors Affecting Humor Usage

Media category	Motivation to process	Pace	Active audience involvement	Clutter/distraction	Intrusiveness	Tools to develop humor	Summary for humor
TV	Low (+)	Fast (+)	Low (+)	High (+)	High (+)	High (+)	√√+
Radio	Low (+)	Fast (+)	Low (+)	High (+)	High (+)	Moderate (0)	√√
Consumer magazine	Low (+)	Slow (0)	Low-Moderate (+/0)	Moderate-High (+/0)	Moderate-High (+/0)	Low (−)	√−
Outdoor	Low (+)	Fast (+)	Low (+)	High (+)	High (+)	Low (−)	√−
Internet pop-ups	Low (+)	Fast (+)	Low (+)	Moderate-High (+/0)	High (+)	Moderate (0)	√−
Newspaper	Low-Moderate (0)/(+)	Slow (0)	Low-Moderate (+/0)	Moderate-High (+/0)	Moderate-High (+/0)	Low (−)	0/√−

(continued)

59

Table 4.1 (continued)

Media category	Motivation to process	Pace	Active audience involvement	Clutter/ distraction	Intrusiveness	Tools to develop humor	Summary for humor
Business and trade publications	Moderate (0)	Slow (0)	Moderate (0)	Low-Moderate (−/0)	Moderate (0)	Low (−)	0
Catalog	Moderate-High (0)/(−)	Slow (0)	High (0/−)	High (+)	Low (−)	Low (−)	0
Direct mail	Low (+)	Slow (0)	Low (+)	Moderate-High (+/0)	Moderate (0)	Low (−)	0
Internet Web site	Moderate	Slow	High	Moderate	Low	Moderate to high (limited by bandwidth issues) (0)	0+
	(0)	(0)	(−)	(0)	(−)	(0)	0+

less support (outdoor, 40 percent; magazine, 39 percent; newspaper, 29 percent; and direct mail, 22 percent). This practitioner view is interesting and consistent with the analysis in Table 4.1. Both provide useful starting points, but neither provides actual evidence of humor's use and performance in different media.

The first part of the question we wish to address is, does the frequency of humor used vary by media type? Research on this matter is limited aside from Weinberger et al. (1995). Their work is the most comprehensive examination of humor in different ad media. They studied magazines, TV, and radio. Their result supports the responses obtained from the surveys of advertising executives noted above. Radio advertising used humor over 30 percent of the time and TV ads over 24 percent. As predicted from the executive survey, magazines ads used humor far less, in just 9.9 percent of all ads. A more recent study (of just *Fortune, Time,* and *New Woman*) found that TV ads used humor 26.22 percent of the time and magazines just 4.95 percent (Catanescu and Tom 2001). This magazine percentage is significantly lower than the earlier study probably because *Fortune* and *Time* tend to be serious publications and advertise products that use humor infrequently. All the results are consistent with the analysis in Table 4.1.

Percy (1997) identifies brand awareness (recognition and recall) as key communication effects in "need arousal," "information search and evaluation," and "purchase" stages of the decision process. Humor, whether delivered through pictures or words, has its greatest effect precisely on brand awareness. Television and radio advertising are both highly attention getting because of production values and the combination of their intrusive nature and the fact that they are action media. In addition, Percy suggests that TV is effective for obtaining both "recognition awareness" and "recall awareness." The absence of visuals in radio is a handicap with recognition awareness but recall awareness is an objective where radio does help. Thus, from an attention and awareness perspective, it is not surprising to find a high percentage of ads in TV and radio using humor. Magazine and newspaper ads require active reader participation, and as a result do not command attention as effectively as TV and magazines, though there is opportunity for some recognition-awareness for both through visual presentations. Recall awareness may be fostered with repetition of advertising in daily newspapers.

Perhaps the devices to execute humor in print are more limited and the fundamental philosophy of using print may be different. It is also possible that Krugman's view of higher-involvement print media may diminish the impact of peripheral and generally nonessential cues like humor, making it less effective because audience processing is more intense and selective. Further, as suggested in Table 4.1, humor is harder to execute in print because of fewer tools in the executional arsenal. In addition, its impact on the audience may be neutralized through more vigilant processing. Such differences would explain the enormous disparity in usage found between magazines versus radio and TV.

Of course we have looked at a very narrow set of media for which there is some hard evidence of significant humor usage. But what about outdoor, direct media and advertising or the fast-emerging Internet? Unfortunately, there are no parallel studies that have tracked the usage of humor in these other media. Instead we only have the speculation of industry observers. Take for example this from a story by direct marketer Beth Negus Viveiros (2003).

> Did you hear the one about the copywriter who created hilarious direct mail packages . . . ? If you said no, don't feel left out of the loop. Humor is one of the classic taboos of DM copywriting, a tactic felt best left to general advertisers and late-night talk show hosts. While some marketers—like the political magazine *The Nation*—have been able to get a giggle and a response, the traditional mantra that funny does not equal money remains.

The writer attempts to combat the taboo but she laments that the notion that humor cannot be effective in direct marketing is false. "Often, humor isn't used even where one might expect it. New York–based Corporate Comics creates comic books for clients to use as promotional tools and mailing pieces. But even in 'funny books' like these, humor is a rarity, utilized more to make a point about the client's competition rather than as a main theme" (Viveiros 2003).

Quoting some leading names in the industry, Viveiros (2003) points out common misgivings about humor in direct mail. "People don't really care about making something funny," says Joe Kolman, publisher of Corporate Comics. "They care about making something that sells." Another cautions that those who delve into humor also need to take care not to look silly. "People who depend on humor for impact often lapse into foolishness, talking dogs, desperate novelties. These are attention-getters, but they are poor salespeople," he says. "The relationship between gaining attention and actually marketing is one of stopping somebody on the street and actually selling them something. It's an introductory proposition" (Viveiros 2003).

"Humor is very subjective, and if [your audience] doesn't get the joke, or it annoys or offends them in some way, you've really done damage," agrees copywriter Ken Scheck. "It's hard enough to get people to read direct mail, and if you annoy or offend them, you're making a hard task even more diffi-cult" (Viveiros 2003).

As for clients, they do not usually welcome the idea of humor. "You have to hit the nail pretty well, and then sometimes you have to sell the idea," says Scheck, because the campaign is very serious to them. "They don't want you writing jokes."

This skeptical view of using humor in direct mail is of course consistent with the survey of practitioners cited earlier where only 22 percent felt hu-mor and direct mail was a good match. In Table 4.1 we give direct mail a neutral grade of 0 along with trade publications and catalogs, while we scored Internet Web sites 0+. Extrapolating from the survey of practitioners and the content analysis of Weinberger et al. (1995), if statistics were available, we would expect the use of humor in these media to be less than in magazines, and probably in the 5 to 8 percent range or lower. As a relatively new advertising medium, the Internet may see increasing use of humor. The Web has the poten-tial to use the tools available to television and radio and add interactivity. Some advertisers have begun to harness the potential of the Web for humor. Ameri-can Express produced a series of short films featuring Jerry Seinfeld with an animated Superman that were available only on its Web site. Burger King de-veloped the "subservient chicken." This Web site featured a man in a chicken costume who would appear to respond to the visitor's commands. The Web has also become a source of "viral ads." Typically these are humorous ads that often push the limits of taste. Although these ads are often disavowed by the associated advertiser (see Chapter 9 for a discussion of the Ford Ka ads), it appears that some have been tacitly approved and allowed to "slip out."

Another medium that has not been formally studied but where the indica-tors for the use of humor appear relatively strong is outdoor. In Table 4.1 we give outdoors a ✓–. From the 1930s to the 1950s, Burma Shave signs across America used the power of word play to create humorous and memorable ads that have become advertising icons. There are numerous examples of hu-morous award-winning outdoor ads posted on the Outdoor Advertising Association's Web site. The Chick-fil-A and Virgin Atlantic ads (Exhibits 4.1 and 4.2) are both wonderfully playful and humorous examples of the use of humor in outdoor advertising. Practitioners rated outdoor and magazines as virtually identical in their suitability for using humor. In Table 4.1 outdoor has all the same preconditions as TV and radio for humor with the exception of fewer "tools to develop humor." Unlike TV or radio, there is no ability to generate humor with audio or with the dynamic interaction of characters. On the other hand, words, color, and pictures provide a considerable opportunity

Exhibit 4. **Chick-fil-A**

"Eat Mor Chikin" cow campaign for Chick-fil-A restaurants. Used by permission. The cows and "Eat Mor Chikin" are registered trademarks of Chick-fil-A Properties, Inc.

Exhibit 4.2 Virgin Atlantic

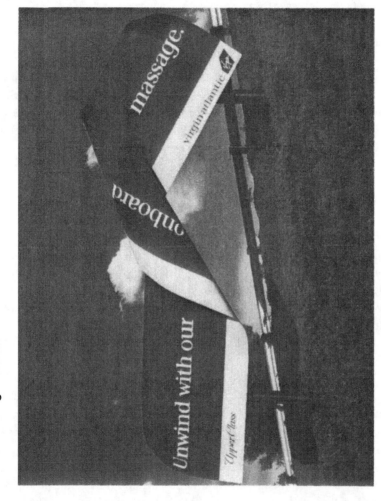

Virgin Atlantic Airways/Agency: BBDO Net#Work.

to capitalize on the similar preconditions that favor TV and radio. The ✓– for outdoor is a relatively strong rating and similar to consumer magazines, whose use of humor overall is in the 10 percent range and as high as 18 percent for lower-risk/frequently purchased/experiential products. If we had available a survey of humor for outdoor, we might expect similar or higher usage levels, particularly for product categories such as alcohol.

Where Is Humor Effective?

We have addressed the issue of the amount of humor used, but the bigger issue of its impact is quite another. What "impact" means is itself a nontrivial question that can be addressed by any number of metrics ranging from attention, affect, recall, comprehension, beliefs, liking, attitudes, or actual behavior. Given this array of potential effects the evidence to date about the impact of humor in advertising is extremely limited. In Table 4.2 we provide a broad overview of thirty-three published studies that have tested humor in four different media. Most of the studies are from controlled laboratory studies, but there are a few that used industry data with their time-tested measures examined across a large pool of products and audiences. As we can see, with the exception of Markiewicz's dissertation in 1972, serious empirical investigations in the public domain about the impact of humor in advertising really did not begin until the 1980s. Even Sternthal and Craig's 1973 review of humor in advertising was based almost entirely on related work in non-advertising settings and on results from a proprietary industry study.

Print

There are ten print studies listed in Table 4.2, most of which are controlled laboratory experiments. Two of the ten studies used industry data collected by Roper/Starch in the form of several post-exposure measures of recall/ attention and held attention in their three primary measures of Noted, Associated, and Read Most. There is a significant positive effect of humor over the general pool of ads in the same publications and for the same products as registered on their measures of Noted (0.96) and Read Most (1.37) (attention and held attention), and a negative impact on the Associated (–0.83) (recall comprehension) measure. The general result is that humor in magazine ads enhances attention (Noted and Read Most) but appears to hinder comprehension. The impact of humor is more nuanced when product and type of ad (humor or message dominant) is used, as we will see in chapters 5 and 6. The

Table 4.2

Studies of Humor Effects in Different Media

Magazines	Television	Radio	Direct mail
M1. Brooker (1981) 0 Persuasion (mild humor) + Source liking (weak)	T1. Murphy, Cunningham, and Wilcox (1979) + Unaided ad recall (in serious program) – Unaided product recall 0 Aided recall	R1. Cantor and Venus (1980) – Comprehension	DM1. Markiewicz (1972) + Persuasion (of soft sell messages)
M2. Madden and Weinberger (1982)[a] + Attention – Recall of brand	**T2. McCollum/Spielman (1982)[a] + Attention, persuasion	R2. Madden (1982) + Attention, persuasion, comprehension (related humor only)	DM2. Gelb and Pickett (1983) + A_{ad}, credibility, source liking, intent
M3. Sutherland and Middleton (1983) 0 Recall + Attention – Credibility	T3. Belch and Belch (1984) 0 Unaided recall, persuasion + Source liking	R3. Lammers, Libowitz, Seymour, and Hennesey (1983) Comprehension + Persuasion, source liking (males not females)	DM3. Scott, Klein, and Bryant (1990) + Behavior (for social events)
M4. Wu, Crocker, and Rogers (1989) + Attention + Comprehension (high involvement) 0 Source liking	T4. Stewart-Hunter (1985) 0 Recall (brand name)	R4. Duncan, Nelson, and Frontczak (1984) + Comprehension	
M5. Smith (1993) + A_{ad}, A_b (with weaker claims)	T5. Stewart and Furse (1986)[a] + Attention, comprehension	R5. Duncan and Nelson (1985) + Attention, source liking 0 Persuasion	

(continued)

67

Table 4.2 (continued)

Magazines	Television	Radio	Direct mail
M6. Zhang (1996) + A_{ad}, A_b (low need for cognition)	T6. Speck (1987) + Attention, comprehension, persuasion (3 of 5 measures), source liking (4 of 5 measures)	R6. Gelb and Zinkhan (1986) – Recall + Source liking, A_b 0 Intent	
M7. Spotts, Weinberger, and Parsons (1997)[a] + Attention (yellow and white goods) + Recall (brand) (yellow goods)	T7. Chattopadhyay and Basu (1990) + Persuasion, source liking (prior favorable brand attitude)	R7. Weinberger and Campbell (1991)[a] + Recall (related humor)	
M8. Cline and Kellaris (1999) + A_{ad}, A_b (with weaker arguments)	T8. Zhang and Zinkhan (1991) + Recall, source liking	R8. Flaherty, Weinberger, and Gulas (2004) + A_{ad}, A_b (when humor perceived)	
M9. Geuens and DePelsmacker (2002) + A_{ad} (if not irritating but cheerful and interesting)	T9. Unger (1995) + A_{ad}, A_b		
M10. Cline, Altsech, and Kellaris (2003) + A_{ad}, A_b, Affect, less CA	T10. Alden, Mukherjee, and Hoyer (2000) + A_{ad} T11. Chung and Zhao (2003) + Memory (recall) low-involvement goods T12. Woltman-Elpers, Mukherjee, and Hoyer (2004) + Surprise (late)		

[a]Studies using standard industry data from commercial research firms.

eight laboratory studies show a positive impact on attention, A_{ad} (attitude toward the ad), A_b (attitude toward the brand), and source liking. There are mixed results for the various recall/comprehension measures, no effect in one study that examined persuasion, and a negative impact on credibility.

Radio

There are eight humor studies that used radio as the test medium. Just one study (part of a larger radio study by Weinberger, Campbell, and Brody 1994) used syndicated industry data from Radio Recall Inc.'s forty-eight-hour methodology. The conclusion is that humor enhances attention (Execution Recall). In contrast, the measure of comprehension (Recall Index, including five sub-measures of recall), shows a net negative impact when compared to non-humor. Thus, at this global media level, there is evidence that radio ad humor enhances attention and may harm comprehension. The eight laboratory studies support the use of humor to enhance attention, source liking, A_{ad}, and A_b. There is mixed support for enhancing recall (comprehension) and no support for persuasion (intent).

Television

The evidence for humor in TV ads is also good overall, but comes from just the two studies using industry data. The results show an overall gain for attention (Clutter/Awareness) with rather neutral results for persuasion (attitude shift). McCollum/Spielman's *Topline* summarizes tests of hundreds of ads and concludes that humor is an aid when Clutter/Awareness scores are the benchmark (exceeding the norms 75 percent of the time), but attitude shift was less than the norm for humorous ads. Similarly, Stewart and Furse (1986), using 1,000 ads tested by Research Systems Corporation (RSC), show that humor in TV ads positively influences recall and comprehension but not persuasion (no impact). In comparison to the myriad list of executional factors, humor has the strongest impact of all on recall (standardized beta 0.21). When predicting comprehension of an ad message, humor was the second strongest feature (next to brand-differentiating message), with a standardized beta of 0.11. Both the *Topline* and Stewart and Furse studies employed standard industry measures of commercial impact using either actual ads or developmental versions of actual ads. The results of both studies suggest that humor in TV ads has a good chance at aiding recall and comprehension but not persuasion. The other ten TV studies of humor used laboratory tests by individual researchers. Some of these studies tested actual commercials run by advertisers while other studies developed ads specifically for the research project. The results are largely favorable for humor enhancing attention, source liking, A_{ad}, A_b, and persuasion. Results for recall (comprehension) varied depending on the measures used but generally humor either helped or had no impact compared to non-humor. Finally, Woltman-Elpers, Mukherjee, and Hoyer (2004) studied moment-to-moment reactions to TV ads and found that the peaks in perceived surprise just preceded the peaks in perception of humor. Unfortunately, there is no evidence in their study of an examination of connections between humor and higher order outcomes, such liking, A_{ad}, A_b, or persuasion.

Direct Mail

The least studied of the four media listed here is direct mail, with just three published papers. The first was part of Markiewicz's pioneering humor dissertation in 1972 in which a series of small experiments was conducted. Just one of the studies used direct mail and in it she found that humor aided persuasion when combined with a soft-sell message. Gelb and Pickett (1983) found that humor enhanced source liking. Finally, in a structured field test of humor in a direct mail context, Scott, Klein, and Bryant (1990) examined the use of humorous versus non-humorous appeals in community flyers placed in mailboxes. The humor studies of magazine, radio, and TV cited above all employed standard industry data collected by professional research firms. This study of direct mail was a one-time test by investigators trying to determine if humor relevant to an event could increase behavior (attendance). It is the sole study among all those dealing with the media that looks at a behavioral measure of performance rather than measures of attention, recall, comprehension, or persuasion. Each of three field sites tested attendance at a local social or business event. The results indicate the effective use of humor influenced attendance at all three social events but had no impact on the business events. Use of humor in direct mail for an appropriate (nonserious) situation worked while the serious business events did not. This is consistent with the survey of advertising experts cited earlier that recommended against the use of humor for serious products, and also supports direct mail experts who advocate the positive impact of humor for appropriate products.

Do not try to bring humor into the following situations: insurance, loans, health issues, management decisions. Your first reaction may be: 'What

Figure 4.1 **Media Factors and the Challenge Model**

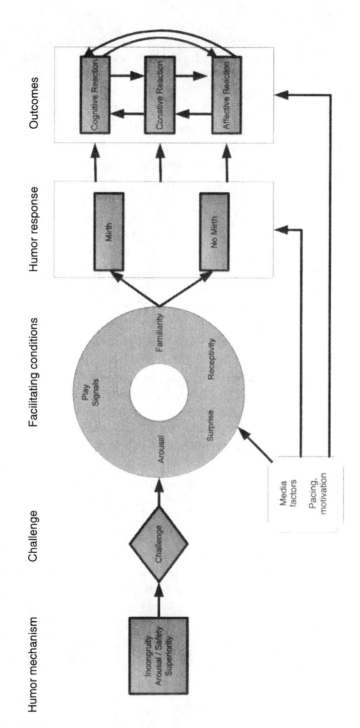

about the Geico commercials?' Yes, they're quite humorous, and yes they have an 800#, but they're more branding than direct response. Take a look at Geico's direct mail—the humor has almost totally disappeared, replaced by tried (and tired) direct mail techniques" (Stein 2002).

Despite the limited support from the several studies of humor with direct mail, there is a long history of taboo against it. Stein (2002) notes that in *2,239 Tested Secrets for Direct Marketing Success,* published in 1998, Denny Hatch and Don Jackson just about avoid the subject totally. There are just three entries dealing with the subject: Milt Pierce, in his "30 Questions to Ask Before Submitting Copy," asks "Is your copy funny or cute? (Avoid humor at all costs)." Craig Huey simply says "Don't use humor." However, Barbara Harrison in her "Break the Rules: Rules of Effective Direct Mail Copywriting" comments "Humor is usually risky, but can prove highly effective."

The direct mail business is replete with stories about success and failure of humor from adamant statements that humor on a mail package will always lose to one without humor, all the way to amazing reports of persistent response rates as high as 100 percent and doubled sales of some products with the use of cartoons. It is puzzling to direct mail creatives who have used humor effectively that many in the industry are still reciting the old "never use humor" rule popularized decades ago by David Ogilvy, Bob Stone, and John Caples. Though there are only a few academic studies of humor in direct mail, the results there are all positive, giving further credibility to the practitioners who advocate using humor such as Stein (2002).

The results of this mini-feud about the efficacy of humor in direct mail highlights the broader questions about humor. What we do know about humor is that its use in different media varies quite widely and that the conditions for its use and execution are more favorable in broadcast than in print. However, at this stage, it is folly to make intractable statements for or against the use of humor in any medium because there is probably more that we do not know than what we have revealed about the impact of humor in different media. Other contingencies related to the product, message, context, and audience all play a role in determining humor's efficacy. All these topics we address in this book.

Finally, Figure 4.1 attempts to visually link the media factors considered in this chapter to the challenge model introduced in Chapter 2.

——— 5 ———

Product Type and Humor

The frequent use of humor in advertising and the tens of billions of dollars spent on executing and placing it in media make it seem that humor is used by almost every advertiser. But is this true, and if so, is humor equally effective for different products? In general, it is well understood in advertising message research that the type of product interacts with executional factors in an ad to affect advertising impact (Stewart and Furse 1986; Sewall and Sarel 1986). This fact has started to be recognized in humor research, which has found that there are large differences in both the use and impact of humor for different products in advertising. For instance, in television advertising Toncar (2001) estimated that in the United States between 21 percent and 48 percent of ads for different products used a humor strategy. Madden and Weinberger (1984) surveyed advertising research and creative executives in the top 150 U.S. agencies about their views on the use of humor and found that only consumer nondurables received strong support for being well suited to humor (70 percent). Using humor with business services, durables, retail advertising, and industrial products received support from between only 24 percent to 37 percent of the executives. In addition, a high percentage of executives expressed the view that such products were specifically ill suited to using humor. The categories with the largest mention from open-ended responses were all consumer nondurables including soft drinks, alcohol products, snacks, and candy. Bauerly (1990) asked consumers directly about the appropriateness of humor with goods and services. The products that were viewed as appropriate were soft drinks, snack foods, computers, automobiles, beer, bowling alleys, restaurants, diaper services, overnight delivery services, and exterminator services. Inappropriate products were laxatives, feminine care products, condoms, cemetery monuments, higher education, and financial and medical services. Nondurable goods are precisely the group of products that Toncar (2001) and Weinberger and Spotts (1989) identified as having the highest usage of TV humor in both the United States and the

UK. The more durable products like computers and automobiles and a business service like overnight delivery cited by Bauerly (1990) may indicate a greater receptivity to using humor in these higher risk and functional categories than has been predicted. In the remainder of this chapter, we examine the conceptual scheme that drives the use of humor and the relative effectiveness of humor when used with different products. We conclude the chapter with other product-related factors that influence the effectiveness of humor with different products.

An ELM Explanation of How Humor Works in Advertising

Though it is important to know how humor is developed, it is as critical for advertisers to understand how humor works on consumers. There has been ongoing discussion in the marketing and humor literature for at least thirty years about how audiences process information. A debate about high and low involvement led to recognition that there is not a one-size-fits-all model. This same pattern persisted in the early humor literature as well, with broad generalizations about how much humor was used and its strengths and deficiencies. Starting in the late 1980s a more situational approach to decision making was developed in the behavioral literature, which spread into advertising strategy and the analysis of humor.

A traditional behavioral perspective, based on a cognitive processing approach more or less following a classic hierarchy of effects perspective, anchored one end of the contingency continuum. The situations in which this approach dominates are in high involvement and high-personal-relevance rational decisions. Here audiences would be more motivated to process information.

At the opposite extreme are decision situations where audiences have a low motivation and perhaps low ability to process communication. The traditional hierarchy of decision making may be reversed and processing is after the fact. A noncognitive theory accounting for this decision making is found in classical learning theory. Applied to music, several researchers (Gorn 1982; Shimp, Stewart, and Rose 1991) have found that effects on attitudes and behavior can occur simply through associating a pleasant stimulus with an unconditioned stimulus. Even in low involvement or low-personal-relevance situations, the simple pairing of humor with an ad and product might operate below a threshold of awareness in much the way that Krugman (1962) suggested that low-involvement learning could occur. Further, thirty years of research (Zajonc 1980; Bornstein 1989) has shown that mere repeated exposure to a stimulus can have a positive impact on liking of the stimulus itself. "The compelling evidence that people have positive affective responses toward stimuli they cannot remember having seen suggests that ads receiving limited attention may nonetheless be effective agents of attitude change" (Janiszewski 1993).

The ELM (elaboration likelihood model) developed by Cacioppo and Petty, and reported in a series of studies (see, e.g., Cacioppo and Petty 1984), is a model of persuasion developed in the 1980s to resolve many of the apparent inconsistencies in the literature. Their contingency model examined the interface between the audience and the message and takes into account the high-personal-relevance setting where the audience is motivated and able to process information as well as the low-motivation situation described above. In the ELM framework the motivation and ability to process a message would vary in the audience while the message could be either focused on the attributes of the persuasion object or on message elements that are secondary to the message. In its simplest form we would have highly motivated audiences with a high ability to process information geared for what the ELM labels "central route" processing. This scenario would be matched with messages dominated by information that would feed this desire from the audience. On the other extreme of this simplified dichotomy would be an audience with a low motivation to process and a low ability to engage in more than peripheral processing using peripheral cues that are not central to the message itself. Such cues as cartoon characters, music, humor, and celebrities could, the ELM argues, help influence the audience in the absence of motivation for more substantive information.

Of course, extreme central processing or extreme peripheral processing exists on a continuum. For humor, and the other peripheral cues, the ELM posits their effect most clearly in the low-motivation/low-ability situation. Weinberger et al. (1995) examined the use and effectiveness of humor on ad recall and recognition for situations that can be conceived as lower or higher motivation to process. Advertisers tend to use more peripheral cues in these lower motivation situations (Spotts, Weinberger, and Parsons 1997; Toncar 2001). Moreover, ads that use humor in a dominant rather than as a supportive role work best in situations where there is the lowest motivation to process ad information. This is consistent with an ELM framework. Further, for these low-motivation situations humor that is embedded in the verbal part of a message-dominant ad detracts from the recognition scores. By the same token, for these same low-motivation situations, humor related to the products and delivered mainly through visual rather than verbal means (image-focused versus message-dominant humor) is very effective for both extremely low-motivation-product situations. Thus, the humor works to aid recognition scores either in situations where the humor dominates or in situations where humor is executed visually in ads that use humor in a secondary role (ad is dominated by a message). In this low-motivation situation, humor used in a secondary role, where the ad is message- and information-focused (rather than visual), is related to somewhat lower recognition scores.

This does not preclude humor from aiding persuasion in high-motivation situations, but its role is to enhance the fun attributes or image of the product so that it is related to the desired image of the product in some fashion. Thus, the humor cue itself becomes an attribute associated with the product. Humor would not be expected to shine at its best in a high-motivation-to-process situation where there is little information and where humor dominates. On the other hand, humor may buttress product or image attributes in these high-motivation situations by acting as a cue itself.

Over the past twenty plus years several behaviorally oriented product typologies have been developed that attempt to recognize the critical underpinnings of the ELM framework, high/low involvement, and some aspect of low and high hedonic value (Vaughn 1980: 1986; Rossiter, Percy, and Donovan 1991; Wells 1989; Weinberger, Campbell, and Brody 1994). Each of the frameworks is built around a matrix in which there is a high-low involvement continuum. The operational definition of low and high varies, but the types of products classified in the upper and lower halves of the matrices are quite consistent. The functionality dimension in these product grids (also referred to as purchase motivations) has considerable consistency across schemes. In each matrix, one half of the decision making involves high functional value and is labeled either "think" or "informational." The other half is high in hedonic value and is labeled "feel," "emotional," "expressive," or "transformational." The point in all of the matrix typologies is that the classifications capture important aspects of consumer decision making. The classification of a particular product or brand is aided by the characteristics of the decision making surrounding it. Table 5.1 is a compilation of features that assist in the classification of a product into one of the four product color matrix (PCM) cells illustrated in Table 5.2.

To be most effective, promotional messages should acknowledge these differences in involvement and hedonic value. The product matrix is presented to highlight the differences between products that need to be considered when developing advertising and humor in particular. The PCM draws on the ELM theory and adds a metaphor of color to highlight the meaning of

Table 5.1

Product Characteristics Within Cells of the Product Color Matrix (PCK)

Product color	Product risk	Purchase motivation	Consumption motives	Emotional benefits	Motivation to process	Focused attention	Processing style	Product type
White "big tools"	Higher	Negative	Functional/rational orientation	Some/long-term	Higher	High	System	Durable/ shopping
Red "big toys"	Higher	Positive	Expressive orientation/usually conspicuous	Many/long-term	Higher	High	Systematic	Durable— nondurable/ often luxury
Blue "little tools"	Lower	Negative	Functional/rational orientation	Few to none/ short-term	Low to moderate	Low	Heuristic	Nondurable/ staple
Yellow "little treats"	Lower	Positive	Expressive orientation/may be conspicuous	Some/short-term	Low	Low	Heuristic	Nondurable/ often impulse

Table 5.2

The Product Color Matrix (PCM) and Prototype Products

Consumer objective	Functional/tools	Expressive/toys
Higher risk	Cell 1 "white goods"	Cell 2 "red goods"
	Bigger tools	Bigger toys
	Large appliances	Fashion clothing and
	Typical cars	accessories
	Business equipment	Hair coloring
	Insurance	Motorcycle
	Auto tires	Sports car
		Fashion luggage
		Jewelry
Lower risk	Cell 3 "blue goods"	Cell 4 "yellow goods"
	Little tools	Little treats
	Detergents and household	Snack foods
	cleaners	Desserts
	OTC remedies	Beer
	Motor oil and gas	Alcohol
	Most non-dessert foods	Tobacco products

products. The colors white, red, blue, and yellow are used as shorthand for the exemplar products that represent each portion of the grid. Along one dimension of the PCM is a "functional tools" versus "expressive toys" dimension and along the other is a low-versus high-risk dimension. Among the products in the low-risk dimension, involvement is lower because many decisions are routine, lower cost, and/or not worth the effort. In the ELM framework these are ads where audiences have a lower motivation or need to process information. Along the "tool and toys" dimension, products filling more functional needs are contrasted with those filling more expressive needs, like wants and rewards (e.g., have hedonic value, emotional benefits, or more positive purchase motivations). A tool is an implement that helps us accomplish a task and achieve a goal, such as safety, health, cleanliness, and work completion (e.g., have less hedonic value or emotional benefits, or have negative purchase motivations). A toy is consumed for its sensory and pleasure-fulfilling properties.

Using the product color matrix, cell 1 is "white" (see Table 5.2). The white product is higher risk, often but not always based on price, and is a "big tool" product that fills a functional need. Refrigerators, washer/dryers, and other such appliances are the prototypical examples of white goods. They are durable and expensive, requiring consumers to shop and compare because of the risk involved with the choice. Of course, other products such as insurance, some automobiles, and many nonroutine business products would also be among the products in this cell. From an information-processing perspective, consumers evaluating white products should have the highest level of motivation to process and attention focused on the ad and the largest amount of working memory allocated to constructive processes, resulting in self-generated persuasion (MacInnis and Jaworski 1989). There are likely to be few emotional product benefits, and executions would be rationally dominant. A typical white good ad using humor is the Volvo ad (see Exhibit 5.1). Here a well-known brand subtly reinforces its well-known safety theme with related humor.

Cell 2 of the product color matrix consists of what are labeled "red" products. Red is chosen because it symbolizes flamboyance and is expressive, and so too are the products that are represented here. The sports car, the motorcycle, the red dress, fancy tie, jewelry, and other conspicuous products representing the individual and having higher risk are red goods. The white and red goods of cell 1 and cell 2 have high risk in common. However, for the white goods the high risk might be dominated by significant financial risk while the red goods are likely to have social as well as financial risk. The BMW ad in Exhibit 5.2 is for a luxury high-performance car, a red product. The humorous incongruity reinforces this car as a male fantasy object even more powerful than sex with a beautiful woman. The use of humor for red products is unusual. What is not unusual is that, like many ads with humorous intent, this ad by D'Adda, Lorenzini, Vigorelli, BBDO, Milan, Italy, is likely to be entertaining to some and highly offensive to others. This aspect of humorous advertising will be addressed in Chapter 9.

White goods are "big tools" while red goods are "big toys." While white goods satisfy a functional goal, red goods help satisfy more conspicuous and flamboyant goals. MacInnis and Jaworski (1989) would characterize this decision making as high in motivation to process, attention focused on the ad, and a high degree of working memory allocated to processing. Unlike white goods, red goods involve role-taking processes that result in empathy-based persuasion. In the Pechmann and Stewart (1989) framework these products involve systematic processing but have many emotional benefits. Therefore, executions may be mixed with rational and emotional product benefits or be slightly weighted toward emotional. The advertising for white and red products would be different in their creative structure and appeals to match the different processing evoked by the products.

79

Exhibit 5.1   **Humorous Ad for Typical White Good: Volvo**

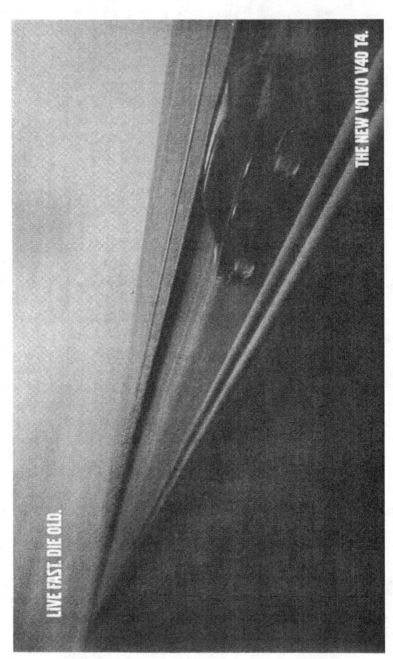

LIVE FAST DIE OLD.

THE NEW VOLVO V40 T4.

Volvo/Agency Forsman & Dodenfor's, 1990.

Exhibit 5.2 **Humorous Ad for Typical Red Good: BMW**

Nuova BMW Serie 3 compact 316ti e 318ti Valvetronic.
Valvetronic: la nuova tecnologia BMW che aumenta la potenza del motore e riduce i consumi.

BMW and D'Adda, Lorenzini, Vigorelli, BBDO, 2002.

Cell 3 of the product color matrix is "blue," representing the low-risk and functional decision-making characteristics of habit buys. Products in this group are "little tools" that are consumable and help accomplish small tasks like cleaning, cooling, personal hygiene, and so on. Blue is the toilet bowl cleaner, the laundry detergent, and the mouthwash that are part of this set of routinized purchases. There are, of course, many products that are not physically blue but share the same characteristics. Staple food items, many health and beauty aids, and over-the-counter drugs all fall into this grouping. As compared to the more risky white goods, consumers are less willing to process information when purchasing these low-risk and functional products. However, because of the functional or tool aspect of the products there is some interest in relevant information. Using MacInnis and Jaworski (1989), the level of motivation to process should be low to moderate, attention focused on the ad, and moderate levels of working memory allocated to processing. The representative operations are either meaning analyses or information integration. The formation of attitude toward the brand is either heuristic or message-based persuasion. Pechmann and Stewart (1989) look at heuristic processing dominating here where there are few emotional benefits. Executions would be expected to be a mixture of rational and emotional with some slight weighting toward rational. The "got milk?" ad in Exhibit 5.3, featuring "Jeopardy" game show host, Alex Trebek, uses play on words to emphasize a rational message about fat-free milk (a typical blue product) having the calcium to beat osteoporosis.

Finally, cell 4 consists of "yellow" goods. These products represent "little toys" that are the day-to-day rewards to which we treat ourselves. Snack chips and beer are the most appropriate color metaphors for the yellow goods, but the list would include other products such as gum, candy, soft drinks, wine coolers, and cigarettes. These products are the low-risk, routine purchases that help make us feel a little better. Yellow goods focus on want satisfaction and expressiveness. Although similar to red goods, yellow goods are not as risky. The ELM framework would classify this product group into a low-motivation-to-process category because of the low risk and routinized nature of the decision making. For MacInnis and Jaworski (1989) these are the decisions with low to very low motivation to process, attention divided, and low-working memory allocated to processing. The representative operations they describe are feature analysis or basic categorization resulting in brand attitudes formed by either mood-generated affect or pure affect transfer. Pechmann and Stewart (1989) see heuristic processing dominating, with advertising executions emotionally dominant. Put another way, the need or

Exhibit 5.3   **Humorous Ad for Typical Blue Good: Milk**

Courtesy of Lowe Worldwide.

desire for consumers to process message-related information about these yellow products should be low and peripheral cues like humor might be expected to be used often and with some success. The Absolut L.A. ad (see Exhibit 5.4) is part of the long-running and high-profile campaign that propelled the brand. The brand is a typical yellow good and the humor is a visual incongruity punctuated by the headline linking the pool and bottle shape to the L.A. lifestyle.

Using Humor With Different Products

Thus, what are the uses and effects of using humor with different products? Clearly, there is no single answer. Some advertisers for white goods, like insurance companies AFLAC, Geico, and Met Life, use a humor and entertainment strategy for what is a high-risk functional product category. How widespread is this counterintuitive use of humor, and is there any evidence about its success?

When Humor Is Used

An analysis based on the PCM breakdown has insights about the use of humor for different decision-making situations (see Table 5.3). The lowest incidence of humor across radio, TV, and magazines was in the red cell of high-risk and expressive toys. Here none of the TV ads, 10 percent of radio, and just 5.5 percent of magazine ads made an attempt at humor. In Toncar's (2001) TV study, ads for this group of products had the lowest use of humor both in the United States (20 percent) and the UK (14 percent). These more expressive high-end products are apparently no laughing matter for most advertisers regardless of the media being used. In contrast to the red cell, the low-risk, "little treats" of the yellow cell had the highest utilization of humor for all three media, with radio at 40.6 percent, TV at 37.9 percent, and magazines at 18.1 percent. Toncar's survey finds a nearly 50 percent use of humor in TV for this product group in the United States and the UK. Furthermore, the lower risk and functional goods of the blue cell use humor less than the yellow cell products but in still far higher proportions than for the products of the red cell. Compared to white goods, the low-risk aspect of the blue goods seems to have an important influence on the decision to use humor. White goods, with their high risk and functionality, had lower use of humor in radio (14.3 percent) and magazines (7.9 percent), but about the same percentage in TV (23.9 percent) when compared to blue goods. In the UK, Toncar (2001) found a relatively high 35 percent in TV ads for this group of products.

84

Exhibit 5.4 **Humorous Ad for Typical Yellow Good: Absolut**

Under permission by V&S VIN & SPRIT AB (publ).

Table 5.3

Frequency of Humor Usage in the United States (in percent)

Consumer objective	Functional/tools	Expressive/toys
Higher risk	Cell 1 "White goods" Bigger tools	Cell 2 "Red goods" Bigger toys
	23.9[a] Humor tv (22)[b] 7.9 Humor magazine 14.3 Humor radio	0.0* Humor TV (21)[b] 5.5 Humor magazine 10.0 Humor radio
Lower risk	Cell 3 "Blue goods" Little tools	Cell 4 "Yellow goods" Little treats
	22.2[a] Humor TV (29)[b] 11.9 Humor magazine 35.2 Humor radio	37.9 Humor TV (48)[b] 18.1 Humor magazine 40.6 Humor radio

[a]Adapted from Weinberger, Spotts, Campbell, and Parsons (1995).
[b]Percentages from Toncar (2001).
Overall sample: 24.4 percent Humor TV, n = 450, cell 1 = 67, cell 2 = 32, cell 3 = 248, cell 4 = 103.
9.9 percent Humor magazine, n = 451 cell 1 = 176, cell 2 = 89, cell 3 = 125, cell 4 = 61.
30.6 percent Humor radio, n = 510, cell 1 = 32, cell 2 = 23, cell 3 = 199, cell 4 = 254.

In general, the result for the use of humor for different products is consistent with what the ELM framework would expect. The higher risk (and involvement) white and red goods use humor less than the lower risk (and involvement) blue and yellow goods. The overall pattern of humor usage is consistent with research and creative executives' beliefs about both the relative value of humor in different media and the appropriateness of humor with blue and yellow products (nondurables). In particular, yellow products, such as soft drinks, alcohol, snacks, and candy, were specifically mentioned by executives in the survey as products well suited to humor. The heavy use of humor in TV ads for white goods runs counter to the ELM and ad executives' opinion about the appropriateness of humor for more durable products.

Of course this result is important because it reflects how advertisers believe the world to operate. We turn next to an equally or more important question of the actual impact of humor with the four PCM product groupings.

The Impact of Humor Differs Across Product Groups

The relatively few humor studies that have tested the impact of humor with different products are summarized in Table 5.4 and one particular study by

Weinberger et al. (1995) is detailed in Table 5.5. For white goods, humor did not work at all for radio, but it did help Noted and Read Most scores for magazines. With blue goods just the opposite pattern was found, with humor in radio ads enhancing ad performance while it reduced the Starch Noted and Associated scores for magazine advertising. For red and yellow goods, humor worked well for radio and enhanced magazine ad scores.

White Goods

For the higher risk and functional white goods, radio humor—regardless of relatedness of humor to the product—performed lower than non-humor on both the Recall Index and Execution Recall. For magazines, there was a net positive impact of humor over Starch norms on the three measures when the attempt at humor was perceived as humorous.

Red Goods

The higher risk and expressive toys in the red cell revealed some interesting contrasts. For the few radio ads in this group that used humor, related humor had a minor positive net effect on the Recall Index and Execution Recall. Unrelated humor tended to have an adverse impact on these scores. Related humor in magazines had a positive effect on Noted and Read Most scores. Unrelated humor had an adverse impact on Read Most and Associated, but it had a positive effect on Noted scores. Similar to the results for magazine ads for white goods, magazine ad humor for red goods tended to be harmful to the Associated measure of recall whether the ads were perceived as humorous or not.

Blue Goods

Advertisers utilize radio and magazine humor much more for the lower risk blue and yellow goods than for products in the higher risk cells. The issue is whether humor has a positive net effect on recall. In radio, related humor has a slight positive impact on both recall measures. Unrelated humor in radio performs about as well as non-humorous ads but not as well as related humor.

For magazines, the results are not as promising, with a negative net impact on Noted and Associated and a positive affect only on Read Most scores. In the blue cell, it does not seem to matter whether the humor is related or unrelated and whether the ads are perceived as humorous. In radio, the

Table 5.4

Studies Directly Examining Humor Use or Effects With Different Products

Author(s) and date	Type of study and subjects	Media	Finding
McCollum and Spielman (1982)	Data-based study of 500 commercials, target audiences	TV	Humor better for established products and is better suited to certain product categories (yellow, not white or red)
Madden and Weinberger (1984)	Survey of U.S. advertising executives, 68 research executives, 72 creative executives	NA	Consumer nondurables best suited to humor treatment
Weinberger and Spotts (1989)	Content analysis study, 450 U.S. and 247 UK commercials	TV	Humor most commonly used for low involvement products (blue and yellow)
Bauerly (1990)	Mall intercept survey, 226 respondents	NA	Soft drinks and snack foods best suited to humor (yellow)
Scott, Klein, and Bryant (1990)	Field experiment, 513 respondents	Direct mail	Humorous ad increased attendance at social events (yellow), but not to business events (white)
Weinberger and Campbell (1991)	Data-based study of over 1,600 pretested ads	radio	Most common use for low involvement products (blue and yellow), most effective for high involvement/feeling (red) and low involvement/feeling situations (yellow)
Toncar (2001)	Content Analysis of 379 U.S. and 467 UK commercials	TV	Confirms highest use of humor in lower involvement products
Chung and Zhao (2003)	Field experiment	TV	Humor enhanced memory recall for low involvement products
Flaherty, Weinberger, and Gulas (2004)	Experiment	Radio	No impact of product type

Table 5.5

Recall Performance of Radio and Magazine Ads

Consumer objective	Functional/tools	Expressive/toys
Higher risk	Cell 1 "White goods" Radio Rel. humor: -6.3% Index, -5.2% Execution Unrel. humor: -3.2% Index, -1.4% Execution Magazine Rel. humor: 2.0 Ntd, -.46 AS, 3.46 RM Unrel. humor: 1.5 Ntd, .01 AS, .49 RM	Cell 2 "Red goods" Radio Rel. Humor: 8.5% Index 5.8% Execution Unrel. humor: -8.7% Index, -7.7% Execution Magazine Rel. humor: .23 Ntd, -1.1 AS, 2.21 RM Unrel. humor: .83 Ntd, -2.3 AS, -.51 RM
Lower risk	Cell 3 "Blue goods" Radio Rel. humor: 1.6% Index, 2.1% Execution Unrel. humor: .1% Index, .9% Execution Magazine Rel. humor: -1.1 Ntd, -2.0 AS, 1.1 RM Unrel. humor: -1.5 Ntd, -2.4 AS, 1.2 RM	Cell 4 "Yellow goods" Radio Rel. humor: 1.5% Index, 1.2% Execution Unrel. humor: -3.0% Index, -1.6% Execution Magazine Rel. humor: 1.5 Ntd, .45 AS, 1.48 RM Unrel. humor: 3.5 Ntd, 2.55 AS, 1.7 RM

Notes:

Rel. humor/unrel. humor: refer to related and unrelated humor.

Radio and magazine scores below are the amount ads differed from norms. Higher numbers indicate stronger performance.

Radio combined : -.97 Recall index, 2.87 Recall execution n = 510.

Radio related humor: 0% Index, 4.0% Execution, n = 297, cell 1 = 13, cell 2 = 20, cell 3 = 126, cell 4 = 138.

Radio unrelated humor: -2.3% Index, 1.3% Execution n = 213, cell 1 = 19, cell 2 = 3, cell 3 = 73, cell 4 = 116.

Magazine combined: .64 Noted, -.84 Associated, 1.07 Read Most n = 567.

Magazine related humor: .32 Noted, -.92 Associated, 1.76 Read Most n = 239, cell 1 = 28, cell 2 = 62, cell 3 = 84, cell 4 = 65.

Magazine unrelated humor: .87 Noted, -.79 Associated, .57 Read Most n = 325, cell 1 = 102, cell 2 = 83, cell 3 = 79, cell N = 60.

89

evidence on the margin favors related humor while in magazines the evidence is slightly negative regardless of humor relatedness. In general, though humor is widely used for this category of products in magazines and radio, the results on attention and recall do not give strong support for humor here.

Yellow Goods

As expected, the yellow goods have the highest incidence of humor use for all the media that were tracked. For magazine ads, the effects are uniformly positive on all three Starch measures. This result becomes even stronger when the humor is actually perceived as humorous and holds whether the humor is related or unrelated to the product. In radio, the effects of humor are positive on both measures, provided the humor in the ads is related to the product. A study of the impact of humor on memory of elements in Super Bowl ads (Chung and Zhao 2003) further supports the expectation from the ELM and practitioners that humor works best with these lower risk products (see Table 5.4).

An article titled "Focus on Funny" produced in McCollum/Spielman's *Topline* research report (1982), which summarized the results of the use of humor in different situations using TV ads, examined 500 light-hearted ads in their research files focusing on their scoring of Clutter/Awareness and Attitude Shift. In general, the Clutter/Awareness scores for these ads equaled or surpassed the norms for ads in general in 75 percent of the cases and equaled the lift gained by the use of celebrities in ads. Use of humor to gain an attitude shift was less than the norm for ads overall and for celebrities. When examined by product, the results become more complex. The use of humor for new product introductory commercials was far less likely to succeed than when it was used with established brands (Clutter/Awareness gain in 63 percent with new products compared to 79 percent with established products). For Attitude Shift, only 47 percent of ads for new products were gainers compared to 71 percent for established products. One-third of the new-product commercials scored at or above the norm on both the Clutter/Awareness and Attitude Shift measures, while 59 percent of established brands met this criterion. A further probing of why this result occurred suggested that

> the attention commanded by the humor seemed at the expense of the product story. Viewers seemingly had difficulty decoding the sales messages. . . . Moreover, introducing your product with levity may suggest to the consumer that you don't take the product very seriously. . . . By contrast, a tried-and-true brand is already established, so that light-hearted advertising for it is less

likely to have a negative impact on the inclination to buy. . . . In sum, humor can present communication impediments and hinder conviction for a product that has not had the opportunity to build a reputation and image. While there are always exceptional cases, our experience has shown that it is advisable to be wary of humor at a product's introductory stage—it could hurt more than help. (McCollum/Spielman 1982, 2)

A further examination of the established products in the McCollum/ Spielman study considered product-humor compatibility. Though neither the ELM nor the product color matrix was used as the framework, the conclusions are similar. First, the study notes that though 59 percent of commercials for established products scored at or above the norm, the rest of the commercials (41 percent) scored lower on both the Awareness and Persuasion measures. The study concludes that the humor-product fit plays an important role. It argues that in certain categories it is self-evident, citing products with such names as Hubba Bubba, Yodels, Doo Dads, Snickers, Butterfingers, and so on. Fun foods, it argues, are naturally compatible with a lighthearted approach as it benefits the image and the way they are used. It notes that frequently these products are aimed at children and teens, who may be more inclined to humor. Such fun products are yellow products or little treats, where we showed that humor is used often and with success in radio and magazines. This does not preclude the successful use of humor in other categories. In the basic food category, which coincides with blue products, humorous commercials aimed at adults and where there is a "sameness" can be successful, but the chances for success are less. In each product category within the blue group there is at least one exception showing a successful brand using humor. The study cites the successful use of humor in cat food ads using a "buffoonish feline character," and Raid's use of cartoon characters. Even with products like luggage, using exaggerated torture tests with apes has been successful. "In all these product fields, our research has shown that humorous commercials have had fairly high success rates because the humor was used with product purpose and was appropriate in meaningful product demonstrations" (McCollum/Spielman 1982, 3). The study found few successes of using humor with banks, real estate, insurance, or financial/ investment services. "High ticket items—automobiles, entertainment systems, and appliances—have seldom been well-served by humorous advertising." These are the white goods, where the use of humor was shown earlier to be relatively low and where humor can work, but the odds of success are lower. For products of high status and emotional value, which the PCM labels red goods, the study argues that humor is used sparingly and that its use trivializes and is inappropriate. This result is consistent with the radio and magazine studies cited earlier.

Known and Unknown Products

An additional way that advertising has been viewed with respect to product is whether the product is known or unknown or new or old. Here the notion of prior brand attitude becomes important because the brand can be viewed as an attitude object with influence on information processing (Petty and Cacioppo 1981). Chattopadhyay and Basu (1990) found that prior brand opinion interacted with the delivery of humor in a TV commercial. The result showed that humor enhanced consumer attitude, purchase intent, and choice for brands for which consumers had a positive prior attitude. However, when initial brand attitude was negative, the non-humorous version of the commercial worked better than the humorous version. Though this study was conducted using pens as the product (typically a blue product at lower price points), there is no evidence that the effect is limited to low-risk and functional products. Related work has examined brand familiarity as a factor governing ad effects (Kent and Allen 1994). Stewart and Furse (1986) specifically studied ad message elements in TV with respect to brand familiarity and brand preference. Overall, their study found that for their sample of largely low-risk (blue and yellow) goods, humor was an important factor in predicting recall and comprehension but not persuasion. In fact, humor had the second highest and most consistent correlations with recall and comprehension for both new and established products.

Conclusion

There is a consistent pattern of humor usage that is related to the changing risk levels and purchase motivations reflected in the different product groups. Higher risk red and white products generally have the lowest levels of humor usage, and lower risk yellow and blue products have the highest. For all three media, there appears to be a consensus among advertisers that yellow goods are most suited to humor, while red goods are the least suited. These conclusions are derived from the frequencies of humor usage for each PCM group,

Figure 5.1 **Product Factors and the Challenge Model**

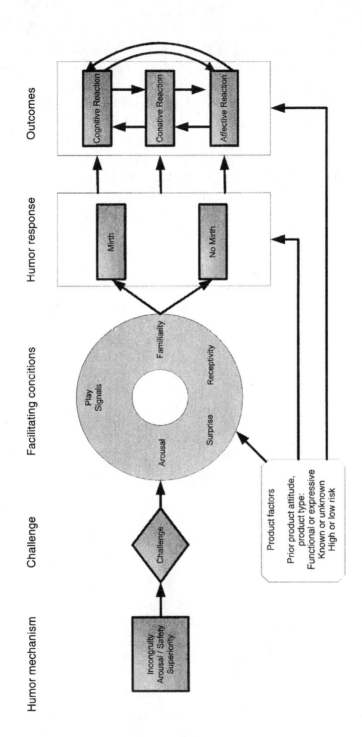

Humor mechanism   Challenge   Facilitating conditions   Humor response   Outcomes

93

where humor was uniformly used most with ads for yellow goods and least for red goods. It has been further found that established products and those with positive prior brand attitudes work better with humor than new products or products with poor prior brand attitudes. Most evident is the few studies that have explicitly studied the impact of humor with different products. Beyond the speculation by advertisers about where humor is appropriate, there is relatively little to guide effective usage for different products. Figure 5.1 links the product factors summarized in this chapter with the general challenge model used in this book as an integrative view of the working of humor in advertising.

—— 6 ——

Humor Type and Message

There are many factors that may be considered pertinent to a full discussion of the message aspects of humor. We start by looking at the position of humor in its general role as an entertainment device. From there we shift to examine the types of humor and the impact of humor on different response variables, and then some of the message contingencies such as humor's relevance and repetition.

The Broad View of Humor

Humor, however we classify it, is part of a broader set of stimuli that may act as peripheral communication cues and that may provide pleasure for an audience. Wyer and Collins (1992) following Long and Graesser (1988) define a humor-eliciting stimulus as "a social or nonsocial event, occurring purposely or inadvertently, that is perceived to be amusing" (663). Though this definition is far broader than many might accept, it points to the important understanding that humor is part of a constellation of message factors that might provoke pleasure, including music, fun people, cartoon characters, animals, children, an upbeat mood, surprise, warmth, and so on. An analysis of humor is incomplete without looking at the relative importance of this broader entertainment construct.

Not surprisingly this topic has been of importance to advertisers for generations and in the 1970s computational technology permitted the type of large-scale testing and analysis needed to learn more about what makes a successful ad. In an advertising context, Leavitt (1970), Wells et al. (1971), Schlinger (1979b), and colleagues at Leo Burnett and Needham Harper Steers explored the characteristics of commercials associated with advertising effectiveness. In an early development, Wells et al. (1971) identified humor as one of six factors to predict commercial effectiveness, with characteristics such as Jolly, Merry, Playful, Humorous, and Amusing loading on the factor.

After more extensive testing, humor became part of a broader Entertainment construct. This stream of proprietary factor testing of TV advertising became known as the Viewer Response Profile (VRP), which identified six stable factors, their names representing a summary of the items loading on a particular factor. One of the six factors was labeled by Schlinger as Stimulation or Entertainment. Schlinger described this as a way to "sugar coat" the persuasive message of an ad. The favorable affect from such ads she argued could be generalized to the brand. The features associated with Stimulation or Entertainment at Leo Burnett evolved in different tests of large samples of commercials. In one study (Schlinger 1979a) the following factor loadings were associated with this Stimulation/Entertainment dimension:

.87	Amusing
.87	Lots of fun to watch and listen to
.86	Playful
.86	Clever and quite entertaining
.83	Exciting
.82	Characters capture attention
.82	Enthusiasm catching
.75	Unique
.67	Tender
.61	Dreamy
−.66	Dull and boring

Olson (1985) utilized the VRP to examine the relationship between the success of new-product introductions and commercial characteristics for TV ads. The result was that two factors, Entertainment and Relevant News, were able to predict product success with about two-thirds accuracy. This blended approach for new products combines peripheral cues, including humor, with message elements. New products, Vaughn (1986) argued, resemble products that require higher involvement and rational process paralleling the ELM high motivation to process.

More recently Woltman-Elpers, Wedel, and Pieters (2003) studied the influence of entertainment and information features in a TV ad's ability to hold attention. A commercial high in entertainment value ensures that consumers continue to view the ad whereas a commercial high in information value induces consumers to stop viewing. Woltman-Elpers et al. add a footnote to Olson's suggestion that a blend of entertainment and information (personal relevance) is most effective for gaining purchase of new products. They demonstrate that high levels of entertainment and information do not work well together and actually discourage continued viewing. Consumers prefer a high level of entertainment and low levels of information. It should be noted that

Table 6.1

Focus of TV and Magazine Ads: Entertainment Versus Factual/Relevance
(in percent)

Consumer objective	Functional/tools	Expressive/toys
Higher risk	TV Entertaining 10.1 Fact/relevance 49.3 Both 36.2	TV Entertaining 6.9 Fact/relevance 68.9 Both 10.3
	Magazine Entertaining .6 Fact/relevance 70.6 Both 28.2	Magazine Entertaining 15.6 Fact/relevance 34.4 Both 34.4
Lower risk	TV Entertaining 20.3 Fact/relevance 43.4 Both 27.9	TV Entertaining 62.0 Fact/relevance 12.0 Both 17.0
	Magazine Entertaining 3.2 Fact/relevance 62.7 Both 31.7	Magazine Entertaining 34.4 Fact/relevance 18.0 Both 37.7

Source: Adapted from Weinberger and Spotts (1993).

the Woltman-Elpers work did not look at higher order effects (i.e., attitudes, intention, behavior) and so it is unclear if purchase behavior, the measure that Olson studied, would have been harmed in their dual condition (entertainment and information). Vaughn (1986) suggested that new products may be initially similar to high-involvement and thinking products, but this is not a category represented in the Woltman-Elpers research. It is an important issue because Weinberger and Spotts (1993) found that a blended approach of entertainment and information is commonly used in many TV and magazine ads (see Table 6.1). At the very least, the Woltman-Elpers research questions (at least for some products) the ability of such a blend in TV ads to hold audience attention.

In support of the notion of a differential impact of humor or other peripheral cues to enhance advertising is work by Aaker and Stayman (1990). They highlight a deficiency in the prior ad testing of the VRP, which tended to treat ads for all products the same when conducting factor analyses. They point out that not all ads may benefit the same from particular ad features. Based on what we saw in Chapter 5, we concur. Their analysis across eighty commercials tested on television revealed five factors they label entertaining/humorous, stimulating, informative, warm, and dislikable, with some evidence for confusing and forgettable dimensions. The entertaining/humorous factor was closely related to ad liking in nine of fifteen clusters of ads in three of fifteen regressions predicting ad effectiveness. "In addition to the humorous adjective, the entertainment/humorous factor included the adjectives clever, original, and imaginative, which provide unambiguously positive views of the ad" (14). Geuens and De Pelsmacker (1998) find that ads that are warm, erotic, or humorous all outperform ads that use non-emotional appeals. They suggest that positive feelings, which they define as interest, lack of irritation, and cheerfulness, have a positive impact on ad and brand recognition and that this is particularly true for the humorous ads.

These results support the supposition of the ELM that peripheral cues should have different effects for situations of higher or lower motivation to process and ability. It is also consistent with the results of Weinberger and colleagues (1989: 1997), which show differential use of peripheral cues and humor as well as differential effects of different types of humor in situations where lower and higher motivation to process would be expected.

Humor clearly can play an important role in determining if an ad is entertaining (and not irritating), but there are many other ways to make an ad entertaining without using humor. Humor is simply one class of stimuli that can be used. Further, Aaker and Stayman (1990) find that even the important entertainment factor is not universally effective (66 percent measured with liking and 40 percent measured with recall) for all ad situations. When applied to advertising, this result and the ELM suggest that humor as a subclass of entertainment devices will not work to enhance liking or recall in all situations. The fact is that neither humor nor any other entertainment device is likely to have a universal positive impact on all measures of success. For instance, a study of reactions to print ads for alcoholic beverages found that though humor did not have an impact on ad-evoked feelings, it did have an impact on ad and brand recognition by increasing interest and cheerfulness and reducing irritation (Geuens and De Pelsmacker 1998).

With this macro perspective of humor as an entertainment device we begin in the succeeding sections of this chapter to sort out what we know about the use and impact of more specific and micro aspects of the humor message itself.

Types of Humor

There are many ways to classify humor. Freud argued that the pleasure obtained from wit comes about either from tendentious or non-tendentious wit. If a message is tendentious, its execution relies on aggression and/or a

Table 6.2

Use of Humor in Business-to-Business Magazine Ads in the United States, UK, and Germany

Humor type	Number of ads	Percentage of ads
Pun	52	34
Warm	28	18
Nonsense	27	18
Aggressive	21	14
Sexual	9	6
Other	12	8
Total	149	100

Source: Adapted from McCullough and Taylor (1993).

sexual focus. Non-tendentious wit is more playful, relying in its execution on absurdities or nonsense. Goldstein and McGhee (1972) explored humor typologies by surveying the humor research (in a non-advertising setting) between 1950 and 1971. The types of humor were most generally categorized as either aggressive, sexual, or incongruous (nonsense). In an early study of humor in magazine ad performance, Madden and Weinberger (1982) found that all 148 liquor magazine ads they examined derived their humor from nonsense with none being sexual or aggressive. Though the survey was not comprehensive, this result is probably indicative that nonsense humor is generally favored by advertisers. It is possible that use of sex and aggression is seen as more risky and thus they are used more cautiously.

Variations of the Freud classification have been used in an advertising setting. A content analysis of business-to-business advertising in magazines in the United States, the UK, and Germany found a surprisingly high 23 percent overall usage of humor, led by the British sample at 26 percent (McCullough and Taylor 1993). Of the humor types found by McCullough and Taylor (1993), three categories correspond directly with Freud's groupings of tendentious (aggression and sexual) and non-tendentious (nonsense) wit (see Table 6.2). "Aggressive" and "sexual" account for a combined 20 percent of the humor. "Nonsense" is listed at just 18 percent, but this low percentage is a bit misleading because "puns" at 34 percent and "warm" at 18 percent are often found to use non-tendentious humor. The combined potential of non-tendentious humor using the sum of "nonsense," "warm," and "pun" is 70 percent. This number is probably a better comparison to the Madden and Weinberger (1982) finding that 100 percent of the consumer magazine ads for alcohol that they employed for their study used "nonsense" to execute humor.

Table 6.3

Use of Humor Devices in U.S. and UK TV Ads (in percent)

Humorous devices	United States	United Kingdom
Pun	4.5[a]/5[b]	14[a]/4[b]
Understatement	2.7/1	2.2/16
Joke	2.7/37	2.2/19
Ludicrous	66.4/45	59.1/37
Satire	26.4/10	33.3/18
Irony	0.9/2	2.2/6
Total number humorous ads	110/220	91/85
Percent humorous	24/28	36/33

[a]From Weinberger and Spotts (1989); [b]from Toncar (2001).

Kelly and Solomon (1975), using a different approach, classified humor according to devices such as "(1) pun—the humorous use of a word or phrase in a way that suggests two interpretations; (2) an understatement—representing something as less than is the case; (3) joke—speaking or acting without seriousness; (4) something ludicrous—that which is laughable or ridiculous; (5) satire—sarcasm used to expose vice or folly; and (6) irony—the use of words to express the opposite of what one really means" (32). Two studies of humorous TV ads in the United States and the UK that used the Kelly and Solomon list of humor devices both found that "ludicrous" was most common, ranging from 37 to 66 percent of all the sample, followed by "satire," which ranged from 10 to 33 percent of the ads in the two studies (see Table 6.3). British ads were found in the Toncar (2001) study to use "understatement" more and "jokes" less than the U.S. ads.

A study of humor in award-winning radio advertising from 1974 to 1988 by Murphy, Morrison, and Zahn (1993) examined ten categories of humor devices that they derived from the work of Kelly and Solomon (1975) and McCollum/Spielman (1982). Their categorization recognizes that often humor involves a combination of devices for its execution. Their results (see Table 6.4) show that "nonsense" is by far the most favored device (64 percent), and that "satire" (37 percent), "eccentric characters" (36 percent) and "frustration" (29 percent) were all used extensively in humorous ads. Their finding that "nonsense" dominates is consistent with the heavy use of non-tendentious approaches found in other studies.

In the only direct comparison of humor devices in different media, Catanescu and Tom (2001) studied different devices in magazines and television. The biggest difference between the use in TV and magazines is that

Table 6.4

Use of Humor Devices in Radio Clio Award-Winning Ads (in percent)

Humor device	1974–78	1979–83	1984–88	Average 1974–88
Nonsense	49	69	70	64
Eccentric characters	33	40	34	36
Word play	12	15	5	10
Sarcasm	13	17	16	16
Satire	28	36	43	37
Parody	27	11	17	17
Stereotype	11	11	12	11
Human relationships	28	24	17	22
Repetition	10	8	7	8
Frustration	32	23	32	29

Source: Adapted from Murphy, Morrison, and Zahn (1993).

Table 6.5

Humor Devices Used In TV and Magazine Advertising (in percent)

Type of humor	Magazine	Television
Comparison	14.5	5.4
Exaggeration	8.5	7.2
Personification	13	15
Pun	18.5	15
Sarcasm	23.5	12.7
Silliness	14.5	28.9
Surprise	8	15.7
Total *n*	201 ads	166 ads

Source: Adapted from Catanescu and Tom (2001).

"silliness" (28.9 percent) and "surprise" (15.7 percent) are almost twice as common in TV as they are in magazines. On the other hand, "sarcasm" (12.7 percent) and "comparison" (14.5 percent) are much more common in magazines (see Table 6.5). It is possible that the different use of these devices in the two media reflect the differing ability to develop humor in print and broadcast. As discussed in Chapter 4, print is limited because of an absence of audio and the dynamic interplay of characters that is possible in TV.

In the most intricate and detailed study of humorous messages, Speck (1987) developed five humor types based on a combination of incongruity, humorous disparagement, and arousal-safety (see Table 6.6). The reader may recall from Chapter 2 that there is some consensus that these are the three

Table 6.6

Speck Humor Types

Humor types	Arousal-safety	Incon-gruity-resolution	Humorous disparage-ment	Perceived humorous (in percent)	Fre-quency of use (in percent)
HTI-Comic wit		X		55* (avg. 3.2/5)	21
HT2-Sentimental humor	X			30 (avg. 2.2/5)	11
HT3-Satire		X	X	53 (avg. 3.1/5)	17
HT4-Sentimental comedy	X	X		60 (avg. 3.4/5)	28
HT5-Full comedy	X	X	X	75 (avg. 4.0/5)	22

Source: Adapted from Speck (1987, 1991).
*Percent who scored > 2 on five-point perceived humor scale.

underlying processes that generate humor. From these three processes Speck (1987: 1991) argues that arousal-safety and incongruity-resolution can create humor on their own, whereas humorous disparagement requires either arousal-safety and/or incongruity-resolution. Unlike the other studies of message type just described, Speck not only examined the frequency of each type of humor but also its perceived humorousness. Table 6.6, adapted from Speck (1987: 1991), illustrates the five humor types that are developed from the basic humor processes. It is noteworthy that the only form of humor not using incongruity-resolution—sentimental humor—is perceived as least humorous. The most complex humor—full comedy—using all three mechanisms is seen as the most humorous. Speck used this framework to test TV ads that represented each of the humor types. His study goes on to further test the effects of each humor type using a comprehensive battery of dependent measures. We will examine the results of this later in this chapter as part of a broader review of the findings in the literature.

Communication Goals and Humor

Though pleasure and amusement may be the audience's reward for viewing or hearing a humorous ad, they are not likely to be the sole or primary reason that advertisers employ humor. There may be an important interplay between the type of humor and its impact on how well a message communicates. In this section we explore this important connection between humor and its effects and, where possible, we examine the more minute relationship between the type of humor and its impact.

The nature of the communication goal set for the message plays a major role in the appropriateness of different types of humor. The issue is an important one and is part of the ongoing broad advertising debate about the appropriate measures of advertising success. We certainly do not aim to settle the debate here, but hope instead to shed light on what objectives seem attainable with humor and when. Vakratsas and Ambler (1999) conducted a cogent review of what we know about how advertising operates. In it they examined seven different frameworks and the support for how they work. An important conclusion is that there is no one hierarchy of effects, but many ways that advertising can be utilized depending on contingencies.

Sternthal and Craig (1973) listed advertising goals and the impact of humor on a set of goals that even at the time reflected the classic view of the traditional hierarchy-of-effects model, namely a linear and largely cognitive view of how advertising works. Though many of their conclusions remain insightful, there have been important changes that bring in the noncognitive and affective reactions to advertising to a greater extent than ever. Weinberger and Spotts (1989) surveyed research and creative executives at agencies in the United States and the UK about their views about what could be attained with humor (see Table 6.7). Both groups agreed that humor is more effective than non-humor at gaining attention, registering brand names, and enhancing mood. The U.S. agency sample was more cautious, expressing that humor could harm comprehension and recall and is not good for complex messages or for gaining persuasion. The goals surveyed here reflect both the traditional, mostly cognitively dominated hierarchy of effects as well as the more contemporary affective perspective.

Pre-attention and Affect

Change began to take place toward a more affectively based response to advertising and then VanRaaij (1989) offered an alternative hierarchy in which affect plays an important role. Here cognition is preceded by "primary affective reaction" (PAR), which serves as a gatekeeper and decides whether the ad is interesting and worthy of further processing. In this framework, liking of the ad or product is a prerequisite to processing information. Deeper cognition in the form of cognitive elaboration then serves to justify and support the PAR, as well as more extensive affective reactions and brand attitude formation. Affective feelings may be evoked more directly than through attitude toward the ad. In this approach, capturing interest and liking become important.

Still another and more radical view that emerged (after the Vakratsas and Ambler 1999 review article) of the influence process conceives advertising

Table 6.7

U.S. and UK Agency Executive Opinions About the Communication Objectives for Humor (in percent)

Communication objective	United States (n = 129)	United Kingdom (n = 29)
Attention		
Better at gaining attention than non-humor	55 agree 12 disagree	66 agree 3 disagree
Comprehension		
Harms comprehension more than non-humor	50 agree 11 disagree	31 agree 38 disagree
Effective at gaining comprehension	38 agree 27 disagree	42 agree 12 disagree
Harms recall more than non-humor	33 agree 41 disagree	14 agree 62 disagree
Effective as non-humor for name registration	65 agree 12 disagree	66 agree 7 disagree
Effective as non-humor for complex points	28 agree 50 disagree	38 agree 28 disagree
Persuasion		
Increases more than non-humor	26 agree 24 disagree	62 agree 7 disagree
To gain yielding	37 agree	42 agree

To gain intention	23 disagree	15 disagree
	29 agree	46 agree
	30 disagree	19 disagree
Enhances mood	54 agree	59 agree
	15 disagree	—
Mood aids persuasion	74 agree	79 agree
	8 disagree	—
Action		
Creates greater sales effect than non-humor at gaining purchase	25 agree	34 agree
	24 disagree	14 disagree
Source credibility	34 agree	35 agree
	33 disagree	27 disagree
Helps enhance	10 agree	21 agree
	44 disagree	17 disagree

Source: Adapted from Weinberger and Spotts (1989).

105

as having an important post-usage impact on customers. Most of the traditional views, including all the variations on communication hierarchies, focus on the pre-purchase period when advertising shapes an audience's thinking before a choice is made. In fact, the radical view directly challenges Vakratsas and Ambler's (1999) conclusion that advertising is more effective before usage experience. The new view presented by Braun (1999) and Hall (2002) suggests that advertising has a critical impact on audiences *after* their experience with the good or service. Here advertising helps shape how the entire product experience is remembered and perhaps how future product decisions are made. The implication is that traditional pretesting of ads and pre-purchase communication exposure testing of advertising may be missing an important effect. Humor, for instance, may have a positive impact on those who have already used a product by positively altering or reinforcing associations and recollections of the actual product experience. If this was the main impact of the ad, and we were to measure the impact of humor in a pre-purchase setting, we might falsely conclude that there was no humor effect.

The increasing recognition is that affect and exposure to messages are connected (Zajonc 1980) in important ways. The mere exposure school of affect suggests that awareness of the advertising is not even necessary for an effect. Hoffman (1986) identified several ways that affective responses may be influenced: (1) a direct affective response to a stimulus, (2) an affective response to the match between the stimulus and a stored concept in the mind, and (3) an affective response to the meaning of the stimulus. A humorous ad might activate any one of these mechanisms to create affect.

A direct affect transfer in an ad below the level of attention was examined by Janiszewski (1993). He provides evidence that pre-attention is important and that trace measurement of attention is not essential to tracking the impact of affective responses. This suggests that perhaps we are being too conservative when holding humor to a purely cognitive standard of impact. Further, if Braun (1999) and Hall (2002) are correct that advertising operates by shaping post-experience recollections, it probably works through one of the three processes suggested by Hoffman.

Even in the earlier reviews of humor there was considerable support for judging humor in part using affective measures. Source-liking deals with noncognitive affect. Sternthal and Craig (1973) concluded that humor enhanced the liking of the source. The more recent advertising humor literature gives similar strong support for enhanced liking through the use of humor, which has been shown to increase liking of the ad (A_{ad}), the source (A_s), and the brand (A_b) (see Table 6.8). Our review indicates that nine of ten studies show a positive connection between humor and source liking. Looking at the more cognitive measures, the same strong positive link between humor and A_{ad} is found, with twelve of thirteen studies supporting humor. For A_b the evidence is strong, with nine positive results, one no finding (Brooker 1981) (mild humor was used), and two negative findings (one used a strong message argument). Unger (1995) and later Cline et al. (2003) specifically modeled and found a positive connection between humor, A_{ad}, and A_b. The Cline work included affect in its model and found that humor works both directly on A_{ad} and also indirectly by heightening affect. This result partially supports VanRaaij's PAR, which argued for a primary role for affect before cognition. Further, Lee and Sternthal (1999) found that a positive mood can be induced by humorous TV ads and that this effect can facilitate and enhance recall by stimulating brand rehearsal. A prior positive or neutral brand experience with superior stimulus learning is consistent with the hedonic contingency view developed by Wegner, Petty, and Smith (1995).

A strong affective response has significant implications and is congenial with a surge of research in the late 1980s and early 1990s in which American advertising research began indicating that liking may be a very important variable in the effectiveness of an ad (Biel and Bridgwater 1990; Haley and Baldinger 1991). In Haley and Baldinger's (1991) comprehensive study for the Advertising Research Foundation, six copy-testing methods were employed to study five matched pairs of commercials with 400 to 500 respondents per cell; thus, a total of nearly 15,000 interviews were conducted for the study. This research showed that two liking measures were the strongest indicators of a commercial's sales success, outperforming all other measures. The overall reaction to the commercial, in terms of liking, was demonstrated to predict which of a paired set of commercials would be the sales winner 87 percent of the time, with an index level indicating an association three times stronger than random chance. A related dichotomous liking measure had a successful prediction rate of 93 percent, albeit with a lower index level. These liking findings provided strong support for the importance of this factor in the effectiveness of an ad. In concert with the Haley and Baldinger finding, Biel and Bridgwater (1990) concluded that individuals "who liked a commercial 'a lot' were twice as likely to be persuaded by it as people who felt neutral toward the advertising" (38). Although in the Biel and Bridgwater (1990) work liking was not confined to entertainment value and included such factors as personal relevance, a finding by Haley and Baldinger (1991) is directly tied to humor. Their study indicates that a positive response to the statement "This advertising is funny or clever" predicts the success of an ad 53 percent of the time, whereas agreement with the statement "This advertising is boring" predicts failure 73 percent of the time (Haley and Baldinger 1991).

Table 6.8

Summary of Humor Study Results With Outcome Measures

Study	Attention	Recognition	Recall comprehension	Source liking	A_{ad}	A_b	Source credibility	Persuasion and intention	Other
Markeiwicz (1972)			0					+ (for soft sell approach only) – (for hard sell)	+ More interesting
Murphy et al. (1979)			– unaided + aided						
Cantor and Venus (1980)			– (for existing products only) 0 (new products)			–			
Brooker (1981)				+ weak effect (mild humor)		0	0	0	
Madden and Weinberger (1982)	+	+	+						
Madden (1982)	+ (related) 0 (unrelated)		0 source recall + retention (related humor, new product) 0 or – (unrelated and/or old product)		+	+	– or 0 trustworthy (related humor or not and old and new)	+	
McCollum/ Spielman (1982)			+				+	+	

Study		– (recall, high involvement, infrequently purchased products)				–/0 credibility, authority, character	
Sutherland and Middleton (1983)		– (recall, high involvement, infrequently purchased products)					0
Gelb and Pickett (1983)			+	+		0	0
Lammers et al. (1983)		– recall (unfamiliar industrial product)	+ men	– women / + men			+ males / – females
Belch and Belch (1984)	0 one or 5 exposures / + 3 exposures	0 aided recall	+			+	+
Duncan et al. (1984)		+ aided recall (when perceived humorous)					
Stewart-Hunter (1985)		0 (brand name registration)					
Duncan and Nelson (1985)	+	+	+	+	+		0
Stewart and Furse (1986)	+	+					
Gelb and Zinkhan (1986)		– (result questioned in Nelson 1987)	+	+			+
Speck (1987)	+	+	+	+		– knowledgeable / + trustworthy (certain humor types)	+ (3 of 5 humor types helped)
Wu et al. (1989)	+	+ (unaided brand recall)	0			0	

(continued)

Table 6.8 (continued)

Study	Attention	Recognition	Recall comprehension	Source liking	A_{ad}	A_b	Source credibility	Persuasion and intention	Other
Scott et al. (1990)								+ behavior-attendance (community social event)	
Chattpad-hyay and Basu (1990)				+ prior positive brand attitude			+		
Weinberger and Campbell (1991)			+ yellow and red products (related humor)					+ yellow and red products (related humor) 0 white and blue products and all unrelated humor	
Zhang and Zinkhan (1991)			+ message recall	+					
Smith (1993)					+ (with weak arguments)	+ (with weak arguments)			
Zhang (1996)					+ (when low NFC)	+ (when low NFC)		+ (when low NFC)	
Unger (1995)					+	+			
Spotts et al. (1997)		+ Starch noted (yellow and white products)	+ (yellow products) – (blue and red products)						
Cline and Kellaris (1999)					+ low involvement product and weak arguments	+ low involvement product and weak arguments			

Study					
Lee and Mason (1999)			+ (humor helped when irrelevant to main message)		+ irrelevant humor reduces negative cognitive responses
Alden et al. (2000)		+ (humor helped when irrelevant to main message)			+ surprise as well as warmth, emotionality, familiarity and ease of resolution
Geuns and DePelsmacker (2002)	0	+ (with ad evoked feelings and warmth)	+ (with ad evoked feelings and warmth)	+ weak (with ad evoked feelings and warmth)	
Cline et al. (2003)		+			– counter arguments + affect
Krishnan and Chakravarti (2003)	+ Claim, humor recall (Moderate humor) 0 Claim, humor recall with high humor				
Chung and Zhao (2003)	+ Memory (low involvement products)				
Woltman Elpers et al. (2004)					+ surprise precedes humor
Flaherty et al. (2004)		+	+		

111

The Haley and Baldinger study for the ARF and the basic work inspired by Zajonc were watersheds for advertising because they finally gave liking and affect legitimacy as they linked directly with an impact on sales. When large industry studies by the research firm Mapes and Ross began to reveal similar evidence, even the late David Ogilvy after years of disparaging the use of humor explicitly recognized its positive potential (Ogilvy and Raphaelson 1982).

Gaining Attention

The pre-attention and affect story for humor is a good one, but traditional attention measures, despite their need for cognition, are able to consistently detect a humor effect as well. It appears that the view of advertisers in the United States and the UK that humor enhances attention is well supported by the available empirical evidence. The handful of studies that have specifically measured attention (see Table 6.8) have found consistently positive effects. In studies of actual magazine ads (Madden and Weinberger 1982), television ads (Stewart and Furse 1986), and radio ads (Weinberger and Campbell 1991) in standard industry ad-testing situations, humor has been found to have a positive effect on attention. Similarly, this attention effect has also been demonstrated in the laboratory (Madden 1982; Duncan and Nelson 1985; Wu et al. 1989). In a thorough test of attention effects in the advertising arena, Speck (1987) compared humorous ads with non-humorous controls on four attention measures: initial attention, sustained attention, projected attention, and overall attention. He found humorous ads to outperform non-humorous ads on each of the attention measures.

Although the results seem to indicate a positive impact on attention, and in general the past thirty years of research largely supports this conclusion drawn by Sternthal and Craig (1973), future researchers should be aware that all humor is not created equal. Related humor, that is, humor directly connected to the product or issue being promoted, appears to be more successful than unrelated humor at gaining attention (Duncan 1979; Madden 1982). In fact, controlling for the relatedness factor makes the findings of the experimental studies in advertising unanimous in their support for a positive effect of humor on attention. This indicates that the mere insertion of canned humor into a given ad is unlikely to have the same impact on attention as the use of a more integrated humor treatment.

Comprehension and Recognition

The literature is mixed on the effect that humor has on comprehension and recognition. Most studies do not measure recognition, opting for other measures such as unaided or aided recall of aspects of the ad, brand, or message. The few studies that have tested recognition report either no effect or a situational impact on just one or two product types (see Table 6.8). We know far too little to draw even tentative conclusions. In addition, there is a long-standing debate about whether some measures, such as Starch Noted scores, are best labeled recognition or recall measures. In fact, the entire study of comprehension has many variants of dependent measures, such as aided and unaided recall of message, executions, brand names, and so on, a handicap when comparing studies.

In a study of 1,000 broadcast commercials, Stewart and Furse (1986) found humorous content to increase the comprehension of an ad. Other studies have found similar positive results (Duncan, Nelson, and Frontczak 1984; Speck 1987; Weinberger and Campbell 1991; Zhang and Zinkhan 1991). However, these studies contrast sharply with the results of other advertising researchers who have found a negative relationship between humor and comprehension (Cantor and Venus 1980; Gelb and Zinkhan 1986; Lammers et al. 1983; Sutherland and Middleton 1983). This negative view of the effect of humor on comprehension is shared by the majority of research executives (64 percent) at U.S. ad agencies.

In sum, of the advertising experiments that attempted to measure the effects of humor on comprehension (see Table 6.8), several lean toward a potential for humor to enhance comprehension. Although these findings certainly fail to resolve the true effect of humor on comprehension, they do call into question the existence of a global negative effect hypothesized by Sternthal and Craig (1973). The picture becomes even clearer when we recognize that the negative results are associated with some product groups but not others (Spotts et al. 1997), such as infrequently purchased products (Sutherland and Middleton 1983) and industrial products (Lammers et al. 1983). In the last two cases humor is not commonly used. With product accounted for, the preponderance of the results about comprehension is positive, with a handful with no effect and just three studies showing negative effects.

This surprisingly consistent result emerges despite a wide range of comprehension measures among the studies. Depending on the specific measure used, recall may be an indication of comprehension or it may merely indicate attention. For example, the Starch Associated score might be viewed as a measure of recognition, recall, or comprehension. More importantly, the measures employed may have an impact on the results found. Studies that employ multiple or summated measures of comprehension (Speck 1987; Weinberger and Campbell 1991) are more likely to find positive or mixed positive effects on comprehension than studies that employ single measures

(Cantor and Venus 1980; Lammers et al. 1983), indicating that a positive comprehension effect may be missed by relatively narrow measures. Further evidence of the importance of measures is found in the work of Murphy and his colleagues (Murphy, Cunningham, and Wilcox 1979). Their study of context effects demonstrates that different measures of recall may produce different results.

Humor type may be an important determinant in comprehension effects. In a study that directly compared the effects of various humor types on comprehension, Speck (1987) found significant differences due to type. His findings indicate that some humorous ads do better, and some do worse than non-humorous ads on descriptive and message comprehension and that this differential performance is attributable to humor type. We will discuss Speck's study in more detail later in this chapter.

Persuasion

Sternthal and Craig (1973) concluded that the distraction effect of humor might lead to persuasion. However, they note that the persuasive effect of humor is at best no greater than that of serious appeals. These conclusions seem to agree with the opinions of U.S. ad executives. Madden and Weinberger (1984) found that only 26 percent of these practitioners agreed with a statement proclaiming humor to be more persuasive than non-humor. While U.S. advertising executives largely agree with the conclusion of Sternthal and Craig (1973), this opinion is in sharp contrast to that of their British counterparts, 62 percent of whom viewed humor as more persuasive than non-humor and only 7 percent of whom disagreed (Weinberger and Spotts 1989).

The literature in marketing and communication has addressed this issue directly, and the evidence for a persuasive effect of humor has become stronger over the years. Speck (1987) found three out of five humor treatments increased two measures of persuasion: intent to use the product and change in perceived product quality (see Table 6.9). Similarly, in an experimental study, Brooker (1981) found a humorous appeal to be more persuasive than a fear appeal. However, neither humor nor fear appeals were more persuasive than a straightforward approach. An examination of TV commercials, published by McCollum/Spielman (1982), found that 31 percent of humorous commercials exhibited above average scores on persuasiveness. This figure represents about average performance when compared to other executional tactics examined, such as celebrities. Stewart and Furse (1986) found no effect of humor on persuasion. Finally, in their study of radio ads, Weinberger and Campbell (1991)

114

found unrelated humor to perform the same or worse on a persuasion measure compared to no humor. Additionally, while related humor was more persuasive than no humor for low-involvement-feeling products (yellow goods), it was found to be less persuasive on high-involvement-thinking products (white goods). Other advertising research also indicates that, much like comprehension, other factors may intervene to moderate the effect of humor on persuasion. For example, although Lammers and his colleagues (Lammers et al. 1983) found a positive effect for humor on persuasion, this effect was present only for males. Similarly, Chattopadhyay and Basu (1990) found a moderately positive persuasive effect for humor. In their study, subjects with a prior positive brand attitude were more persuaded by humorous treatments than were subjects with preexisting negative brand attitudes.

Perhaps the strongest case for a persuasive effect of humor is presented in a study by Scott, Klein, and Bryant (1990), who employed a behavioral measure of persuasion quite different from the attitudinal measures of persuasion used in other studies. They found that attendance at social events (e.g., town picnics) was greater among subjects who received the humorous treatment of an ad than among those who received one of two other types of promotions. The humor treatment was not found to increase attendance in comparison to the other type of promotions at business events (e.g., town council meetings). The support for a persuasive effect shown in the Scott, Klein, and Bryant study must, however, be viewed with caution since it was just one study and was delivered through direct mail rather than in more common general advertising vehicles.

Overall the advertising literature has produced at least ten findings that found a positive effect of humor on persuasion. Five other studies produced equivocal findings. Only two studies, Markiewicz (1972) and Lammers et al. (1983), found a negative effect, and in the Lammers study the negative effect occurred only for female respondents. The Markiewicz study revealed that the addition of humor to a low-intensity soft-sell approach aided the level of persuasion while the addition of humor to a hard-sell approach actually harmed persuasion. This level-of-intensity factor appears to impact the level of persuasion garnered by humorous messages. Though there are relatively few studies that have looked at humor and persuasion, the risk of harming persuasion appears small. The evidence seems to lean more toward the British agency view that humor can aid persuasion than the equivocal American view that it neither harms nor helps (see Table 6.7). Unfortunately, most humor researchers of late have not focused on persuasion, opting to examine liking, A_{ad}, and A_b.

Table 6.9

Usage and Impact of Humor Type in Primetime TV Commercials (in percent)

Differential effects of humor type on communications goals

	Comic wit	Sentimental humor	Satire	Sentimental comedy	Full comedy	Non-humor control
Frequency of use	21	11	17	28	22	
Overall attention	.06[a]	-.02	.07	.06	.27	-.45
Message comprehension	-.15	—	.23	-.01	-.11	-.11
Descriptive comprehension (recall)	-.18	—	.21	-.13	.13	-.04
Perceived source trust	-.1	.00	-.26	.27	-.10	.11
Perceived source knowledge	-.09	-.21	-.05	.23	-.21	.16
Source liking	-.01	.31	-.23	.23	.15	-.19
Ad attractive (A_{ad})	.01	.23	-.08	.29	.05	-.22
Ad seen positively (A_{ad})	.10	.37	-.11	.32	.13	-.35
Enjoyed ad (A_{ad})	.26	.45	.16	.31	.48	-.78
Product quality (A_{b})	.12	-.29	-.18	.09	.21	
Intent to use	.02	-.15	.00	-.11	.18	
Perception humorousness by respondents[b]	.54	-.27	.94	.42	1.49	-1.62

Source: Adapted from Speck (1987).
[a]Numbers represent effect sizes.
[b]Midpoint 0, with -3 to +3.

116

Source Credibility

The results of the few advertising studies examining the effect of humor on source credibility can best be described as mixed (see Table 6.8). The advertising studies exploring source credibility have produced a smooth distribution of results with four studies reporting enhanced source credibility in humor conditions, five indicating neutral or mixed effects, and three indicating a negative relationship. Speck's (1987) work indicates that type of humor used may also influence humor's impact on credibility. Speck (1987) measured two aspects of source credibility: "knowledgeableness" and "trustworthiness." He found that although all sources in the experiment were viewed as moderately knowledgeable, the sources of non-humorous ads were viewed as more knowledgeable than the humorous sources. However, trustworthiness of a source was demonstrated to be enhanced through the use of one specific humor type. "Sentimental comedy," defined by Speck as a combination of two humor processes, arousal-safety and incongruity-resolution, in which the process of empathy-anxiety-relief occurs, was found to outperform other humor treatments and non-humor treatments on measures of trustworthiness (see Table 6.9).

In summary, overall the research indicates that it is unlikely that source credibility is consistently enhanced through the use of humor. This result is consistent with the opinions stated by U.S. and UK advertising practitioners (Madden and Weinberger 1984; Weinberger and Spotts 1989). There is even some evidence that humor may harm source credibility. These studies cast doubt on the tentative conclusion drawn by Sternthal and Craig (1973) that humor enhances source credibility.

Speck's Analysis of Communication Effects

Finally, in a large experimental study of television advertising Speck (1987: 1991) explicitly connected the type of humor and its communication impact. His five humor types noted earlier in this chapter (see Table 6.6) have widely varying effects. Using the effect sizes in Table 6.9, we can easily look at the impact of the different types of humor. Looking first at the positive effects, we see that all five humor types resulted in "enjoyed the ad," a measure of A_{ad}. Other measures of A_{ad} (ad attractive and ad seen positively) were positive for all except "satire." Satire also has a negative impact when we look at source liking, trust, and product quality. Despite a high-perceived humor rating, satire may represent a unique genre that carries with it negative associations that are

117

derived from the disparagement quality that is one of its hallmarks. Consistent with the discussion of attention earlier in this chapter, four of the five humor types had a positive impact and all were much more positive than the no-humor control ads. Sentimental humor had a slight negative effect.

The Speck framework suggests a situational use of humor types. For instance, though it is lowest on perceived humor, "sentimental humor," followed by "sentimental comedy" and "full comedy," works best at achieving positive affect. For source credibility (knowledge and trust), "sentimental comedy" is the only type that outperforms non-humor. This suggests that generally humor may actually harm source credibility.

The impact on recall and comprehension is as mixed as the literature has suggested. Only "satire" helps the two comprehension measures, with mixed or negative results for the other four humor types. Conversely, "full comedy" has the strongest impact on brand attitudes and "satire" and "sentimental humor" perform quite badly.

Thus, which humor type works best? Based on this one extensive TV study, Speck suggests that at just 22 percent of humorous TV ads, "full comedy" may be underutilized by advertisers. It has the strongest perceived humor ratings, which we have seen to be an important aspect of ad humor. Further, it has the strongest general effects on A_b, A_{ad}, intent, source liking, attention, and descriptive comprehension. It performs no worse than non-humor on message comprehension. The key negative is on source credibility.

Key Message Variables

Perceived Humor

There are a handful of message variables that have emerged over time as key influences in the advertising humor literature, none more important than the perception of humor. Unger (1995) found that there is a direct linkage between ad funniness, liking the ad, and liking the product. This affective view places a heavy burden on a humorous ad to actually be perceived by the audience as humorous. A number of recent studies have explicitly tested this aspect of humor and the results are instructive. Cline, Altsech, and Kellaris (2003) show both a direct path effect from perceived humor to A_{ad} as well as an indirect effect on A_{ad} through affect. Both paths indicate both the importance of perceived humor as well as the impact of on A_{ad}. Flaherty, Weinberger, and Gulas (2004) also found a strong affective connection between perceived humor in ads for a variety of different products. Their study in a radio advertising context found that ads perceived as more humorous were seen as more entertaining, useful, novel, and not annoying, and the brand was perceived as good.

Most interesting is that failed humor (an ad that was intended to be humorous but was not perceived that way) had associated with it some important negative features such as annoying, bad brand, and ad not useful. This result reminds us that humor is quite individual and that simply creating what one thinks is humorous is not sufficient. There appears to be a significant risk that because of individual taste, product, or circumstance, humor may not be appropriate and could have unwanted and unforeseen effects. Geuens and De Pelsmacker (1998) punctuate this point in research that found that a lack of irritation together with cheerfulness plays an important role in forming brand impressions, especially in the case of humor. Positive affect appears to be a key here, and if the pre-attention work by Janiszewski (1993) is correct, the affect generated by humor may have important unconscious effects. The message variable humor is therefore linked to the humor elicitation provoked by an ad (Wyer and Collins 1992).

This issue of a positive bounce from ads perceived as humorous and negative associations connected to failed humor places a burden on learning the factors that generate perceived humor or humor elicitation. Most of the studies chronicled have examined created humor rather than perceived humor. The fact is that in many of the studies the level of humor is not high. When manipulation checks are conducted between high and low humor or humor and non-humor, often the ranges are not very wide and in many cases a particular ad may be seen as humorous by some and not by others. A recent exception (Krishnan and Chakravarti 2003) investigated the influence of no-, moderate-, and high-humor treatments on claims and humor recall for unrelated humor. The result suggests that more humor may not always be best. We want ads to be perceived as humorous; after that threshold, the effects may not be linear. In fact, for claim recall, moderate humor outperformed no humor and high humor most consistently during incidental exposure to the ads. On a 7-point scale of perceived humor, the mean for no humor was 2.53, moderate humor 3.77, and high humor 5.06. Even the high humor is not exceptionally high. Recall that the Speck analysis in Table 6.9 found that the "full comedy" ads had the highest levels of perceived humor but performed the worst on message comprehension and did poorly on source trust and knowledge. On the other hand, "full comedy" was the most consistently strong performer on most of the other performance variables. This of course clouds the results because the Krishnan and Chakravarti study did not examine these other important outcome variables and so it is unclear whether high humor like "full comedy" in Speck's work, may have performed well on attention, source liking, intention, and so on if they had been measured.

Thus, what tends to make an ad perceived as humorous? A particularly important line of work by Alden, Mukherjee, and Hoyer (2000) developed a model and empirical testing that focuses on the relationship among incongruity, surprise, perceived humor, and attitude toward the ad. First they suggest that higher incongruity leads to more surprise. They provide evidence that the degree of surprise triggered by an ad is partly governed by what a comic might call a setup. For incongruity to exist an existing condition needs to be reversed or violated. Thus, Alden, Mukherjee, and Hoyer include "schema" familiarity as a key factor. This schema might be preexisting and shared wisdom of the audience's past experience or knowledge or it can be set up more directly by the ad itself. Woltman-Elpers, Mukherjee, and Hoyer (2004) conducted a moment-to-moment (MTM) analysis of TV ads and found that MTM surprise precedes MTM humor. That in turn predicts overall humor perception. This helps confirm the theorized connection between surprise and perceived humor, but what about the elements that move an audience from surprise to perceived humor? Alden and his colleagues show that warmth, playfulness, and ease of resolution are ingredients that help determine whether an ad is perceived as humorous. At least for the types of TV ads studied, this research provides important insight and may provide a model for how advertisers might pretest ads. The caution is that different types of humor may work differently and that their study focused just on humor that uses incongruity. As we saw in Table 6.9 from Speck's work, the effects of humor vary considerably. Even his four humor types that used incongruity differed in their perceived humor and in their effects on the varied outcome measures. Most all of the Speck's humor styles had a positive impact on A_{ad}, a result Alden and his colleagues also found. However, it is with the higher order effects that greater differences occur. As we know, A_{ad} is not the end of the story and it suggests that a greater battery of dependent measures needs to be examined to give more guidance about whether incongruity, surprise, and level of humor are linear. For instance, is humor its own virtue, where more is always better than less or none? This may not always be the case because a factor such as relatedness of the humor may become important.

Relatedness

Speck (1987) discusses several kinds of relatedness of humor and the message. First, there is intentional relatedness, which defines whether an ad's humor is dominant or whether it is subordinate to the message. Spotts, Weinberger, and Parsons (1997) utilized this framework to examine magazine advertising and found that 55 percent of the ads using humor were humor dominant. Unfortunately, with the exception of yellow low-involvement and fun products, the use of humor dominant ads did not perform well. Message-dominant ads where humor is subordinate and linked to either an information focus or image focus were used less often. The yellow products and also the white high-involvement and rational products seemed to benefit from a connection of humor and a connection to visuals in the ads. There was no consistent gain for any products when humor was related to information in the message-based ads.

A second type of relatedness that Speck outlined based on structural relatedness focuses on where in an ad the message elements come in a humor-dominant ad or where the humor comes in a message-dominant ad. In print this might mean page location and in a broadcast ad whether the elements occur at the start or end. Beyond Speck's own work, this is not an aspect of humor that has received significant attention in the advertising literature.

The third type of relatedness is thematic relatedness, which focuses on the connection between the message content or the product and humor. This is what most researchers mean when they refer to whether humor is related or not to the humor. The more general advertising literature has examined this issue and has concluded that meaningful connections between elements in an ad and the message improves message memory (Friedman and Friedman 1979; Edell and Staelin 1983). This suggestion seems quite intuitive, yet there has been relatively little study of the concept. Based on a few studies, Weinberger and Gulas (1992) argued that if we control for this type of relatedness some of the conflicting findings in earlier studies vanish. The few advertising studies that have directly tested thematic relatedness (Madden 1982; Weinberger and Campbell 1991; Altsech, Cline, and Kellaris 1999; Cline and Kellaris 1999; Lee and Mason 1999; Krishnan and Chakravarti 1993) have not always found that related humor is superior to unrelated humor. From Table 6.10, which summarizes these studies, we can see that there is some evidence that related humor can help attention, arousal, and intention; may assist recall and persuasion for more emotionally consumed products; aids A_{ad} and A_b (for ads with strong message arguments); and aids message and humor recall. The contrary findings suggest that unrelated humor boosts A_{ad} and A_b for low-involvement products and weak message arguments (Cline and Kellaris 1999). It also helps A_{ad} and A_b and reduces negative responses (Lee and Mason 1999). It should be noted that the Lee and Mason study also found that related humor outperformed the unrelated, though they both had positive effects on A_{ad} and A_b. Krishnan and Chakravarti conclude "that more relevant humor stimulates additional and separate rehearsal as well as humor-claims links, facilitating encoding and rehearsal" (241). In the first of their studies (Krishnan and Chakravarti 1993), the researchers found unrelated humor can also aid recall of message claims and recall of the humor executions. More generally, they suggest that the effects of incidental exposure to advertising may be understated by cognitive measures of recall and recognition. The pre-attention and affect literature that we touched on earlier would support this contention. The implication for an emotional element like humor may be that its subconscious effects might be poorly detected.

Repetition

Of course repeating commercials in an advertising campaign is a popular practice with the belief that greater opportunity for exposure improves awareness and recall. There is a large body of mainly psychology research suggesting that mere exposure effects (Zajonc 1968, 1980) enhance liking. This would argue for more repetition. However, the most comprehensive and prominent work about repetition is Berlyne's (1970) two-factor theory, which consists of a habituation phase of exposure, sometimes called wear in, and a second phase, when boredom sets in as wear out occurs. In the early stages more exposure is helpful. Cacioppo and Petty (1979) found that moderate levels of repetition were optimal, apparently striking a balance between the necessary wear-in phase where positive cognitive responses increase and before wear out begins, when negative cognitive responses develop and where some believe inattention develops and dominates. A delay in wear out may be possible when ad messages are more complex, making processing more difficult and thus delaying the tedium of repetition (Anand and Sternthal 1990).

The influence of repetition has been a topic in the advertising literature for decades (Zielske 1959), the results of which were cogently summarized by Vakratsas and Ambler (1999). They state in a summary table that "in low-involvement situations, repetition of different versions of an advertisement prevents early decay of advertising effects." And, they continue, "recall and attitudes can be maintained at a high level if an advertising campaign consists of a series of advertisements" (31). Campbell and Keller (2003) found that ads for unfamiliar brands exhibited wear out at lower levels of repetition than ads for familiar brands.

Table 6.10

Relatedness and Humor

	Unrelated humor	Related humor
Madden (1982)	− attention, arousal (compared to related humor) + attention, arousal, intention + intention − recall (existing product)	
Weinberger and Campbell (1991)		+ recall, persuasion (for high and low involvement and feeling products— Yellow and Red products)
Altsech, et al. (1999)		+ A_{ad}, A_b and intention (with strong arguments)
Cline and Kellaris (1999)	+ A_{ad} and A_b (with low involvement product and weak arguments)	
Lee and Mason (1999)	+ helps A_{ad}, A_b and reduces negative responses 0 than non-humor	+ A_{ad}, A_b compared to unrelated humor
Krishnan and Chakravarti (2003)		+ claims and humor recall compared to unrelated humor

Note: Relatedness here refers generally to thematic relatedness of humor to the message, product, arguments, or other central ad elements.

The importance of repetition for ads using humor is accentuated by the issue of perceived humor. If ads loose their ability to generate a humor effect, the evidence of failed humor that we touched on earlier in the chapter is that there may be negative consequences. Belch and Belch (1984) found that humorous ads decayed at the same rate as non-humorous ads, but that the optimal level was three exposures, with five being too high. There is some evidence that humorous ads may wear out faster than non-humorous treatments over repeated exposures (Gelb and Zinkhan 1985). This finding has intuitive appeal because the surprise element is often present in humor and is a key to humor success (Alden, Mukherjee, and Hoyer 2000); Woltman-Elpers, Mukherjee, and Hoyer 2004) is likely to become less surprising with continued repetition. Zinkhan and Gelb (1990) concluded, "not all humorous commercials (comedy acts) 'wear out' with repetition; some seem to get better, as anticipation of what will be presented evokes an anticipatory humorous response" (440). Of course, it is possible for humor to persist. Consider *M*A*S*H* or *I Love Lucy,* which remain funny for decades. However, also consider that these programs represent varied humor executions and that the repeated viewing of a particular episode may not occur for months or years. Seeing it again has a familiar wear in before wear out has a chance to occur. Like Bill Murray in *Groundhog Day,* watching the same *M*A*S*H* episode over and over is likely to lead to wear out quite quickly. As ad scores on liking diminish, Haley and Baldinger (1991) found 73 percent of the products involved had sales failures. The potential for wear out carries with it the likelihood that liking will diminish, possibly leaving products vulnerable.

Wyer and Collins (1992) interpreted humor effects through the lens of elaboration. If humor has high elaboration potential, it wears out more slowly because it has more implications. They argue that all jokes become stale after a while. It is possible that more complex humor triggers greater elaboration and forestalls the boredom of wear out. This would suggest that ads that use very simple and noncomplex humor might wear out faster. The clear implication from the broader advertising literature is that varied executions of the same ad—adding complexity and variety—delay the boredom. Based on Campbell and Keller's work (2003), this may be particularly true for unfamiliar brands to forestall their faster wear out.

Conclusion

We know that humor is part of a larger entertainment construct that can be triggered by any number of devices that may be emotional or not. Humor in advertising seems to be dominated by non-tendentious humor that is not sexual or disparaging. Most ads seem to use incongruity either by itself or in combination with disparagement or arousal-safety. The greatest perceived humor was seen in ads labeled "full comedy" by Speck, which used incongruity, arousal-safety, and disparagement. The effects of humor even in this high humor condition are not all positive. Generally, the positive effects of humor are on attention, affect, source liking, A_{ad}, and A_b.

The connection to repetition is that humor can wear out. The broader advertising literature suggests that varied executions and more elaborate ads may delay the effects. There seems to be a growing body of evidence that surprise and humor are linked and that surprise is derived from complexity.

Figure 6.1 **Message Factors and the Challenge Model**

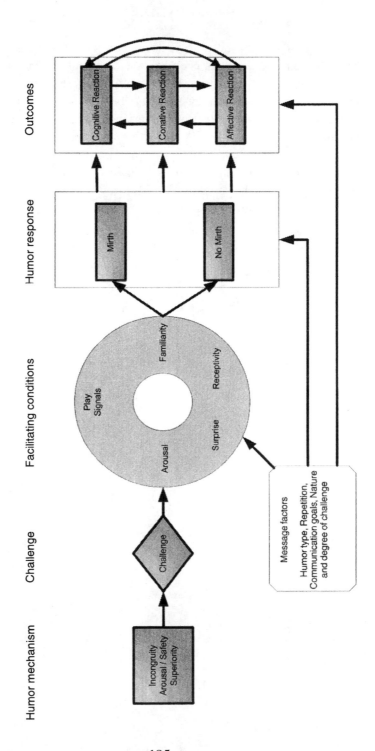

The delicate balance that needs to be developed is that the complexity needs to capitalize on a situation that people recognize as outside the norm and the resolution needs to come easily. However, as suggested by the repetition literature, resolution that is too easy may not be elaborate or complex enough to prevent rapid wear out. Either clever variations that keep the audience off guard or a complexity within the execution may help delay any wear-out effect. Finally, it appears that a warm and playful context to the humor seems to facilitate its creation and enhance A_{ad}. Figure 6.1 links the message variables covered in this chapter to the challenge model and serves put the message factor in perspective.

——— 7 ———

Context Issues

In humor, timing is critical. Critchley (2002) states that humorous timing consists of two temporal dimensions: "duration" and "instant." He uses the analogy of the rubber band to illustrate these dimensions. Duration—the stretching of the band—is the setup of the joke. Instant refers to the snapping of the band, in other words, the punch line. Critchley's (2002) work provides a model that aids in the discussion of humor types such as incongruity-resolution as outlined earlier in this book. Incongruity is a type of "duration" and resolution is a type of "instant."

Yet timing has a third dimension as well, which we will call "moment." Moment refers to placement of the humor in time and space. An attempt at humor in a given moment may be successful while exactly the same humorous execution in another moment may fail. In the days following the tragic shootings at Columbine High School in Littleton, Colorado, the syndicated cartoon *Zits* featured a high school student who tells his parents that he has narrowed his career choices down to "paramedic or professional assassin" (Kennedy 1999). This cartoon was actually written and submitted to the syndicate weeks before the Columbine massacre. Many of the over 700 newspapers that carried the strip modified or pulled the comic prior to publication. However, due to oversight or poor judgment, it did run unaltered in many newspapers, including the *Boston Globe* (Kennedy 1999). If the cartoon had appeared on the day that it was written, it is likely that many readers would have found it humorous. However, by the time the cartoon made it to print the moment had changed and what was a well-intentioned attempt at humor appeared to be a mean-spirited demonstration of insensitivity. The moment was not appropriate for this particular "joke."

Moment can be critically important in an attempt at humor. However, it is best analyzed as a part of the broader construct of context. Context includes moment, but also includes other aspects of the situation as well.

Whether or not something is humorous depends in very large part on the context. Indeed, the context may create the humor. For example a workplace gripe, not intended as humor, could elicit a humorous response from onlookers if they can see that the boss is in earshot, but the speaker does not. In a different context, with no boss present, no perception of humor would occur. Similarly, signs, traffic and others, that are innocuous when viewed individually, can create humor when viewed together. Numerous examples of these appear on various humor Web sites but the veracity of these examples is difficult to independently confirm. Nonetheless, it is likely that at least some of them are real. Juxtaposition is also a frequent source of humor on cinema multiplex signs when multiple film titles combine to create humorous combinations.

The Importance of Context in Advertising

The role of context on advertising effectiveness has been widely studied (see e.g., Goldberg and Gorn 1987; Kennedy 1971; Murry, Lastovicka, and Singh 1992; Soldow and Principe 1981). Kennedy concluded in 1971 that ads were not independent of program context. Norris and Colman (1992) stated the case for context effects more broadly: "The same source delivering the same message to the same audience on separate occasions might produce very different effects depending on the differing programming or editorial contexts in which the message appears" (38).

Norris and her colleagues have studied context effects extensively (Norris and Colman 1992, 1993, 1994; Norris, Colman, and Alexio 2003). Norris and Colman (1992) found that the more subjects were involved with the editorial content of a magazine, the less they were able to recall about the ads contained in the magazine. They found a similar negative correlation in studies of television advertising (Norris and Colman 1993, 1994). However, when respondents were examined in a seminatural viewing environment in which they were able to select from four television programs, the correlations were reversed (Norris, Colman, and Alexio 2003). In this study, respondents' self-ratings of involvement, entertainment, and enjoyment of programming were positively correlated with ad recall, A_{ad}, A_b, and purchase intention. Interestingly, the study also found that high self-reports of program involvement were correlated with better recall of ads in the first of two commercial breaks whereas high self-reports of program enjoyment were correlated with better recall of ads in the second commercial break (Norris, Colman, and Alexio 2003). In another study of television advertising, Tavassoli, Shultz, and Fitzsimons (1995) found an inverted-U relationship between viewer involvement and recall and A_{ad}. An increase in viewer involvement, from low to moderate, resulted in an increase in ad effectiveness measures. However, an increase from moderate to high involvement resulted in decreased measures of ad effectiveness. Based on the work that has been done, it is apparent that context effects are complex and the study of these effects presents many methodological challenges.

The issue of context becomes more important with new media such as the Internet where automated ad placement and dynamic Web content create shifting sand in which to place ads. This can lead to problems. There are anecdotal reports of pop-up ads appearing on Web sites at inopportune times. It has been reported that a United Airlines ad appeared on a September 11, 2001, news Web site displaying a photo of the burning World Trade Center, an ad for hot air balloon rides reportedly appeared on a news Web site story about a hot air balloon crash, and an ad promoting an online IQ quiz that featured a famous humorous photo of Albert Einstein sticking his tongue out was reportedly attached to a news story regarding a brain-damaged woman. In another context, the ad is likely to have been perceived as humorous. This placement, however, likely elicited a different response. Given the fluid nature of Web sites it is difficult to independently confirm whether or not any of these specific placements occurred, however, it seems likely that the filters used by ad servers are imperfect and that inopportune placements can, and likely do, happen.

Context is a multidimensional construct. With regard to humor in advertising, there are four important dimensions of context that affect the use of humor: source context, media context, micro-social context, and macro-environmental context.

Source Context

As we previously noted, humor cannot be understood in a vacuum. Whether or not something is humorous is largely dependent on factors outside of the humor execution itself. Presidential candidate Richard Nixon's 1968 appearance on *Laugh-In* was not funny because of the line he delivered. "Sock it to me" was an oft-repeated catch phrase of the show. Nor was it funny because of his great delivery, although the wooden nature of the delivery may have helped. It was funny simply because the source of the line was Richard Nixon. At the time it was very rare for national political figures to appear on entertainment programming, particularly a pop-culture show such as *Laugh-In*, known for its irreverence. Additionally, among political figures, Nixon would

129

seem to be the least likely candidate for such an appearance since he was perceived by many to be humorless. Aristotle claimed that "the secret to humor is surprise." Nixon's performance was a surprise.

Decades later, Robert Dole carried the role of politician as comedian into the realm of advertising. After his failed presidential bid, Dole appeared as a spokesperson for the impotence drug Viagra in what many viewed as a courageous act. This serious ad provided a powerful setup for a later humorous ad in which the "little blue friend" that helps Dole "feel vital again" turns out to be a can of Pepsi (Michaelson 2001). The ad is made more humorous because, like Nixon's public image, Bob Dole's was largely one of dour seriousness. It is interesting to ponder whether the lighter side of Bob Dole, which was displayed in humorous advertising for Pepsi and Visa, could have helped his political aspirations if it had been evident prior to his failed presidential bid.

A similar source effect may occur with advertisers. A humorous ad may be more effective if it is used by an advertiser that is generally associated with serious or sentimental advertising or if it is used in a category where humorous advertising is little used, thus creating surprise. For example, Paul Wellstone's successful campaign for a U.S. Senate seat in 1990 employed a set of quirky television commercials. Since campaigns for the Senate are rarely known for humor, the light humorous technique in the Wellstone ads had more of a humorous effect than it likely would have had if used in a beer or soft drink ad, where humor is more commonly used. However, since the source dimension of context is very similar to issues addressed elsewhere in this book, in sections on source effects and product effects, we will focus our attention here on the other aspects of context.

Media Context: Humor in Advertising and Advertising in Humor

The interaction between advertising and the media in which it is contained is complex. This complexity is demonstrated in a study conducted by Feltham and Arnold (1994). This was not specifically a study of humorous advertising. The variable of interest, programming, and advertising consistency was conceptualized in terms of logos and pathos. However, logos were manipulated through the use of a humorous camera ad (low logos) and a rational camera ad (high logos), thus giving some insight into effects of humorous advertising. The authors found that television advertising that was consistent with the programming in which it was contained, based on measures of logos and pathos, resulted in lower recall but higher A_{ad}, A_b, and purchase intention. This suggests, paradoxically, that ad/program consistency lowers recall and enhances persuasion. So consistency can have a negative or positive effect depending on the communication outcome sought.

Although many studies suggest an interaction effect between program environment and commercials contained within that environment (see e.g., Coulter 1998; Goldberg and Gorn 1987; Kamins, Marks, and Skinner 1991; Mathur and Chattopadhyay 1991), several studies that examined context effects with a specific focus on humor found no significant effects (Cantor and Venus 1980; Madden 1982; Markiewicz 1972), or found very limited effects (Murphy, Cunningham, and Wilcox 1979). These findings are counterintuitive. If context affects advertising, as most research findings indicate, why would humorous ads be immune from these effects? Based on these puzzling findings and the inconclusive research of the time, in 1992 we called for more research on context effects as they relate specifically to humorous advertising (Weinberger and Gulas 1992). Our call was answered (Perry et al. 1997a; De Pelsmacker, Geuens, and Anckaert 2002).

In an experimental study that manipulated level of ad humor and level of program humor, Perry and his colleagues conclude, "Overall, the more humorous a commercial is, the greater the benefit for a product advertiser. The more humorous a program is, however, the more dangerous it may be for advertisers to include their humorous commercials in the program. This is because it seems the commercials must boast a higher level of humor than would otherwise be necessary, in order to be recalled after exposure to a high-humor program" (Perry et al. 1997a, 36).

Before the reader draws a broad general conclusion from this finding, it should be noted that the Perry et al. (1997a) study also uncovered gender effects and complex interactions that suggest further research is necessary on this issue.

Another study that specifically evaluated the interaction of humorous television commercials and humorous programming was conducted by Furnham, Gunter, and Walsh (1998). In this 2×2 experimental study, six humorous or six non-humorous ads were inserted into either humorous or non-humorous programming. This resulted in four conditions:

- Humorous program with humorous ads
- Humorous program with non-humorous ads
- Non-humorous program with non-humorous ads
- Non-humorous program with humorous ads

The study found that overall unaided recall of advertising was stronger for ads contained in the non-humorous programming than in the humorous programming regardless of ad type. However, the study also found that unaided recall for the humorous ads was enhanced by the non-humorous programming and unaided recall of non-humorous ads was slightly higher in the humorous programming than in the non-humorous programming. The authors conclude, "humour with humour does not fare as well as humour with non-humour" (Furnham, Gunter, and Walsh 1998, 565).

De Pelsmacker, Geuens, and Anckaert (2002) conducted the most comprehensive study to date on this issue. Their research design included three types of media context: humorous, warm, and rational. Each of these types was operationalized in both a television format (ten-minute program excerpts) and a print format (ten-page mock magazines). Ads were selected similarly. Six television ads, two humorous, two warm, and two rational, and six print ads, two in each category, were tested. The study also examined levels of involvement and age of respondents. This complex study produced complex results.

> For low involvement persons, ads embedded in similar contexts appear to lead to better understanding and a more positive affective reaction. . . . In high involvement situations, the contrast effect . . . and the resulting perception of novelty and unexpectedness appear to stimulate consumers to process the advertising stimulus even more. . . . However, the congruency effect only leads to significant effects on two components of A_{ad}. Cognitive elaboration, measured as the perception of informativeness of the ad and ad content and brand recall, is not influenced by the interaction between congruency and product category involvement.
>
> (DePelsmacker, Geuens, and Anckaert 2002, 58–59)

The study also found an age effect. For older respondents, highly appreciated context was associated with positive advertising evaluations. Additionally, ad content and brand recall was higher when ads were embedded in congruent context. The authors posit that this finding may be due to diminished processing resources and the concomitant reliance on contextually based processing strategies.

Micro-Social Context

Zhang and Zinkhan (1991) found that humorous ads are perceived as more humorous if the audience consists of more than one person. While it is possible to enjoy humor alone, it appears that the experience is enhanced by a social setting. This effect is so powerful that even a simulated social setting enhances enjoyment.

Martin and Gray (1996) found that a radio comedy show was perceived as more humorous by participants of an experiment when recorded audience laughter was present than when it was not. Participants in the recorded laughter condition were also found to laugh more than participants in the control condition. This effect is not lost on the producers of television comedy programs, which often film before live audiences or have added laugh tracks to provide a "social" setting for viewers at home.

Humorous ads viewed with others are likely to be perceived as more humorous than humorous ads viewed alone. Although marketers generally have little control over the social setting in which ads will be seen, there are some advertising vehicles that produce predictable viewing situations. With the average Super Bowl party hosting seventeen people, the Super Bowl is a bigger at-home party occasion than New Year's eve (Kanner 2004). Kanner quotes noted advertising executive Jerry Della Femina: "Humor works because the Super Bowl is one of the rare occasions when TV is watched by groups" (6).

The social effect of humor also has methodological implications. Pretesting of advertising is often done using groups of respondents. Similarly, academic studies evaluating humorous ads often do so in a group setting. This methodology may inflate the perceived humor of a given execution, which may affect the results of the study. This issue will be discussed more fully in Chapter 8.

Macro-Social Context

Advertising During the Great Depression

The Great Depression is aptly named. Between 1929 and 1933 the gross national product (GNP) in the United States dropped from $103 billion to $55.7 billion (An 2003). In 1929, unemployment in the United States was 3.2 percent. In 1930 it had increased to 8.7 percent. It would increase again in 1931, again in 1932, and yet again in 1933, when it peaked at a staggering 24.9 percent. The unemployment rate did not drop below 14 percent until 1941 (U.S. Census Bureau 2003) and the outbreak of World War II. This ten-year period of double-digit unemployment rates marks the bleakest economic period in modern U.S. history. Such widespread economic hardship had a broad impact on American culture and society, including the entertainment of the era. "The balancing act for film-making was to both reflect the realism and cynicism of the Depression period, while also providing escapist enter-tainment to boost the morale of the public" (filmsite.org 2004). It is reason-able to expect that it also affected advertising executions during the period. Although a humorous ad could provide a welcome escape, the reality of the economy suggests that this was not a time for frivolity.

There does appear to be empirical evidence of a more serious approach to advertising during the era. In an analysis of advertising visuals of the 1920s and 1930s, An (2003) found a statistically significant difference in the use of literal visuals and symbolic visuals. Literal visuals communicate factual in-formation about a product whereas symbolic visuals communicate through abstract associations such as lifestyle, metaphor, aesthetics, or storytelling (An 2003). An (2003) found that ads of the 1930s differed from those of the 1920s in that those of the later period were more likely to use literal visuals, which the author attributes in part to the economic insecurities of the time.

As noted in Chapter 1, the appropriateness of humor in advertising was an issue of much debate in the 1920s and 1930s. This debate was due in large part to the growth of "scientific" methods in advertising. But it no doubt was also influenced by the business cycle.

In an illustration of both the seriousness and silliness of the era, the hard-sell approach taken by many advertisers during the period was mocked in contemporaneous advertising satire that appeared in *Ballyhoo,* a popular magazine of the time:

> Slenderine did it! Miss Susie Susskopf of Little Falls, Ohio, weighed 430 pounds on April 1, 1931. She was torn down socially, unpopular at parties, and while she could sing like Helen Morgan, nobody would let her sit on the piano. Discouraged she jumped into the Hudson River and caused the famous flood of 1931. Things went from bad to worse for Susie, until one day a friend told her about Slenderine. On April 15, 1931, Susie had re-duced to 60 pounds, had won the bathing beauty contest at Atlantic City and married a millionaire. Sounds almost impossible, doesn't it? Well, it is. Slenderine: it is nice on codfish balls, good for squeaky shoes, and keeps woolen underwear from shrinking. (*Ballyhoo,* January 1932, reprinted in McFadden 2003, 126)

Advertising Post–9/11/2001

The respective roles of October 29, 1929 (Black Tuesday), and September 11, 2001, in shaping American history and culture are best left to historians. However, it is clear that the events occurring on both dates had wide-ranging effects. The cost of replacing the destroyed and damaged physical capital in New York City alone has been estimated at $21.6 billion (Bram, Orr, and Rapaport 2002). The loss of television advertising revenue in the week following the attack has been estimated at $313.2 million (Raine 2003). The costs to the U.S. economy as a whole through the loss of life, drop in stock prices, diminished travel, increased security and military expenditures, has been in the hundreds of billions. Economically, this is unlike any other date since 1929. The event also had a profound effect on the American psyche.

The days and weeks following September 11, 2001, saw a decrease in public expressions of humor. The September 24, 2001, issue of the *New Yorker* was published without cartoons for only the second time in the publication's history, the first being August 31, 1946, after the bombing of Hiroshima (Tugend 2002). Bob Garfield cautioned advertisers in a September 17, 2001, editorial that humorous ads may be construed as irrelevant in a post–9/11 environment.

> We can argue endlessly about how many people you can risk offending before your mordant wit or raunchiness is deemed beyond the pale. At this moment in history, however, the pool of the thin-skinned isn't 25,000. It is 250 million.
>
> Tread lightly. For certain, for the next weeks and months, there can be no airplane jokes, no New York jokes, no military jokes, no injury jokes, no death jokes, no cop jokes, no fireman jokes. That alone will cramp the industry's style. But it is not just that. Levity itself will be viewed with suspicion and distaste. As the airwaves gradually resume programming and ad traffic, many a fist will be shaken at the indecency of content that 10 days ago seemed delightful. (Garfield 2001, 29)

It appears that many advertisers took heed of this advice. For several months following 9/11 it appears that marketers took a more somber approach to advertising (Howard 2002). However, in the absence of a detailed longitudinal content analysis across media and product, which to our knowledge has not been conducted, it is impossible to ascertain the true level of humor usage pre– and post–9/11. Nor has any study been done, to our knowledge, that specifically addressed the effectiveness of humor in advertising from a pre- and post–9/11 perspective.

Ad-Induced Context

Although the focus of this chapter is the effects of context on humorous advertising, it should be noted that context effects have two other

135

conceptualizations with regard to humorous advertising. First, humorous ads provide a context for the medium in which they are contained. Perry and his colleagues found that the entertainment value of a television program is increased by humorous ads contained in the program (Perry et al. 1997b; Perry 2001). This effect has been generally overlooked in academic research. Although the effect is tangential to the focus of this book, it might be useful in media analysis. Broadcasters could perhaps influence program ratings by encouraging the use of humorous advertising. For example, there is evidence that the viewership of the Super Bowl is enhanced by the entertainment value of its commercials (McAllister 1999). Although the Super Bowl is a unique broadcast, a similar effect might be present for other programs as well.

Broadcast ads are generally shown in pods of several commercials at a time. The "batting order" within the pod establishes context as well. A humorous ad that follows another humorous ad may perform differently than a humorous ad that follows a warm sentimental ad.

Finally, there is a micro level of context within the ad itself. The humorous ad provides the context for the product and brand information contained in the ad. This context is distinctly different from that of a non-humorous ad. It has been posited that contextual information, such as an affective response to a humorous ad, is stored along with the information contained within the ad (Shapiro and Lang 1991), thus providing a mechanism for humor effectiveness. However, since the theoretical mechanisms of humor have been addressed earlier in this book, we will not reopen this issue here.

Conclusion

As we have done in many previous chapters, we include here a visual connection between the topic covered in the chapter with the challenge model that we introduced in Chapter 2 as a means of connecting disparate aspects of humor (Figure 7.1). In spite of the significant body of research on context, many questions remain regarding context effects (Moorman, Neijens, and Smit 2002). Additional work needs to be conducted in this area. Specifically, research regarding context should be expanded to include new forms of context such as product placement and Internet advertising. With this expanded view of context, research should explore interactions with regard to audience factors such as age and gender, need for cognition,

Figure 7.1 **Context and the Challenge Model**

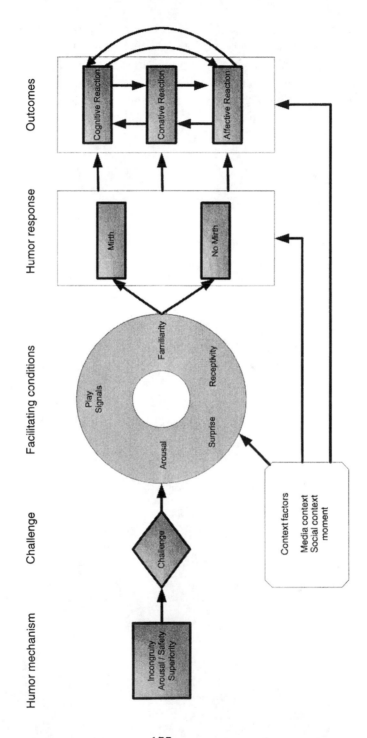

involvement, existing brand attitudes, and other variables. Product/context interactions should also be explored. Differences with multiple exposures over time (i.e., the same ad in a given television program each week) is another aspect of context worthy of research. The study of these issues raises methodological challenges. But humor research is rife with method-ological challenges, as we will see in Chapter 8.

8

Research Methodology Issues

E.B. White said, "Analyzing humor is like dissecting a frog. Few people are interested and the frog dies of it." We respectfully disagree with White on his first point. If few were interested, you would not be reading this book and the dozens of studies referenced here would not have been conducted. However, we cannot argue with White on his second point. It is difficult, perhaps impossible, to analyze humor without destroying the humor. Of the scores of studies reviewed for this book few would be considered even marginally humorous. But then it is not the intention of the authors of these works to be humorous, nor is it our intention. It is their intention to be illuminating, and this is a difficult task in the case of humor.

In some ways analyzing humor is akin to analyzing sunsets. Was today's more beautiful than yesterday's, or more awe inspiring? Can the beauty of a sunset be captured by meteorological research? Perhaps astronomy, physical geography, optics, physics, or some other discipline would provide a better perspective on the subject. In any case, we are not likely to fully understand the essence of a sunset via science. Furthermore, in the process of analysis we may lose appreciation for the beauty that motivated the research in the first place. If we examine each individual element of a flower, or a butterfly, or a waterfall we may not see any beauty. Yet, as a whole the beauty is apparent. Similarly with humor, if we examine the "joke" removed from the context, or change the source, or change the moment, or change the audience, in order to facilitate study, we may change the nature of the humor and kill the frog in the process. We are thus faced with a dilemma. It is difficult, perhaps impossible, to fully understand humor without manipulating it in some way. However, if we manipulate it in any way, we have changed it and we may no longer be studying what we think we are studying.

There is, however, science in sunsets and waterfalls and frogs. There is also science in the creation of humor and there is certainly science in the study of it. The science we are referring to here is Kuhn's (1970) notion of science. That is, a science of paradigms. For example, the superiority theorists (e.g., Gruner 2000) can find aggression, or other forms of superiority, in even the most light-hearted humorous executions. The incongruity theorists (e.g., Nerhardt 1977), similarly tend to find incongruity in all humor. Some even find humor in all incongruity. We are not attempting here to disparage the work of the scholars of these schools of thought, nor any other, but rather we wish to note that research done within a particular paradigm is likely to be supportive of that paradigm. More broadly, some humor researchers approach the issue via linguistics, and others via psychology, sociology, or physiology. Caron (2002) even makes the case that "evolution" should serve as a theoretical paradigm for humor research. Whatever the perspective taken, most find empirical evidence that supports their position.

Research methodology issues are complicated by the fact that the construct of interest itself is open to interpretation. We have used the term "humor" throughout this text, although some might argue that what we are really referring to is "comedy," which they view as a different construct than humor (Stern 1996). Caron (2002) uses the term "the comic" to refer to research on laughter, smiles, and the comic situations and artifacts that create them. He contrasts this term with humor, which he feels is more narrowly defined. Thus the nature of the conceptualization of humor also affects the nature of the research undertaken to explore it.

Humor is not unique in this regard. As Kuhn (1970) noted, it is the course of "normal science" to work within a paradigm. We too are working within a paradigm in the construction of this book. The work that we have reviewed here is predominately rooted in the positivist perspective. This perspective is consistent with the majority of the research done on humor in advertising. Yet it should be noted that we carry our own methodological baggage to the project. We both have a personal leaning toward the positivist approach. This leaning undoubtedly affects our research, and our evaluation of research, as it is reflected in this book.

As we have noted earlier, humor research occurs in many disciplines and uses many methodologies. Each of the methods used to study humor has its advantages and disadvantages. In discussing these advantages and disadvantages it will be necessary to revisit many of the topics covered earlier in this book, namely: audience factors, product factors, context issues, and wear out. In addition to these issues there are other methodological concerns that face humor researchers. We will address those here as well.

Advertising Research

The challenges of advertising research date back to the roots of advertising. The oft-quoted axiom, "I know that half of my advertising is wasted but I do not know which half," is most commonly attributed to department store pioneer John Wanamaker (see e.g., Liodice 2004; White 2002). The quote has also been attributed to William Wrigley (Caples 1974) and to "one of the world's largest manufacturers" (Reeves 1961: 1977). It is likely that all to whom it has been attributed made this observation, each perhaps believing it to be an original insight. Countless others have probably held similar beliefs. The statement resonates with many because of the difficulty in measuring advertising effectiveness. Reeves (1961: 1977) posits that one of the most popular myths of business is to attempt to measure the effectiveness of an advertising campaign based on sales results. Obviously, good advertising should have a positive influence on sales, but sales are the result of far more than just advertising. Caples (1974) offers seventeen ways to test advertising. His list is by no means exhaustive. The complexity of measuring advertising effects remains a pressing concern as noted by Bob Liodice of the Association of National Advertisers (ANA), a person that *Advertising Age* listed as one of "10 Who Made a Mark on Marketing" in 2004 (*Advertising Age* 2004a).

> Marketing accountability is one of the most important subjects we have in front of us at the ANA—and for very good reasons. Too often, the marketing industry had been blistered by criticism of our inability to connect "the cause" with "the effect."
>
> We believe so much in this subject that we, at the ANA, will be raising the marketing accountability "bar" at every opportunity. We applaud the work of our comrades at the Radio Advertising Bureau, the Advertising Research Foundation, the Interactive Advertising Bureau and others for their efforts to help the industry raise that bar.
>
> We really are making strides to guessing less and measuring more. We, as an industry, have a long way to go. (Liodice 2004)

Advertising has been in existence in one form or another since the very beginnings of formalized trade (see Chapter 1), yet we are still not able to tell with sufficient certainty whether or not a given ad was successful. This is because advertising research is notoriously complex. Did the ad reach our customers and potential customers? Did they attend to it? Did they understand it?

141

Did they remember any of the copy points? Did they like it? Did they believe it? Did they remember it? Did they see it enough times? Did they see it too many times? Did they see it at the right time? What other information do the customers have about our product and our company? What information do they need? What are our competitors saying? The answers to these and many more questions need to be answered to assess advertising and the questions are not independent of each other. Humor in advertising, of course, is a sub-discipline within both humor research and advertising research and thus it carries with it the methodological complexities of each field.

Doctoral Dissertation Research Methodology

As with any intellectual product, there is a range of quality among doctoral dissertations. Generally speaking, however, dissertations represent the high-water mark of research in a field at the time that they are performed. Not only do dissertations capture a full review of the literature, they also utilize state of the art methodology. This methodology is designed in light of all of the research conducted to date on a given issue. The methodology is proposed and defended before a dissertation committee consisting typically of senior members of the faculty. Dissertations are prepared by students at premier research institutions, under the direction of the research faculty. For many scholars, the dissertation represents the largest single research project of their academic careers and thus dissertations form the basis of many articles published in the top academic journals. We can therefore look to dissertations for insights into high-quality research methodology.

Numerous dissertations have been conducted that specifically explore humor in advertising (Bauerly 1989; Bender 1993; Cline 1997; Kennedy 1972; Madden 1982; Markiewicz 1972; Michaels 1997; Speck 1987; Zhang 1992). Each of these dissertations used an experimental design. Details regarding the methodology of selected dissertations are shown in Table 8.1. The experimental method has distinct advantages over other methods but it has its limitations as well.

Lab Studies Versus Field Studies

With the notable exception of Scott, Klein, and Bryant (1990), most humor studies have been conducted in a laboratory setting of one sort or another (see Table 8.2). For purposes of advertising research, a laboratory can be a marketing research facility, a college classroom, a conference room, or any

Table 8.1

Humor Studies: Selected Doctoral Dissertation Research Methodologies

Dissertation	Method	Subjects
Madden (1982)	2 x 2 x 3 factorial design	326 undergraduate sophomore and junior business and communication students at the University of Massachusetts (158 men and 168 women). Tested in groups of 20 in separate language laboratory booths with subjects randomly assigned to one of two treatments for each of the 20 person sessions. Gender was balanced in each treatment condition.
	Examined Product (mature, new) Context (humorous, non-humorous program) Humor (product-related, product-unrelated, non-humor) **Dependent variables** Attention Comprehension Retention Message reaction Attitude toward the product Behavioral intention Thought listing task **Stimulus** Radio ad for traditional milk (mature) and sweet acidophilus milk (new) professionally produced. Ads for both products represented as from the California Milk Advisory Board.	

(continued)

143

Table 8.1 (*continued*)

Dissertation	Method	Subjects
Speck (1987)	6 x 5 factorial	182 undergraduates from junior and senior marketing classes at Texas Tech University. Gender was balanced in treatment groups (92 men and 90 women). Testing took place in groups of 6–20.

Examined
Humor type (comic wit, sentimental humor, satire, sentimental wit, full comedy, non-humor)

Product category (fast foods, snacks, drinks, personal goods, high/big ticket)—selected to be gender neutral

Dependent variables
Attention
Recall
Comprehension
Wearout
Attitude to the source
Attitude to the ad
Attitude to the product

Other factors
Perceived humor

144

Bauerly (1989)

Stimulus
Thirty humor-dominant television
ads taped from actual broadcast were
shown to groups of subjects in pods of
ten ads. Two control ads remained in
constant position with test ads rotated.
All ads were viewed before questioning began.

286 undergraduate college of business students
at Western Illinois University

2 x 2 x 2 between subjects factorial
design

Examined
Product class congruity (congruent,
incongruent)
Target of humor (product, users)
Program context (humorous, serious)

58 percent male

Gender examined as a blocking variable

Measurements
Thought listing task
A_{ad}
A_b
Recall

Stimulus
Television commercials for fictional
brands professionally produced
for the study

(continued)

145

Table 8.1 (*continued*)

Dissertation	Method	Subjects
Michaels (1997)	2 x 2 x 2 factorial	344 undergraduates at Wayne State University
	Examined	
	Humor (present, absent)	
	Self-monitoring (high, low)	
	Argument type (quality-based, image-based)	
	Product type (social, non-social)	
	Dependent variables	
	Perceived attention	
	Comprehension	
	Persuasiveness	
	Originality	
	Price willing to pay	
	Purchase intention	
	Liking of ad	
	Liking of brand	
	Confidence in judgments	
	Stimulus	
	Print ads for fictional brands produced for the study	
Cline (1997)	*Experiment 1*	253 undergraduate marketing students at the University of Cincinnati
	2 x 2 x 2 factorial design	
	Examined	51 percent female
	Humor strength (high, low)	
	Humor claims relevancy (high, low)	
	Need for levity (NFL) (high, low)	

146

Stimulus
Magazine ads for fictional brands produced by the researcher for the study

Experiment 2
2 x 2 x 2 factorial design

Examined
Humor expectancy (high, low)
Humor claims relevancy (high, low)
Need for Levity (NFL) (high, low)

Stimulus
Magazine ads for fictional brands produced by the researcher for the study

263 undergraduate marketing students at the University of Cincinnati

52 percent female

other controlled facility that has been enlisted for purposes of the research. Regardless of the physical nature of the lab itself, the lab setting has broad implications.

Although it is possible to conduct field experiments, the lack of control afforded by the field setting may allow for confounding variables to intervene in the study. Field studies, by their nature, are often quasi-experimental (no randomization) or nonexperimental. On the other hand, laboratory settings facilitate the use of experiments.

In the laboratory, the researcher can eliminate, or control for, most confounding variables. The ads, the context, and the nature of the exposure are all controlled. Respondents are selected and assigned to conditions. Distractions are minimized. In a laboratory setting, a researcher can "force" exposure to advertising.

The tight controls available to experimental researchers and the ability to randomly assign respondents to conditions allow for detailed hypothesis testing. Researchers can then vary elements of interest while holding other aspects of the condition constant. For example, in Flaherty, Weinberger, and Gulas (2004) the experimenters were able to construct ads that used either incongruity (I) or incongruity-resolution (IR) for each of four different products, for a total of eight ads (see Table 8.3). The researchers were also able to control the audience exposure to the ads. All of the respondents were presented with the advertising stimuli in a consistent manner. Although it is theoretically possible to conduct a similar experiment in the field, the cost of doing such a study would be prohibitive and even with an unlimited budget the controls would be lacking.

Experiments are a popular research tool for studying humor in advertising because the control they offer allows for testing of causal relationships. However, the experimental methodology has substantial drawbacks as well. The laboratory is a very unnatural setting for advertising exposure. In a laboratory setting, respondents generally attend to advertising if presented with experimental stimuli. In the real world, consumers can leave the room while broadcast ads are on, change channels, talk with other people in the room or on the phone, multitask by engaging in other behavior while marginally attending to media, or simply ignore ads. Indeed, as noted earlier consumers often take active steps to avoid exposure to advertising such as zapping and zipping.

In experimental studies, care is generally taken to disguise the hypotheses. Researchers also typically measure hypothesis guessing as a post-experimental check. However, even if hypothesis guessing has not occurred,

Table 8.2

Methodology in Selected Humor Studies

Author(s) and date	Type of study	Sample	Advertising studies		Finding	Comment
			Medium	Product or service		
Brooker (1981)	Experimental study	240 participants	Print	Toothbrush and influenza vaccine	Mild humor ourperformed mild fear but did not out-perform straightforward ad	
Chattopadhyay and Basu (1990)	Experimental study	80 adults	TV	Pens	When prior evaluation of a brand is positive humorous ad more effective in changing consumer attitudes and choice behavior	
Lammers (1991)	Experimental research	111 business undergraduates	Radio	Evatone Soundsheets (business-to-business product)	High self-monitoring men positive and high self-monitoring women negative humor effect	Subjects engaged in systematic rather than heuristic processing
Murphy, Morrison, and Zahn (1993)	Data-based study	1 coder reviewed 566 Clio award-winning radio commercials	Radio		Trend toward increasing use of humor by Clio award-winning advertisers	Award-winning commercials from 1974–1988

(continued)

149

Table 8.2 (continued)

				Advertising studies	
Author(s) and date	Type of study	Sample	Medium	Product or service	Finding	Comment

Author(s) and date	Type of study	Sample	Medium	Product or service	Finding	Comment
Alden, Hoyer, and Lee (1993)	Data-based descriptive study	Ads from United States, Germany, Thailand, and Korea	TV		Humorous communications from diverse National cultures share certain universal cognitive structures, specific content likely to be variable along major normative dimensions	
Unger (1995)	Experimental study	44 Fins and 68 Americans	TV		Cross-cultural support for use of an affect-based model to assess the effectiveness of humor in persuasion	10 ads from Clio award tapes and an international agency's sample reel
Zhang (1996)	Lab experiment	240 business undergraduates	Print	Camera	More effective with audience members with low need for cognition, attitude toward the brand mediated by attitude toward the ad	
Toncar (2001)	Data-based descriptive study	848 U.S. and 282 UK ads	TV		Use of humor influenced by culture	TV ads from United States and United Kingdom compared

Geuens, and De Pelsmacker(2002)	Experimental research	510 Belgian males and females	TV	Paper handkerchiefs, Insurance, a snack, and travel	Direct effect on attitudes of individuals low in need for cognition and indirect influence on individuals high in need for cognition	
Chung and Zhao (2003)	Recall survey	Respondents in Chapel Hill, NC, and Minneapolis, MN	TV		Positive relationship on memory and attitude, more effective in low-involvement products	Post–Super Bowl telephone interviews
Cline, Altsech, and Kellaris (2003)	Experimental study	501 undergraduates	Print	Coffee	Favorable response from individuals with higher levels of need for humor	3 studies conducted
Flaherty, Weinberger, and Gulas (2004)	Experimental study	338 business graduate students, ages ranging from 22–63 years	Radio	Dishwasher, luggage, chocolate bar, light bulb	Incongruity-resolution (humor type) seen as humorous by more respondents than incongruity	
Nonadvertising Studies						
Prerost (1975)	Education experiment	180 adults	Print		Preference for sexual humor over neutral humor and aggressive humor, humor natural vehicle for expression of an aggressive mood	Aggressive and sexual, closely related for males, females prefer neutral humor in nonarousal conditions

(continued)

Table 8.2 *(continued)*

Nonadvertising studies

Author(s) and date	Type of study	Sample	Medium	Finding	Comment
Wierzbicki and Young (1978)	Education experiment	165 male undergraduates	Print	IQ positively related to comprehension; no significant interaction between intelligence and difficulty level; complexity positively related to appreciation; difficulty of processing negatively related to appreciation	30 cartoons used
McGhee and Lloyd (1981)	Lab experiment	57 boys and 54 girls, ages ranging from 38–87 months	Print	Boys' humor enhanced by the victimization of a less similar person, finding for girls consistent but no preference for the opposite sex	
Herzog and Larwin (1988)	Education experiment	516 undergraduates	Print	Fit and originality only predictor variables with significant relationships to appreciation	64 black and white captioned cartoons used
Prerost (1995)	Lab experiment	360 adults	Print	High sexual desire subjects showed greater enjoyment of sexual humor but males showed highest levels of appreciating aggressive humor	
Martin and Gray (1996)	Lab experiment	40 undergraduates	Radio	Added laughter had a positive effect on both spontaneous and retrospective measures of humorous response, no gender effect	

Study	Method	Sample	Medium	Findings	Notes
Herzog (1999)	Education experiment	46 undergraduates	Print	Males liked sexual humor more than females regardless of victim gender, but hostile humor with male victims was rated higher by females, while with female victims showed opposite patterns	Cartoons, booklets used
Nevo, Nevo, and Siew Yin (2001)	Education experiment	119 undergraduates, ages between 19–26	Print	Humor behavior is generally universal, very few gender differences	Subjects of Chinese origin, results compared to that of Israel and United States
Cann and Calhoun (2001)	Education experiment	405 males and females	Print	High sense of humor social asset, generates positive expectations	2 studies conducted
Kelly (2002)	Lab experiment	140 undergraduates	Print	Individuals with a sense of humor less likely to worry	
Greenwood and Isbell (2002)	Lab experiment	140 undergraduates	Audio-tape	Men high in benevolent sexism found dumb blonde jokes more amusing and less offensive than women or men low in hostile and benevolent sexism	
Grisaffe, Blom, and Burke (2003)	Education experiment	20 male and 13 female college soccer players		Use of humor by coach resulted in higher likeability	
Lowis (2003)	Data-based study	366 adults	TV	No regional, no gender differences in humor response scale scores	36 cartoons, small increase in scores with age for work-related cartoons but not for gender bashing in either direction

the very nature of the experimental setting typically encourages cognitive processing—processing that may not occur in a natural setting. In most experiments the respondents know that they are participating in a study. Although they may not know the details of the study, they do typically know that they are being observed. In fact, it would be difficult to conduct an experiment with totally naïve subjects. Institutional review boards at universities are highly unlikely to permit any research in which informed consent of participants could not be demonstrated. Since virtually all scholarly research is conducted by researchers with an affiliation to a college or university, this effectively prohibits any type of fully disguised study. Disclosure requirements are likely less stringent for researchers at agencies and marketing research firms, but research conducted at these institutions is likely to be focused on a particular client and may not be generalizable beyond the study. Furthermore, this research is likely to be proprietary and thus not shared with the research community.

Since study participants generally know they are being observed, they may alter their behavior to present a more socially desirable picture of themselves, to aid the researcher, or to sabotage the experiment. Regardless of the response, it is likely to be different in at least some degree from the behavior that occurs without observation. This has important implications for humor research since the ELM model suggests that response to advertising differs by level of involvement. In an experimental study, the study itself may raise involvement above what it would be in a natural setting.

Audience Factors

Most published research regarding humor in advertising has employed college student subjects (see Table 8.2). This reality is driven by convenience and cost considerations rather than theory. After all, college students are a relatively easily accessible resource for most academic researchers. Although reflexively derided by some journal reviewers, there is nothing inherently wrong with the use of a student sample. College students are legitimate consumers of a wide range of products and they are legitimate consumers of media. This subject pool may be particularly appropriate for certain types of products and certain types of advertising where college students comprise the target market. Also, student subjects are generally acceptable for theory-testing research (Calder, Phillips, and Tybout 1981). This being said, it must be noted that most consumers are not college students. Since reactions to humor can be very audience dependent (see Chapter 3),

Table 8.3

Example of Radio Scripts: Dishwasher Ads

	Incongruity-Resolution (IR) humor		Incongruity (I) humor
Manager:	You asked to see the manager sir.	Manager:	You asked to see the manager sir.
Customer:	Yes. You don't sell Pirmin **dishwashers** here do you? I don't understand it. Everyone loves Pirmin don't they, hon?	Customer:	Yes. You don't sell Pirmin **dishwashers** here do you? I don't understand it. Everyone loves Pirmin don't they, hon?
Wife:	Uh huh.	Wife:	Uh huh.
Manager:	Well, you see sir . . .	Manager:	Well, you see sir . . .
Customer:	They are dependable, quiet and clean the toughest pots and pans. Did I mention . . .	Customer:	They are dependable, quiet and clean the toughest pots and pans. Did I mention . . .
Manager:	Sir . . .	Manager:	Sir . . .
Customer:	. . . the ten-year warranty?	Customer:	. . . the ten-year warranty?
Manager:	Sir . . .	Manager:	Sir . . .
Customer:	It takes the hassle out of doing the dishes.	Customer:	It takes the hassle out of doing the dishes.
Wife:	They are great.	Wife:	They are great.

(continued)

155

Table 8.3 (continued)

	Incongruity-Resolution (IR) humor		Incongruity (I) humor
Customer:	So why don't you sell Pirmin **dishwashers** here?	Customer:	So why don't you sell Pirmin **dishwashers** here?
Manager:	This is a bank, sir. The appliance store is next door.	Manager:	But sir. I have been trying to tell you, we do sell Pirmin. Let me show them to you.
Customer:	Oh.	Customer:	Wonderful.
Announcer:	Pirmin **dishwasher**, accept nothing less.	Announcer:	Pirmin **dishwasher**, accept nothing less.

Source: Flaherty, Weinberger, and Gulas (2004).

Note: Words in bold were altered to accommodate the attributes of the three other products: luggage, light bulb, and candy. Everything else was identical.

caution must be used when projecting findings from a college student sample to a broader audience.

A greater methodological concern, however, comes not from the nature of a student sample but from the manner in which student samples are often used. Typically ads are tested on multiple students at a time, either in preexisting groups (i.e., classes) or in randomly assigned groups created by the experimenter. In either case, participants are exposed to ads in the presence of others. Sometimes these others may be strangers and sometimes they may be acquaintances. Exposure to humor among friends may elicit a different response than exposure to humor among strangers. In either case, the group setting can, and likely does, affect response.

Naturally occurring exposure to advertising often occurs when consumers are alone: listening to the radio while driving, watching TV alone, reading a magazine, surfing the Web, and so on. Response to advertising under these conditions may be very different than response to advertising while in a group. In Chapter 7 we noted that humorous ads are perceived as more humorous if the audience consists of more than one person. Indeed, producers of comedy television shows often add a laugh track to broadcasts because even an artificial social setting can increase perceived humor. In fact, reactions to humor in a group setting may be quite complicated. Usage of humor in group settings has important gender interactions. Research has shown that overall men and women use similar types of humor. However, women tend to use self-deprecating humor when with other women but not when in mixed-gender groups. On the other hand, men infrequently use self-deprecating humor when in all-male groups but do use this form of humor in mixed-gender groups (Crawford 2003). It is likely that reactions to humor differ based on the composition of the group with regard to gender, age, and other factors. A joke that would cause one to laugh with one's friends may cause one to be uncomfortable if one heard it in a group that included one's parents. It is also possible that the size of the groups has an effect on reaction to humor. A group of five may have a very different dynamic than a group of twelve.

Product Factors

Researchers examining humor in advertising have typically captured or created ads to be used as experimental stimuli. Generally studies have been designed around one or two products (see Table 8.2). If more than one product is used in a study, then "product" must be treated as a factor. Given the nature of experimental research, a product factor with many levels (e.g., ten products) adds considerably to the complexity and the cost of a study. Thus it is not surprising that few researchers have chosen this path. Yet the choice of the product to be used in a study is not a trivial matter. As discussed in Chapter 4, product selection can influence reaction to humorous advertising. This is particularly true with regard to issues such as new product versus existing product, high-involvement product versus low-involvement product and functional product versus expressive product. From a methodological perspective, single-product studies raise concerns. This is not to say that all single-product studies are flawed. However, care must be taken in evaluating the results of such a study to ensure that the findings are not an artifact of the product employed in the manipulation.

Comparable Executions

In order to study humorous advertising experimentally or quasi-experimentally, humorous ads must be compared with non-humorous ads. There are two basic ways to do this. A researcher could "capture" actual ads from the marketplace (humorous and non-humorous), for use in the study or alternatively, ads could be created specifically for the research project. A related approach in which existing ads are modified to suit the needs of the study is also used. Regardless of the approach taken, methodological issues arise. We will examine each approach in turn.

Actual captured ads add a sense of realism to a study. If participants see ads for products that they are familiar with, they will process information in familiar ways. That is to say, they will act in a manner that approximates their true behavior. Or at least they may be likely to do so. However, with real ads, for real products, research participants may enter the study with prior brand and product knowledge. This can affect their response to the advertising in question. If a consumer loves Coke, he or she will react differently to a Coke ad than a consumer who hates the product.

Companies and products that a consumer is familiar with have an existing position in the consumer's mind. Ads will be perceived within the context of that image. It is likely that most consumers have seen ads for both Wal-Mart and Target. Although the companies have many similarities, the advertising for each firm has a distinctive tone. A consumer could react positively to a Target ad that would generate a negative response if the source were Wal-Mart and vice versa. Finally, a humorous ad may work well with a product that a consumer is already very familiar with since the consumer really does not need any product information. The same ad may fail with an unfamiliar product.

With the use of real ads we have to ascertain to what extent a research subject's response is based on the given ad in the given study and to what extent it is due to preexisting attitudes. It will be difficult to make this determination. Of course, we could screen respondents by prior exposure and prior brand attitude. Alternatively, we could also use ads for real products that participants are not likely to have been exposed to. For example, some studies employ ads for regional products from regions outside the area in which the study is being conducted. By removing prior exposure, we have controlled for its effect. Practically speaking, this is the same as creating a fictional product. In the eyes of the respondent we have created a "new" product. It is well established in the advertising literature, and understood in advertising practice, that people react differently to new product advertising than they do to advertising for existing products. Thus we are faced with a Hobson's choice. We can use ads for familiar products, which will carry existing brand image with them and other baggage that will influence the results, or we can use ads for unfamiliar products (fictional products, new products, or out-of-market products), which will influence the results since this is equivalent to new product advertising.

If we create ads from scratch for a research project or modify existing ads, we have also introduced a methodological challenge. Created ads eliminate the baggage that real ads bring to the study. However, unless the ads have been professionally produced at a level of quality similar to that of real ads, we are likely introducing additional "noise" into the study. U.S. consumers are very media savvy. Fake ads may lead to hypothesis guessing. Additionally, ads with low production values are not likely to be viewed positively. Comparing an amateurish humorous ad with an amateurish non-humorous ad may give us some insight into humor effects, but this insight may not be externally valid.

Custom designing ads for a study allows a high level of control. Other factors can be held constant while the factors of interest are manipulated. However, this process is not as straightforward as it seems. In the study referred to in Table 8.3 (Flaherty, Weinberger, and Gulas 2004), the researchers created ads that used either incongruity (I) or incongruity-resolution (IR) for each of four different products, for a total of eight ads. This was accomplished by modifying an existing award-winning ad. The fictional brand name Pirmin was used in the study. The use of the name Pirmin eliminated bias from any prior brand perceptions and allowed the same name to be applied to each of the four products. Care was taken to keep the ads as parallel as possible. The same professional actors were used for all eight versions of the ad and the variations across conditions were designed to be minimal. As shown in Table 8.3, the only difference between the I ad and the IR ad is the last line of dialog from the manager. However, this change does add a net eight words to the IR ad. This difference is very slight. But when one considers that the ads are eighty-nine words and ninety-seven words respectively, it means that the IR ad is nearly 9 percent longer than the I ad. We do not believe that this 9 percent difference had any significant effect on the results of the study. It does illustrate the challenge of creating parallel ads however. The Flaherty, Weinberger, and Gulas (2004) study also points up the difference between attempted humor and perceived humor, which we will address in a later section.

Whether ads are captured or created, it is unlikely that an experimenter can truly hold other factors constant while manipulating factors of interest. As previously mentioned, a change in length was an artifact of a change from I to IR in the Flaherty, Weinberger, and Gulas (2004) study. However, both I and IR are relative terms. For example, an ad that features Donald Trump driving a cab presents an incongruous situation, as would an ad that featured the Trump Tower driving a cab. The incongruity of the second situation is considerably greater than the incongruity of the first. This may have a significant effect on findings. However, both ads would likely be classified as using incongruity, and perhaps not further differentiated. To our knowledge neither ad has been done, nor is either likely to be done. But, this situation illustrates that researchers working with humor need to use manipulation checks and measurements to ensure that they are aware, to the extent possible, of every aspect of an experimental manipulation.

Speck (1991) makes a convincing argument that real ads should be used for humor research and to control for extraneous variables by comparing a group of humorous ads against a group of non-humorous ads. He suggests that prior experience with the ad, the brand, or the product category can be controlled with pretesting and the use of covariates. He further posits that humor type is a critical variable that should not be overlooked. We have no argument with the logic of Speck's recommendations. However, we know of no researchers who have followed these recommendations fully. To do so would be a massive undertaking. Speck identifies five humor types. He suggests the use of multiple executions of each type to allow for blocking and the use of covariates to control for "prior experience with the ad, the brand, and/or the product category" (Speck 1991, 36). However, as we have noted earlier, product can be a very important factor, thus the ad sample would need to represent an array of products. If twelve ads are selected for each humor type, to allow for just three ads in each cell of the PCM for each humor type, and twelve non-humor ads are selected for comparison, seventy-two ads would have to be tested. This would likely require well over a thousand respondents to allow for sufficient statistical power to evaluate all of the variables and covariates in this study. Assuming the resources were available for a study of this size, it still might not be possible. Speck (1987) notes that some humor types, such as full comedy, are relatively little used in advertising and use of humor in advertising for certain categories of products is rare (e.g., high-risk expressive items). Given this, it therefore may be difficult to find sufficient numbers of suitable ads to study.

Context Issues

Humor is subjective and situational. What is funny to one person may not be funny to another. What is funny today may not be funny tomorrow. Most advertising researchers pay relatively little attention to context. This can be a significant oversight. As discussed in Chapter 7, context plays a very important role in humor. Holding context consistent across conditions can protect internal validity but may not ensure external validity.

As noted in Chapter 7, context includes the construct of moment. This also affects research methodology. Although it might be possible to completely replicate a chemistry experiment that was conducted in 1940, it is not likely that a similar replication could be done with a humor-in-advertising study. What was considered funny in 1940 is very different from what is considered funny today. One need not go back that far in history. As noted in Chapter 7, "moment" can change in an instant. It could change from one experimental session to the next. Although it is likely that an experimenter would be aware of events like the Columbine High School shootings if they took place during the course of an experiment, other more subtle occurrences may change the moment without the researcher's knowledge.

Attempted Humor Versus Perceived Humor

What constitutes humor? What constitutes non-humor? In our own empirical research we have found via manipulation checks that some respondents find humor in the "non-humor" condition. Occasionally respondents see no humor in the intended humor condition. Some respondents may perceive humor, while others perceive an "attempt at humor," a subtle but important difference. Still others may not even recognize the attempt.

As we will discuss in Chapter 9, attempts at humor may offend some members of the audience. Comedy is not always rooted in comity. If offense is taken, it is unlikely that the humor will have its intended effect.

Table 8.4

Issues to Consider in Testing Humor

Context	Audience	Product	Message	Media	Measurement
Humorous versus serious (editorial content or other ads)	Gender, age, national or racial differences	Fictional versus real	Type of humor	Magazine	Before or after product experience
Schema familiarity	Individual need for humor	New versus old	Amount of humor	TV	Field or lab setting
Warmth	Prior attitude toward humor object	Serious versus fun	Amount of incongruity, arousal, aggression	Radio	Moment to moment reactions
Clutter	Need for cognition	High/low and rational/experiential	Amount of surprise	Outdoor	Pre-attention effects
Moment	Self-monitoring		Relatedness of humor to message	Direct	Attention
			Dominance of humor	Internet	Affective responses, including mood, liking, and VRP type responses (including negative and offensiveness)
				Other	
			Location of humor		Recall and comprehension measures A_{ad}, A_{source}, A_b
			Relatedness of humor to visual or words		Persuasion
			Repetition		Behavior

The issue of perceived humor is important methodologically. If a study is comparing humor with non-humor, it is obviously important that the two conditions differ in perceived humor. But if the humor condition generates a humor score that is statistically significantly higher than the humor score in the non-humor condition, does that mean it is funny? Researchers are often satisfied by the contrast between the two conditions. This is a mathematically valid conclusion. However, in reality no true humor condition may exist.

Wear Out Revisited

Some have argued that humorous ads decline in effectiveness with repetition (Gelb and Zinkhan 1985; Zinkhan and Gelb 1990). This claim certainly appears to have face validity. We typically do not laugh at a joke if we have heard it before. Although a humorous ad is not quite the same as a cocktail party joke, humorous ads do appear to exhibit a different wear out pattern than non-humorous ads. Belch and Belch (1984) found that evaluations of humorous messages were more favorable between the low and moderate exposure levels and became negative between moderate and high exposure. This was in contrast with "serious" ads, in which evaluations decreased between low and moderate exposure levels and remained constant or increased between moderate and high exposure levels. This is an area where more research needs to be conducted. Naik (1999) proposed a half-life model of advertising. It could prove very enlightening to use this model in a comparison of humorous and non-humorous ads.

Conclusion

Research on humor in advertising is methodologically very challenging. It carries with it the challenges of humor research and those of advertising research, which are both challenging in their own rights. These challenges have not deterred numerous researchers from entering the fray. Each of these studies has limitations, since any research design requires trade-offs. Thus it may be best to draw conclusions from a group of studies, rather than an individual study. Table 8.4 is a listing of the many variables that we have touched on in this book. If one were to match topics from each column with the varied topics in other columns it is not difficult to underscore the many gaps that exist in our knowledge of humor in advertising. We hope this book has made strides toward uncovering what we do know about the topic as well as revealing the many areas that need exploration.

—— 9 ——

Entertaining Some—
Offending Others

Entertaining Some

Advertising as a Comic Art Form

As we have noted elsewhere in this book, humorous advertising is entertaining. Humorous television commercials have been featured as content on numerous television specials and humorous ads formed a significant portion of the content of the Fox television series titled *World's Funniest*.

Humorous ads are the core of several Web sites, including funnyplace.org and visit4info.com, and are a prominent feature on several advertising industry Web sites, such as agencypreview.com, ad-rag.com, and thespecspot.com. On the last of these, humor dominates the Web site. Thespecspot.com is a creative showcase for individuals involved in television advertising, and those who wish to be. Although the spots presented there have not been aired by advertisers, they are designed to demonstrate the creative talents of the agencies and individuals who created them. The spots on this site are overwhelmingly humorous in intent. An analysis of spots available on thespecspot.com Web site was conducted on June 26, 2004, and again on January 7, 2005. This analysis revealed a strong preponderance of humorous ads (see Table 9.1). Additionally, the three ads receiving the highest visitor ratings were all humorous in intent.

As noted in Chapter 1, humor has become a mainstay of Super Bowl advertising, perennially the most expensive advertising airtime in the world. Indeed it would be difficult to imagine the Super Bowl without humorous advertising. Budweiser's frogs and lizards and other humorous advertising executions presented over the years are as much a part of the history of the

Table 9.1

Spots Available by Genre on thespecspot.com, on Selected Dates

Genre	Number of spots June 26, 2004	Number of spots January 7, 2005
Action	0	5
Celebrity spokesperson	0	1
Comparison	0	0
Music based	0	1
Drama	1	1
PSA	1	5
Demonstration	2	2
Fashion/beauty	2	4
Graphical	2	3
Slice-of-life	3	7
Satire/parody	6	7
Comedy	32	71
Other	3	7

game as Adam Vinatieri's game-winning field goal in Super Bowl XXXVIII or Scott Norwood's missed field goal in Super Bowl XXV. Super Bowl advertising has, in fact, taken on a life of its own. Super Bowl ads have risen above commercial discourse to become a sanctioned form of entertainment (McAllister 1999). Budweiser and other advertisers have even promoted upcoming Super Bowl ads weeks in advance with teaser ads (McAllister 1999), in much the same way that upcoming entertainment programs are touted. Super Bowl ads are a cultural phenomenon that fosters rare cooperation among competing television networks. McAllister (1999) notes a particular example of this occurring in 1997 when ABC's *Good Morning America* did a Super Bowl ad preview and extorted viewers to "enjoy the spots" on game day even though the Super Bowl aired on Fox that year. It is difficult to imagine other situations where a network would encourage viewers to watch a competitor's broadcast, yet there are many examples of this occurring with the Super Bowl and with Super Bowl advertising.

Super Bowl ads are a news story in their own right. They are regularly reviewed in print and broadcast media. *USA Today* has annually published the results of its "ad meter" since 1989. In the seventeen years of ad meter history, humorous ads took the top ranking in all but three. However, this is not surprising since the ad meter is an entertainment measure. The ad meter methodology makes no attempt to measure recall, A_b, purchase intent, or any other traditional advertising metrics other than liking. While this methodology may be lacking from a business perspective, it is another illustration of the extent to which advertising is considered a form of entertainment. Super Bowl ads, in particular, are expected to entertain, and generally that entertainment occurs in the form of humor.

The Effect of Technology

The drive to entertain in advertising is growing as new media options continue to be added to what appears to be a nearly saturated media environment. Satellite radio now provides millions of listeners with radio choices far greater than anything previously available. Sirius offers over 110 channels and the 122 channels offered by XM include 68 commercial-free music channels. DIRECTV offers over 225 channels of television entertainment. For the discriminating viewer, Dish Network offers America's Top 180, a package that features, presumably, only the "best" 180 channels of programming out of the more than 200 channels available. The average household in the United States now receives 100 television channels, up from 27 channels in 1994 (Bianco 2004), and up dramatically from the 3 to 5 channels that served most households in the pre-cable era. Yet even this degree of media choice is apparently insufficient. A recent study indicated that 67 percent of teenagers aged 13 to 17 sometimes surfed the Internet while watching television, 66 percent read magazines while watching television, and 34 percent listened to the radio (Leonard and Burke 2004). In this media environment, there is little tolerance for interruption by advertising, particularly ads that are boring.

For over twenty years Jan Miner, in the character of Madge the Manicurist, told shocked customers that they were "soaking in it," in reference to Palmolive dish washing liquid. Using this theme, Garfield (2003) notes that we are not just "exposed to TV advertising; we're soaking in it" (186). Garfield is correct. But it is not just TV advertising we are soaking in, it is all media, and by extension, all forms of advertising and promotion. The broad social implications of this can be left to sociologists and cultural anthropologists. It does, however, have important implications for advertisers, especially as new technologies help consumers to separate advertising from programming more effectively than ever before.

TiVo and other makers of digital video recorders (DVR), sometimes referred to as personal video recorders (PVR), provide technology that allows viewers to largely avoid television advertising. Initial proposals for TiVo included a thirty-second skip button (Donaton 2004). Although advertising executives were successful in keeping this button off of the TiVo remote control, the remote allows fast forward speeds, which effectively turn an entire advertising pod into a blur. However, TiVo announced in November of 2004 that in the spring of 2005 "billboards" would pop up as viewers fast forward through ads (Piccalo 2004). In this move TiVo is attempting to provide some form of ad blocking, a feature clearly favored by subscribers, while appeasing advertisers, who ultimately support the production cost of most programming.

TiVo and similar technologies have proved to be a hit with consumers, with the industry growth rate projected to be 47 percent annually during the period from 2004 until 2008 (Bulik 2004). DVR/PVR technology may be in 20 percent of the nation's households by 2007 (Leonard and Burke 2004). Furthermore, from a demographic and psychographic perspective, these households are likely to be the 20 percent that advertisers crave most. Some have argued that TiVo may do to the advertising industry what Napster did to the recording industry, thus killing the TV spot as we know it. A contrary view holds that traditional thirty-second spots can hold their own if they are sufficiently entertaining to avoid being skipped by TiVo subscribers (Leonard and Burke 2004). Recent data show wide differences in TiVo ad skip rates by product category. Ads for beer were skipped 31.9 percent of the time and movie trailers were skipped 44.1 percent of the time. On the other hand, ads for fast food were skipped 95.7 percent of the time and mortgage finance ads were skipped 94.7 percent of the time (Bianco 2004). The overall TiVo ad skip rate is approximately 70 percent (Bianco 2004). Of course, even a 31.9 percent skip rate is major concern to an advertiser.

While the fate of TiVo as a specific product offering is yet to be determined, the onslaught of media, and the growing availability of technology like TiVo, is forcing advertisers to focus on entertainment value or develop other methods of capturing the attention of consumers who are increasingly media savvy and increasingly capable of avoiding advertising messages.

Targeting With Humor

Some target audiences are harder to reach than others. Young audiences are heavy users of media, when broadly defined to include Web sites, blogs, cable television shows, and the like. Yet paradoxically they may be difficult to reach. They have grown up in the world of 100+ television channels, time shifting, zipping and zapping of ads, first with VHS recorders and now with TiVo and other DVR/PVR devices. Personal computers and the Internet have been a part of their lives since childhood. They are very media savvy. Undivided attention is usually brief, if it exists at all. In addition to the dual media use noted above, 56 percent of teens instant message while watching television (Leonard and Burke 2004). Yet this evasive audience is very desirable to a wide range of advertisers.

Based on recent studies, it appears that television viewership is in decline, particularly in certain demographic groups, such as men aged 18–34 (Greppi 2003). However, in an online survey of a 600–member panel of respondents aged 16–24 years conducted May 3–17, 2004, television commercials were selected by 54 percent of respondents as the advertising medium that they are most likely to pay attention to. This was followed by samples handed out at events, noted by 22 percent of respondents.[1] Magazine ads finished third in the study, selected by 11 percent of respondents (Blue Fusion 2004). Furthermore, 73 percent of survey respondents said that advertisements were somewhat influential or very influential in their purchase decisions. When asked about the type of ads they prefer, 8 percent chose informative, 21 percent chose sexy, and 71 percent chose humorous (Blue Fusion 2004). Austin and Aitchison (2003) go much further in this line of thinking. They posit that youth in Asia, the primary focus of their work, believe that brands themselves, not just brand advertising, have a "duty" to entertain.

In an attempt to entertain younger audiences, advertisers have created some very edgy ads that push the limits of taste. The Chino Latino restaurant in Minneapolis, which targets consumers in the 18 to 34 age range, has developed a reputation for this style of advertising, including billboards featuring scatological humor such as, "Mild, medium & 'excuse me, I have to go to the bathroom'" and "The best thing about take-out: Your own bathroom." This is similar to a campaign by Hacienda Mexican Restaurants that featured an outdoor billboard with the slogan "Less artsy. More fartsy." Garfield (2003) notes an ad campaign for Rally's restaurants that targeted young men with double entendre penis humor.

Online ads for the Ford SportKa, a car billed as the "Ka's evil twin," show the vehicle defending itself. In one ad, the car's hood springs up to kill a pigeon that is attempting to land on it. In another, a curious cat climbs up on the car and peers in an open sunroof, which slides closed decapitating the cat with the decapitated body sliding to the ground. Ford has disavowed the second ad, claiming that it was a rejected concept that was not intended to be distributed, and notes that no animals were harmed in either ad since computer generated images were used (Mikkelson and Mikkelson 2004). However, many have found both ads to be tasteless.

For targeting young men, edgy humor may be a reasonable strategy. Those with a broad sense of humor are unlikely to be offended by humor even when it features death, disease, suffering, and other sensitive topics (Herzog and Bush 1994). Additionally, males are more likely to respond favorably to sick humor and tendentious humor than females (Herzog and Karafa 1998), and female respondents' appreciation for cruel humor has been found to peak at a lower level of cruelty than male respondents (Herzog and Anderson 2000). However, this strategy has risks and raises important ethical considerations, as will be addressed in later sections and in Chapter 10.

After the 2004 presidential election advertisers took particular note of the cultural implications of the outcome (Teinowitz 2004). Many voters expressed concern with cultural issues (Lampman 2004; Zuckerman 2004). "'There is going to be greater scrutiny on decency and that could play into advertising and what is indecent in programming and advertising,' said Dick O'Brien, exec VP of the American Association of Advertising Agencies" (Teinowitz 2004, 1). This appeared to be reflected in the 2005 Super Bowl. While the 2004 Super Bowl featured humorous ads that showed a dog biting a man's crotch and demonstrated the unpleasant effects of horse flatulence, the 2005 Super Bowl featured a distinctly less edgy form of humor (Vranica 2005b; Vranica and Steinberg 2005).

During the presidential campaign, much was made of "red states" and "blue states" terminology that entered the popular lexicon. The assignment of colors red for Republican and blue for Democrat appears to be arbitrary. Indeed, Reagan states were marked in blue by TV news commentators in 1980 (Ward 2004). Originally used to project votes from the Electoral College, the terms have become broadly associated with opposing sides in a cultural rift that appears to exist in the United States. There appears to be a geographic component to this cultural divide, with the Northeast, Upper Midwest, and West Coast generally blue, and the Lower Midwest, South, and Mountain States generally red. This suggests that a humorous ad that might be appropriate in the Northeast may be problematic in the South. Coincidentally, the colors may be well chosen for our purposes, since it would seem that residents of the more liberal leaning blue states may have a greater tolerance for "blue" humor than the more conservative leaning red states.

Humor in Award-Winning Advertising

A study of award-winning radio ads found that between 1974 and 1988 62 percent of U.S. Clio Award–winning radio ads used humor (Murphy, Morrison, and Zahn 1993). Additionally, there was a statistically significant upward trend in the data. On average humor usage in the 1974–78 period was 47 percent compared to 63 percent in the 1979–83 period and 76 percent in the 1984–88 period (Murphy, Morrison, and Zahn 1993). More recently, a humorous direct mail campaign for Virgin Atlantic won the top award in the direct marketing category at the Cannes Lions International Advertising Festival in 2004 (Sanders 2004). Of the forty-three ads on the 2001 Clio Gold Winners reel, thirty-one of them were humorous in intent (*Best of 2001:* 2002). In fact, humorous ads are highly represented in virtually every advertising awards competition. As indicated in *The Gunn Report,* a compilation of results of twenty-two advertising competitions around the world, humorous campaigns are highly awarded, as indicated in Table 9.2 (Gunn Report, 1999–2003). Although the merits of the awards system in advertising is an issue of some debate (see e.g., Helgesen 1994; Palmer 2003; Rentas-Giusti 2003), the very fact that there are twenty-two advertising competitions to be summarized by the *Gunn Report* is an indication that they play a role of some importance in the advertising industry.

The Polarizing Potential of Humor

It is axiomatic to say that people like humor. People also like food. With food, what may bring delight to one may bring disgust to another. Such is the case with humor. As discussed elsewhere in this book, what is perceived as humorous by one individual may not be perceived as humorous by another. In fact, humor is a potentially polarizing phenomenon, with the same humorous execution garnering both extremely positive and extremely negative reactions.

A 2004 humorous television campaign by Six Flags amusement parks struck a chord with viewers. The ad featured an old man, or more likely a young man or woman made up to look like an old man, dancing to the song *We Like to Party* by the Vengaboys. The dancing man character was invited to be a guest on ABC's *Good Morning America,* merchandise related to the character became a popular item at the parks, "Mr. Six" became a popular blog topic, and the five-year-old background music became a popular song download. One of the ads in the campaign captured the top likability score in the *Advertising Age* Quarterly Recall Report (*Advertising Age* 2004b). Yet this apparently successful campaign illustrates the potentially polarizing nature of humor, as some comments selected from the rateitall.com Web site indicate (www.rateitall.com). Overall, the ad received a rating of 4.3 stars out of a possible 5 based on ratings by eighty-seven respondents. Most found the ad very entertaining:

Table 9.2

Most Awarded TV Commercials and Campaigns in the World, by Year

Year	Advertiser	Campaign	Humorous intent
2003	Peugeot 206	"Sculptor"	yes
2002	Reebok	"Sofa"	yes
2001	Fox Sports	"Alan & Jerome"	yes
2000	Guinness	"Surfer"	no
1999	Outpost.com	"Band"/"Forehead"/"Cannon"	yes

Hilarious stuff! Every time I see him dance with that goofy expression on his face, it makes me laugh.

LOVE that commercial. No matter what I'm doing, after I've seen that commercial, I just FEEL better. And I would LOVE to know the genius who put it together.

The Old Man character is such a GoofBall, he crackes [sic] me up!!!

That weird looking man dancing like crazy is a hoot! I love it.

On the other hand, some found the ad highly irritating:

Makes me want to throw a rock through the TV.

Pure crap to seduce the infantile American to goo goo over a retarded old man.

Gah! So creepy—he gives me nightmares. Reminiscent of that horrid fireman character Jim Carrey used to play on *In Living Color*.

Too scary . . . too freaky. . . . He gives me the chills. . . . This is the kind of old man you warn your kids to stay away from!!!!!!

Although the Six Flags campaign indicates that even a widely popular campaign will have detractors, this mild campaign generated relatively mild criticism. The negative reaction to a humorous campaign can be much more extreme, as we will discuss in a later section.

Offending Others

Offensive by Definition

As we discussed earlier, superiority theorists such as Gruner (1997) argue that all humor is based on the concept of "winners" and "losers." Often the

171

"losers" are associated with some group via gender, age, ethnicity, or the like. People associated with these groups are thus likely to be offended. Similarly, humor targeting a particular individual, a public figure, or an individual in a comedy club audience for example, can offend the target and those who have an affinity with the target. Indeed, from the superiority theorist perspective one might argue that humor must have at least the potential to offend someone or it is not humor.

In a related vein, Saroglou (2002) posits that religion and sense of humor are a priori incompatible. He argues:

> [F]rom a personality psychology perspective, religion associates negatively with personality traits, cognitive structures and social consequences typical to humor: incongruity, ambiguity, possibility of nonsense, low dogmatism and low authoritarianism, playfulness, spontaneity, attraction to novelty and risk, lack of truthfulness and finality, affective and moral disengagement, loss of control and order as implied by emotionality, and finally transgression, especially transgression of prohibitions related to aggression/dominance and sexuality. (205)

Saroglou (2002) does suggest that optimism-positivism is one personality trait that is positively associated with both sense of humor and religiousness. However, he concludes that it is likely that religious people have a good sense of humor "*despite* their religiosity; and not necessarily *because* of it" (206, italics in original).

Saroglou's work suggests that humor is antithetical to religiosity from a personality psychology perspective. In general, religion teaches nonaggression, chastity, and respect. This is in conflict with the tendentious, sexual, disrespectful nature of much humor. Religion is concerned with the sacred, and humor with the profane. While religion is reverent, in some measure all humor is *irreverent*. Religion is founded on certainty, security, truthfulness, and "truth." Although humor can sometimes arrive at a form of truth, it typically uses surprise, deception, aggression, and other irreligious tools to get there. Religion is about making sense of the universe, and it requires a certain level of closed-mindedness (Saroglou 2002). Therefore, "it seems reasonable to suspect that religion may not be attracted to a celebration of incongruity, ambiguity and most importantly, possibility of nonsense" (Saroglou 2002, 195). Thus even the most playful humor, nonsense, and silliness can be viewed as a challenge to the seriousness of religion.

Religiosity is a component of the lives of most Americans. In a recent study, eight in ten respondents in the United States identified with some

religion and 54 percent reported living in households where they, or someone else, belong to a church, synagogue, temple, or mosque (Paul 2002).
If Saroglou (2002) is correct, it suggests that humor is a priori incompatible, at least to some extent, with the personality psychology of the majority of Americans.

We have adopted challenge theory as the perspective for this book rather
than the superiority theory or the personality psychology perspectives taken
by Gruner (1997) and Saroglou (2002), respectively. Challenge theory allows for incongruity-resolution and other forms of humor processes to occur
without "winners" and "losers." However, the potential to offend still exists.

Anyone who has ever visited a comedy club or watched a comedic film
knows that vulgarity is a staple of humor. Scatological references and pro-
fanity are commonplace in many forms of humor. These techniques are less
common in advertising humor, but their use is growing, as we will see in the
following sections.

Offensive in Practice

Barnes and Dotson (1990) defined the construct of offensive advertising as
two dimensional. One dimension of offensive advertising deals with the promotion of intrinsically offensive products, the other dimension concerns offensive executions. It is the second of these that is our concern here. As
advertisers struggle to break through the increasingly cluttered media environment, many have turned to shocking advertising appeals. Some research suggests that ads that are incongruent with social norms attract attention and are
more likely to be retained in memory (Manchanda, Dahl, and Frankenberger
2002). However, violation of social norms may also lead to offense.

Racist Humor and Other Forms of Insensitivity

Trade cards were a popular form of advertising from the 1870s through the
1890s (Crane 2004). These cards were a cross between advertising fliers,
business cards, and post cards (Chan, Park, and Shek 1997). The cards typically contained commercial information on one side of the card. The other
side sometimes contained a product- or service-related illustration or a picture
or illustration that was unrelated to the product or service but designed to be
interesting or entertaining (Chan, Park, and Shek 1997). Unfortunately, that
entertainment sometimes took the form of racist humor. Trade cards often illustrated Chinese, African American, Irish, Jewish, Italian, or German char-

acters in a stereotypical manner as the butt of a joke. These ads were racist by design. Although modern mainstream advertisers would be unlikely to take this path, modern advertising can be very insensitive.

Just for Feet: A Cautionary Tale

Just for Feet was a fast-growing shoe retailer in 1998 when the company decided to make its first attempt at national brand advertising. This was not to be a timid, halfhearted attempt. The company chose no less of an advertising vehicle than the Super Bowl to make its big-time advertising debut with an ad created by a big-time agency, Saatchi & Saatchi. What a debut it turned out to be.

The ad showed what appeared to be a group of white men riding in a Humvee tracking a barefoot black Kenyan runner.[2] The "hunters" drug the man and while he is unconscious they force a pair of running shoes on to his feet and drive away. The runner awakens shouting "no, no" and tries to shake the shoes from his feet. Not surprisingly the ad caused a great deal of outrage. Bob Garfield, the advertising critic for *Advertising Age,* was one of the first to publicly suggest that the ad was racist and neocolonial (Garfield 1999). Indeed, Garfield reports that upon seeing the ad the Friday before the Super Bowl he called the ad agency in disbelief to see if they really intended to run it (Garfield 2003).

Surprisingly, Just for Feet itself suggested that the racism charge was valid, but that the racism was not their fault. In a court filing claiming malpractice by Saatchi & Saatchi, Just for Feet stated:

> As a direct consequence of Saatchi's appallingly unacceptable and shockingly unprofessional performance, Just for Feet's favorable reputation has come under attack, its reputation has suffered, and it has been subjected to the entirely unfounded and unintended public perception that it is a racist or racially insensitive company. . . . The ad creates the impression that the footwear retailer is "racist, culturally insensitive and condescending, [and] promotes drugs. (Shalit 1999, 2)

It is nothing short of amazing that Just for Feet, a company whose customer base included a large minority component (Cuneo 2000), would not only approve the "Kenya" ad, but spend nearly $7 million on air time, production cost and pre-promotion of the ad with teasers (Shalit 1999).

In 1998 Just for Feet had sales of $775 million and ranked number six in the *Fortune* magazine list of "America's Fastest Growing Companies" (Shalit

1999). Industry analysts predicted that the chain would soon hit $1 billion in annual sales (*SGB* 2000). Then the "Kenya" ad ran. The ad ran once in Super Bowl XXXIII on January 31, 1999. The outrage followed immediately. On March 15, 1999, the CEO of Just for Feet, Harold Ruttenberg, filed the malpractice lawsuit, which was resolved out of court. By September 1999 Ruttenberg was replaced as CEO by Helen Rockey and in November of 1999, less than one year after the Kenya ad, Just for Feet filed for bankruptcy. To be sure, Just for Feet had other difficulties—the chain had expanded quickly and had inventory problems (*SGB* 2000), and executives of Just for Feet have pleaded guilty on securities charges (United States Department of Justice 2004). But the controversy surrounding the "Kenya" ad is unlikely to have helped the firm with its core customers, and may have contributed to the firm's demise.

Nike Just Did It

It would be reasonable to assume that the object lesson of Just for Feet would deter large advertisers from engaging in heroically insensitive advertising. However, this assumption would be wrong. In 2000, Nike ran an ad for its Air Dri-Goat in *Backpacker* magazine. The ad copy stated in part:

> How can a trail running shoe with an outer sole designed like a goat's hoof help me avoid compressing my spinal cord into a Slinky on the side of some unsuspecting conifer, thereby rendering me a drooling, misshapen, non-extreme-trail-running husk of my former self, forced to roam the Earth in a motorized wheelchair with my name, embossed on one of those cute little license plates you get at carnivals or state fairs, fastened to the back?

It is likely that many in the Nike target market found the ad humorous. However, the ad also offended many. Nike pulled the ad and issued an apology. However, some in the disabled community were irritated even more by the apology (Vogel 2004; Ragged Edge Online 2004). The apology included the phrase "*confined* to a wheelchair" (italics added). This terminology is offensive to many in the disabled community, and in their apology Nike noted that the company had a "Disabled Employee Network," which suggested tokenism and/or condescension to some.

Unfortunately for Nike and its agency Wieden & Kennedy, the Air Dri-Goat controversy came shortly after it was forced to pull another campaign in which a "chainsaw-wielding madman chases a female runner" (*Advertising Age* 2000). Apparently some also failed to see the humor in that particular execution.

Sexist Humor in Advertising

A study of offensive advertising conducted in Hong Kong found that "sexist attitudes" were most often cited as the reason that an ad was considered offensive (Prendergast, Ho, and Phau 2002). In the United States there has been no shortage of sexist advertising, particularly in the case of beer. In the early 1990s Stroh Brewery promoted its Old Milwaukee brand with a series of humorous ads in which the "Swedish Bikini Team" would arrive, Old Milwaukee in hand, to rescue men from boredom. While many found the ads to be humorous, others found them to be highly offensive. Indeed five female employees of Stroh Brewery filed a sexual harassment lawsuit against the brewer due to the ad campaign. They argued that, "the ads foster a work environment that encourages sexual harassment. 'These ads tell Stroh's male employees that women are stupid, panting playthings'" (*Time* 1991, 70), and "portrayed women as 'giggling, jiggling idiots who have large breasts and small minds'" (TV Acres 2004).

The beer and bimbo issue was reignited in 2003 in an ad campaign by Miller Lite. In "Catfight," women tear off each others clothes and wrestle in wet concrete in what turns out to be a male fantasy of a beer ad within the ad. "Miller executives say the spot is a hit with its target audience: 21- to 31-year-old beer drinkers. 'They see the ad for what it is: a hysterical insight into guys' mentality,' says Tom Bick, Miller Lite brand manager" (McCarthy 2003, 1B). However, approximately 200 TV viewers e-mailed complaints to Miller regarding the ad (McCarthy 2003), which was part of a campaign that included a pillow fight featuring Pamela Anderson.

A 2004 advertising campaign for Molson provided "tools" designed to be helpful to their customers (see Exhibits 9.1 and 9.2). It is likely that many in the Molson target audience found this campaign entertaining. However, the campaign was highly offensive to others. The Marin Institute, an alcohol policy organization, urged consumers to complain about the ads to Molson via e-mail and provided a prewritten complaint letter for consumers to send to Molson Coors Chairman Eric H. Molson with a copy to be sent to the Federal Trade Commission.

Dear Mr. Molson:

I am writing to register a complaint regarding a Molson advertising campaign running on the Web and in several young men's magazines. The "Friends" campaign provides fake business cards, wallet photos and stickers intended to help men trick women into bed.

Far from meeting contemporary standards of good taste, these ads are offensive, cynical and irresponsible—and violate several provisions of the Beer Institute Advertising and Marketing Code. By endorsing deception in order to "start a conversation that really goes somewhere" Molson promotes lying as the first step in making "friends."

There is no doubt that the ultimate goal of the deceptions suggested in these ads is getting one of those "sexy gals" or "hotties" into bed. Given the strong association between alcohol and sexual assault, including rape, I am surprised that you would want to associate your product with trickery that is just a few steps removed from date rape.

I urge you to immediately withdraw the "Friends" campaign and issue an apology for creating this irresponsible campaign. I also ask that you formally acknowledge that the new Molson Coors Brewing Company will adopt the Coors Advertising Complaint Evaluation process and abide by the Beer Institute Advertising and Marketing Code in the future.

Sincerely,

(*Source*: Marin Institute 2004)

"Bob Wheatley, a Molson spokesman, said the ads do not promote deception, but instead present the brand in a humorous light that makes it stand out against the competition. It's about 'beer being a very social beverage and connecting the voice of the brand to the user's lifestyle,' Mr. Wheatley says. 'No one really takes it seriously.'" (Lawton 2004).

The term "sexist advertising" has historically referred to advertising that demeans or objectifies women. The examples noted above, and Exhibits 2.5 and 5.2 presented earlier, are but a few of the countless illustrations of this phenomenon. Conversely, there has been a recent trend toward misandry in

Exhibit 9.1 **Molson "Business Cards"**

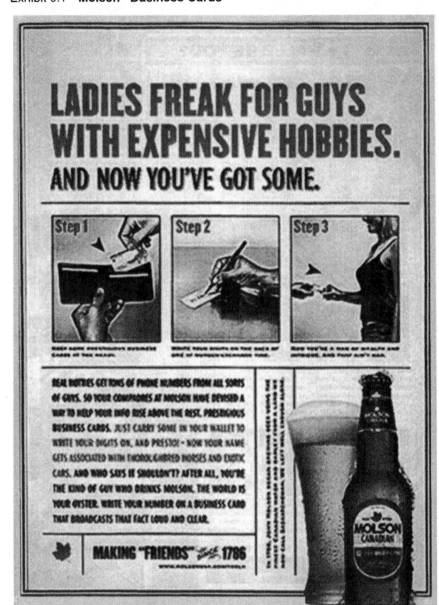

178

Molson USA, 2004.

Exhibit 9.2 **Molson "Wallet Photos"**

Molson USA, 2004.

advertising. Some have posited that this is part of a larger cultural phenomenon (Nathanson and Young 2001). An in-depth examination of this issue is beyond the scope of this book. However, in the case of humor in advertising, the trend appears to be driven largely by the fact that men are safe targets. It is now considered inappropriate to make fun of women, blacks, gays, immigrants, and other historically common targets of humor. But no such prohibition exists on making fun of white heterosexual men.

Comedian/actor Jim Carrey noted in an interview, "I don't mind making fun of stereotypical WASP guys or bigots. That's something that has to be done" (Nathanson and Young 2001). Stewart and Kennedy (2001) quote an executive from J. Walter Thomson: "It is now absolutely acceptable to show men as thick, as incompetent, as sex objects, as figures of fun, because it has become politically correct to do so."

Misandric ads now constitute a significant subgenre of humorous advertising. Some recent examples include:

- In an ad for the Dodge Grand Caravan minivan, a hapless man fumbles about while trying to fold a child's stroller. Meanwhile a woman quickly and efficiently reconfigures the minivan's seats. Ultimately she confidently takes the stroller from the man and places it in the van in the space she created by folding the seat down while he stands by looking utterly helpless.
- In an ad for the Verizon Wireless, a dad tells his daughters how they can call him as much as they want with the family plan. In response the daughters stare at him vacantly. The mom says they can also use it to call their friends; this generates a very excited reaction. In the excitement the dad asks for a group hug but he is ignored by the mom and daughters, who leave the room.
- In another Verizon ad, this one for DSL service, a hapless dad is attempting to help his eight-year-old daughter with her homework. It is apparent that she knows more than the dad. The mom arrives to rescue her and tells the dad to wash the dog. When he hesitates, she tells him to "leave her alone." Upon further hesitation, she sharply demands his exit from the room and he jumps to comply.
- In a digital camera ad, a man walks through a grocery store trying to match photos in his hand with items on the shelf. We then see a woman taking pictures of items in the pantry presumably because the man is incapable of following a list, or making choices on his own.

- In an ad for a family board game, a man asks a woman, "How much does a man's brain weigh?" She answers, "Not much." (Abernethy 2003)

In fact, although many of those complaining about the Molson "friends" campaign view it as demeaning to women, the case could be made that it is men who are actually the butt of the joke. The campaign suggests that men are interested in nothing other than sports and "nudie magazines"; any other interests need to be manufactured to pretend that they have more depth (see Exhibit 9.3).

Preston (2000) quotes an article in *Irish Times* in which John Waters states "that for 'about 30 to 40 percent of television advertising: take a middle-aged, straight, white male, put him with a woman, any woman, and make him look stupid/ignorant/incompetent.'" Although it does not appear that Waters's estimate is based on anything resembling empirical data, misandric advertising does appear to be widespread and it is becoming noticed as such. The European Advertising Standards Alliance (EASA) cautions advertisers about this tactic. "There has recently been a tendency, in some countries, for advertisements to reverse traditional stereotypes, portraying women as dominant, resourceful and capable and men as foolish, immature and inept" (EASA 2004).

In Ireland, the UK, Australia, and Canada, misandric advertising has become a small but growing source of consumer complaints. Indeed, in 1997 "there were almost as many ads drawing complaints about the depiction of men as there were ads drawing complaints about the depiction of women in English Canada" (Advertising Standards Canada 1997, 3). However, it appears that the potential cost of offending men in advertising is relatively low. Herzog and Karafa (1998) found that female respondents rated ads "demeaning to women" much lower than male respondents did (means of 1.96 and 3.18, respectively). However, there was no gender difference with regard to rating ads in the "demeaning-to-men" category, which were rated generally positively by both male and female respondents (means of 3.15 and 3.04, respectively). Thus men are safe targets.

Formal Complaints

In the United States the regulatory environment is very complicated, with overlapping governmental authority for advertising regulation. At the federal level, the Federal Trade Commission, the Federal Communications Com-

Exhibit 9.3 **Molson "Stickers"**

Molson USA, 2004.

mission, the Food and Drug Administration, the Securities and Exchange Commission, the U.S. Postal Service, and several other agencies play a role in advertising regulation. Self-regulation is addressed by the Better Business Bureau (BBB), comprised of regional bureaus and advertising review councils as well as the National Advertising Division (NAD), and the National Advertising Review Board (NARB). There are also a host of trade organizations, such as the Direct Marketing Association and the Distilled Spirits Council, that provide some form of advertising self-regulation.

In some other countries advertising regulation is more centralized. In the United Kingdom advertising complaints are formally handled by the Office of Communications (Ofcom), which regulates all communications industries in the United Kingdom and thereby regulates television and radio advertising. The Advertising Standards Authority (ASA) administers the self-regulation standards for nonbroadcast advertising set by the Committee of Advertising Practice (CAP). Similar governmental and industry bodies exist in Ireland, Canada, and Australia. The data collected by these organizations provide interesting insights into consumer reaction to advertising. Table 9.3 indicates the number of ads that consumers registered complaints about and the top three complaint categories as reported in the 2003 annual report of Advertising Standards Canada.

It appears that there are two main drivers of complaining behavior: deceptive advertising and offensive advertising. Unfortunately, statistical data are not reported regarding whether the offending ad used a humorous approach or not. Nor are details provided regarding ads for which the complaints were not upheld. Descriptions are reported for complaints upheld.

Based on the descriptions provided, it does not appear that any of the forty-five ads cited for accuracy/clarity issues used a humorous approach. Typically these ads could be described as deceptive. With regard to "offensive" ads, it appears that one of the three ads in which "safety" was the issue of concern had humorous intent and that four of the nine ads with "unacceptable depictions and portrayals" were intended to be humorous. Of the seven ads for which the Advertising Standards Bureau of Australia upheld complaints in 2003, four featured an attempt at humor (Advertising Standards Bureau 2004).

Six out of the ten most complained about ads and advertising campaigns in the United Kingdom in 2003 used a humorous approach (Advertising Standards Authority 2003). These included a World War II–themed campaign from Shepherd Neame Ltd. for Spitfire brand beer. The campaign featured ad copy such as "No nazi aftertaste," with the tag line "the Bottle of Britain."

Table 9.3

Complaints to Advertising Standards Canada, by Year and Complaint Issue, Top Three Complaint Categories

Issue	Number of ads charged with offense	Number of complaints upheld
Accuracy/clarity	68	45
Safety	4	3
Unacceptable depictions and portrayals	59	9

ASA received sixty-six complaints regarding this campaign. The campaign was criticized for "being xenophobic, offensive, and trivializing the events of the Second World War" (Advertising Standards Authority 2003, 15). The complaints were not upheld. An ad for easyJet that featured a photo of a woman's breasts clad only in a bra under the headline, "Discover weapons of mass distraction" drew complaints that it was offensive, demeaning to women, and that it trivialized the war in Iraq. The ad generated 190 complaints, however, "noting the humor in the advertisement, the ASA considered that the ad was light-hearted and unlikely to cause serious or widespread offence" (Advertising Standards Authority 2003, 7).

The campaign for the Channel Four TV series *Six Feet Under,* which featured spoofs of cosmetic ads using models made up to resemble corpses, generated 122 complaints stating that the ads were offensive and shocking. The ASA did not rule on the issue of offensiveness. However, it upheld the complaints. The ASA ruled that because the identity of the advertiser and the product was unclear the ads were misleading.

While it is clear that many humorous ads are offensive, it is interesting to note that the fact that the ads are intended to be humorous is commonly used as a defense for their offensiveness. The "weapons of mass distraction" ad ranked as the third most complained about ad in the United Kingdom in 2003. A spokesperson for easyJet defended the ad by stating that it was "the latest in a series designed to be 'topical, humorous and irreverent,'" (BBC 2003). This defense was echoed by the ASA. Similar defenses are found for virtually every ad charged with being offensive. The "humor defense" is interesting, given that it is likely that many of those offended by a given ad recognize that the ad is an attempt at humor, albeit, an offensive attempt at humor.

Notes

1. In the survey, "sampling" was listed as an "advertising medium" not as a sales promotion tool as it is typically defined.

2. Actually the trackers included a black man and a Latina woman, but their appearance on screen was very brief and easy to miss.

——— 10 ———

General Conclusions and Research Directions

We have covered a great deal of ground in this book, which we will not try to recount here, but we will highlight what we currently understand and also what still needs to be researched. The preceding chapters make it clear that much work remains to be done to fully understand the impact of humor in advertising. We know that "humor plays an essential role in many facets of human life including psychological, social and somatic functioning" (Mobbs et al. 2003, 1041). This is not surprising since the benefits of humor appear to have a neurological basis (Mobbs et al. 2003). Given this, it is axiomatic that humor is found in all human cultures.

Since humor has a significant role in human behavior, it is natural that humor would have a role in marketing communications. Indeed, the use of humor can be traced back to the very beginnings of marketing communications (see Chapter 1). Yet, throughout much of its history, the use of humor in advertising has engendered controversy. This is due, at least in part, to the possible polarizing effects of humor (see Table 10.1) resulting from the potentially negative as well positive effects.

Although issues related to humor in advertising still stir debate, there has been a general shift in attitude toward a more positive view of humor in advertising. David Ogilvy famously changed his opinion on the use of humor. In his widely read work, *Confessions of an Advertising Man* (1963), Ogilvy exhorted, "Be serious. Don't use humor or fantasy" (136), and "Good copywriters have always resisted the temptation to entertain" (114). He reversed his position in 1982 by reporting research findings that suggested that humor, "pertinent to the selling situation," improved the performance of television ads in changing brand preference (Ogilvy and Raphaelson 1982, 15). Perhaps the early critics of humor, such as Claude Hopkins, were wrong. Or

Table 10.1

Selected Possible Humor Actions and Reactions

Humor action	Possible positive results for advertiser	Possible negative results for advertiser
An advertiser pokes fun at itself or products	Entertainment value in ad; possible affect transfer builds liking of advertiser.	Entertainment gets in the way of information. Product and /or advertiser "become" the joke, eroding brand image.
An advertiser pokes fun at its competitors	Entertainment value in ad; possible affect transfer builds liking of advertiser. Competitor becomes a joke eroding competitor brand image.	Advertiser is seen as mean-spirited, causing a negative backlash against the advertiser. Consumers remember the competitor's name but not the advertiser's.
An advertiser pokes fun at an individual or group	Entertainment value in ad; possible affect transfer builds liking of advertiser.	Depending on the target of the humor and the nature of the humor, the advertiser may be seen as rude, crude, insensitive, or in the extreme, sexist or racist.

perhaps they were correct for their era. After all, the culture has changed considerably since Hopkins published *Scientific Advertising* in 1923. Of course, the nature of advertising has also changed as has the nature of consumers and the nature of media.

Media choices have grown exponentially in the years since Hopkins, making it easy for an advertiser to be lost in the clutter. Technological changes such as VCRs, TiVo, satellite radio, iPods, and the Internet allow for consumers to have more control of media consumption. Technological changes have even caused some to posit that advertising, as we have known it since the dawn of the television era, is an endangered species. "Advertising is on its deathbed and it will not survive long, having contracted a fatal case of new technology" (Rust and Oliver 1994, 76). More than a decade has passed since Rust and Oliver's diagnosis and advertising still exists. But it is clear that technological developments are shaking the foundations of the industry (Cappo 2003; Donaton 2004; Klaassen 2005). These changes may lead to greater use of humor as marketers work harder and harder to gain and hold the attention of consumers, in which case humor may become an even more important tool.

How Humor Works

It is difficult to recap all of what has been covered in the previous nine chapters, but there are a number of statements that we can make about humor. We start with the final version of the challenge model (see Figure 10.1), introduced in Chapter 2 and developed in Chapters 3 to 7. We posit in the model that humor is generated by combinations of the three humor mechanisms of incongruity, arousal, and superiority. The most common mechanism used to generate humor in advertising is incongruity, though we argue that the common element that unites all means of generating humor is the notion of "challenge" to the normal order. This normal order or schema familiarity is one of the facilitating conditions that must be present in an audience in order for it to recognize what it has seen or heard is a departure from the norm. The challenge in our model can arise from any one of the humor mechanisms, but it is in their combination that we find prototypical humor styles. Speck's work that we discussed in Chapter 6 argues that there are five humor types that emerge from the combination of incongruity, arousal, and disparagement mechanisms. We suggest that the amount of challenge that results may or may not be humorous depending on the presence of facilitating conditions including familiarity, as noted above, as well as play signals (including warmth),

Figure 10.1   **The Challenge Model of Humor: A Complete View**

Humor mechanism   Challenge   Facilitating conditions   Humor response   Outcomes

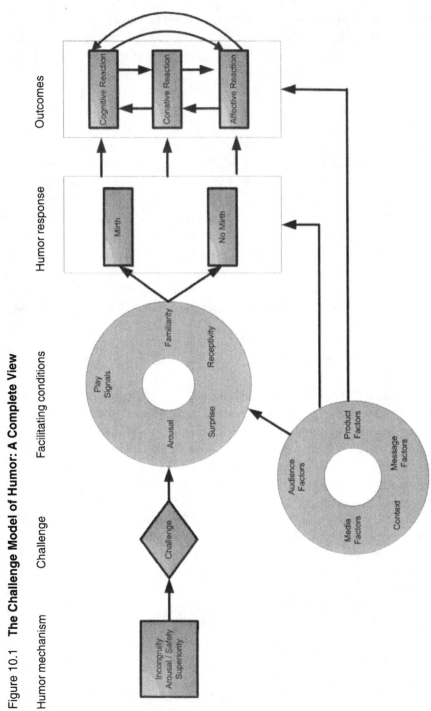

receptivity toward a humor attempt, the amount of surprise and arousal. The humor response in the model of mirth or no mirth is a proxy for a wide range of responses from gladness, gaiety, merriment, laughter, amusement, cheer, grins, happiness, fun, pleasure, and lightheartedness. The higher order outcomes in the model of affect, cognition, and conation can be either positive or negative and constitute the real proving ground for advertising attempts at humor. Speck's study of five humor types with TV ads demonstrates that perceived humor varies widely and that higher order effects are not always consistent. For example, satire, a combination of disparagement and incongruity mechanisms, was perceived humorous by about half of his sample and registered a score of 3.1 out of 5 on his humor scale. These ads had a positive impact on message and descriptive comprehension as well as enjoyment of the ad. However, there were *negative* consequences on perceived source trustworthiness, source liking, product quality, and whether the ad was seen as positive. These are probably not the kinds of outcomes that would endear an agency to its client if these were some of the goals sought from the advertising.

What Humor Can Do

Humor can be a very serious matter. It can be used to entertain, to enlighten, and to persuade. Humor can also offend, confuse, and distract. Which of these diverse outcomes occurs in a given situation can be predicted with some degree of confidence. "Humor is not mere nonsense. Rather, it is a particular form of controlled, rule-bound nonsense" (Crawford 2003). These rules suggest how humor is created (see Chapter 2). Similarly, "rules of thumb" suggest the likely outcome of a particular application of humor in advertising in achieving a particular advertising outcome. Humor research is plagued by many complexities, as mentioned throughout the book. We will summarize many of these contingencies in the sections that follow.

Audience Issues: Who Can We Reach With Humor?

Some of the studies that have found a gender effect for response to humor (e.g., Lammers 1991; Lammers et al. 1983) may in fact have found a gender effect for a particular humorous execution. Men and women both respond positively to humor in general but they differ in the appreciation of different types of humor (Duchaj 1999; Lowis 2003; Prerost 1995; Whipple and Courtney 1981). Gender issues as they relate to the use of humor in advertising are complex. We discussed these issues in detail in Chapter 3 and we do not wish to reopen this discussion here. However, advertisers and advertising researchers should note that men and women might respond differently to a given humorous execution.

Advertising practitioners were found to believe that humorous ads are best suited to younger target audiences (Madden and Weinberger 1984). Again, this may be more of an artifact of how humor is executed rather than an attribute of the audience. A humorous ad that works well with twenty-year-old respondents may work poorly with sixty-year-old respondents. This may not be due to a lack of a sense of humor in sixty-year-olds, but due to differences between twenty-year-olds and sixty-year-olds. Humor is found on seniorsite.com but it is not the same humor that is found on collegehumor.com. This is not surprising. The two targeted age groups differ in many ways. They have different cultural reference points, different concerns, different interests, and different physiology. They may also have different languages. Although a twenty-year-old and sixty-year-old may both speak English, in important ways they may not share the same language. Slang is very generational. This was made very clear to the Metropolitan Transportation Authority (MTA) in New York City recently. The clothing manufacturer Akademiks placed ads on MTA buses featuring either a suggestive photo of a woman or a photo of a couple, and the phrase "Read Books, Get Brain." MTA officials were unaware that "get brain" was teen slang for oral sex. According to a spokesperson for Akademiks, "It's coded language, city slang. Teens know what it means but the general public doesn't" (*New York Daily News* 2004). The MTA pulled all of the ads once they became aware of the hidden meaning. "'It's sad that a company and its advertising agency would appear to be promoting a good cause while instead using vulgar street phrases to demean women,' fumed MTA spokesman Tom Kelly" (*New York Daily News* 2004).

Age and gender are not the only audience factors that can affect response to humorous ads. Educational level, culture, and subculture can all influence reaction to humor. Additionally, personality variables such as need for cognition, level of self-monitoring, and need for levity have potential roles, which have been addressed in studies during the past decade. These factors may interact with each other in complex ways. Each of these audience factors also interacts with source factors.

In Chapter 3 the dispositional theory of humor was discussed (Zillmann and Cantor 1976: 1996). This theory suggests that the preexisting disposition toward a disparaged humor target will affect the perception of humor regarding the target. The preexisting disposition with regard to the disparaging agent will also affect the perception of humor. As an example, a highly sexist man is likely to perceive a joke disparaging women as funny. He is also unlikely to respond positively to any joke presented by a radical feminist.

We also introduced the commonality principle in Chapter 3, which is a related yet somewhat different thesis. The commonality principle suggests that commonality, or lack of commonality, among audience, agent, and target will affect the perception of humor. A Jewish comedian who is telling jokes that disparage Jews to a Jewish audience is more likely to elicit a humorous response than a non-Jew telling the same jokes to the same audience.

Although the two cases described above are not directly applicable to advertising, they are nonetheless relevant to advertising. If an advertiser disparages someone we do not like, we are likely to find it humorous. In contrast, if an advertiser disparages someone we like, we will not likely find it humorous, unless, perhaps, we view the advertiser as "one of us." In this case, the joke among "us" is acceptable. The dispositional theory and the commonality principle indicate that an advertiser must have a clear understanding of the target audience and of the audience's perception of the advertiser in order to successfully execute a humor strategy.

In conclusion, humor can be used with any audience. However, one must understand the audience completely. Commonality aids in this understanding. The more commonality the humor agent (source) shares with the humor audience the more likely the humor execution will be successful.

Media and Context Issues: Where Should We Use Humor?

Humor is used quite differently in different advertising media, with 25 to 30 percent of ads on broadcast media using humor while the percentage in magazines is about 10 percent and probably considerably lower in direct mail. It is likely that the types of products advertised, the active and passive nature of the medium, and range of devices used to generate humor in each medium help drive the volume of humor employed in each medium.

As discussed in Chapter 4, broadcast media are ideally suited to the use of humor. Radio and TV provide a wide arsenal of tools to execute humor, including humorous tone of voice, sound effects, and in the case of television, humorous visuals. In broadcast advertising, the advertiser also controls the pace of the ad. This allows for the use of comic timing, which is an important element of humor. Audiences also have little motivation to process information from broadcast ads, in contrast to print and direct mail, so peripheral processing is more likely to occur. Under peripheral processing conditions, humor is likely to lead to successful outcomes.

Media do more than simply carry messages. The media can add value to the message. The 2003 Radio Mercury Award Grand Prize winning ad was "Dinner Date," an ad for the National Thoroughbred Racing Association. In the ad, an announcer narrates a date in the manner of a horse track announcer calling a race. The names of the "horses" correspond with aspects of the date. This ad works primarily because of the nature of radio. Indeed, it is difficult to envision a successful execution of this ad in another medium. Similarly, the "Bear Fight" television ad for John West Red Salmon works because the medium makes it appear, in a visually convincing manner, that "John West," the fisherman, acquires the choicest salmon by engaging in a boxing/kick-fighting match with a bear who is fishing on the banks of a river. The slapstick humor in this ad could not be reproduced in print or in any other format.[1]

With the exception of the growing list of Web sites that feature ads as content, ads do not occur independently, they occur in some context. While advertising context has been studied extensively, relatively little work has specifically explored context as it relates to humor in advertising. More problematic is that the work that has been done on this issue has produced ambiguous findings that suggest that context may interact with involvement and other audience factors. In general, it appears that humorous ads perform better in a non-humorous context than they do in a humorous context. However, it is likely that contrast between ad and context is an inverted U-shaped function, with a moderate level of contrast superior to high or low levels of contrast. For example, *Saving Private Ryan, Shindler's List, Sophie's Choice,* and *The Passion of the Christ* certainly all qualify as non-humorous contexts, but it is very doubtful that a humorous ad placed in any of these contexts would perform very well. While we can speculate on the shape of the contrast function, to our knowledge it has not been empirically examined.

In conclusion, if the media plan calls for primarily broadcast media, a humorous strategy may be appropriate. On the other hand, if the media plan is dominated by print, it is less likely that a humorous strategy will succeed. In addition, advertisers should be aware of the context in which the ad will be viewed. This context includes not only the immediate media environment but also the broader issues of context such as the micro- and macro-social context of the ad (see Chapter 7).

Product and Message Issues: For What Should We Use Humor?

Although the ultimate goal of all marketing communications is sales, relatively few marketing communications messages are sales oriented. Instead the advertising serves some other marketing purpose: to build awareness of a product or brand, help position a brand, attempt to reposition the competition, or accomplish other communications goals. Messages are structured differently based on the outcomes desired. Humor in advertising tends to benefit some outcome measures more than others and some products more than others. Also, as we have stressed repeatedly, all humor is not created equal. There are many humor types, such as satire, comic wit, full comedy, and so on, which are discussed in Chapter 6. This makes for a complex picture, but looking across multiple studies we can draw some important conclusions.

Some products are better suited to a humor strategy than others. Products that are high in risk (financial risk, performance risk, etc.)—in particular, high-risk expressive products such as sports cars, sailboats, expensive jewelry, and the like—are generally not well suited to the use of humor. There is some tantalizing evidence that related humor provides some advantage for these products in radio advertising, but in general they seem to be much better served by a non-humorous approach to marketing communications.

On the other hand, humor works well for the little treats of life such as beer, snack food, soft drinks, and so on, the so-called yellow goods. These differences are reflected in humor usage and in measures of advertising effectiveness. In radio, TV, and consumer magazines humor is used most frequently with yellow goods. In the United States this is as high as 41 percent for radio, 38 percent in TV, and 18 percent in magazines. In the UK the use of humor exceeds 50 percent for these low-involvement/expressive products. The positive impact of humor on Starch recognition scores in magazines and on various recall scores in radio is strongest for yellow goods.

Humor is used frequently in ads for low-involvement/functional blue goods, but the effects are mixed. Though 35 percent of radio ads use humor, it is only ads using related humor that provide an advantage. For the 12 percent of magazine ads that use humor, there is no consistent advantage and some evidence for a negative humor effect.

Humor used in white good magazine ads provides an advantage over Starch ad norms as long as the ads are not humor dominant or message dominant. They should be image focused. Radio ads for this type of product do not appear to be successful for aiding recall or persuasion.

There are also differences within the color categories. Humor is best suited to audiences that have a positive prior brand attitude. This suggests that humor is probably not a good strategy to revive a brand with a poor image.

The results for humor and new products are mixed from two studies using industry data testing TV ads. The McCollum/Spielman test found that established products were bigger gainers from humor than new products. However, even for new products 59 percent of the audience had positive clutter/awareness scores. Results were lower (47 percent) for an attitude shift with new products. Stewart and Furse (1986) found that humor with new products had a strong effect when recall was measured, a smaller but positive effect with comprehension, and no effect on persuasion. In general, the effects on established products were the same. Both studies agree that the odds of humor working with new products to shift attitudes or persuade are low, but that the odds are much better with awareness, recall, and comprehension.

With regard to outcome measures, there is strong evidence in magazine, radio, and TV studies that humor most often improves attention, attitude toward the ad (A_{ad}), and attitude toward the advertised brand (A_b). There is further strong evidence in studies conducted in magazines, TV, and direct mail that liking of the source of the advertising is enhanced with the use of humor.

The impact of humor on comprehension, persuasion, and source credibility is mixed when we look at the many studies conducted in different media. The strongest support for a general, positive comprehension and recall effect comes from the large Stewart and Furse (1986) regression study of TV ads.

Humor is entertaining, and as we discussed in Chapter 6, entertainment value is a predictor of success of an advertising campaign. We hasten to note that an "attempt at humor" is not the same as "humor." Entertainment value comes from the perception of humor, not the perception of attempted humor. A "humorous" ad that fails is much like a joke that fails. The teller is generally better to have not made the attempt. Similarly in advertising, not only does this failed attempt at humor fail to deliver the benefits of a humorous ad, it performs worse than a non-humorous ad (Flaherty, Weinberger, and Gulas 2004).

Incongruity humor is the most commonly used humor device in advertising. Recent work has linked the amount of incongruity to the amount of surprise and perceived humorousness in advertising. In addition, the full resolution of an incongruity is related to higher levels of perceived humor.

The amount of perceived humor seen in an ad appears to be a key determinant of A_{ad} and A_b and may also govern higher order effects of humor. This would suggest that pretesting advertising is crucial because ads that fail to amuse may prove to be annoying and have unintended negative consequences.

Wear out of humor may occur after three to five repetitions but there is suggestion that positive effects can be sustained much longer with varied humor executions. This suggestion makes particular sense in the context of the research showing that greater surprise triggers stronger humor effects. As a single execution of humor is seen more, the surprise would decline while varied executions with novel surprise should sustain the humor effect for a period until the basic concept becomes stale.

There are mixed results regarding the importance of relatedness of the humor to the product and ad message (thematic relatedness). Related humor appears to outperform unrelated humor, but the results are based on only a few scattered studies.

What Humor Cannot Do

Humor is not a panacea. Advertisers should not use humor as a replacement for a sound marketing communications strategy. Humor, if used at all, should be part of an overall communications strategy. A recent ad for Starburst candy created by TWBA/Chiat/Day featured a high school art student stopping a fellow student, the object of his affection, in the hallway. He takes her to an art classroom to show her his creation, a likeness of her that he has created from Starburst candy. To her horror, he kisses, and then devours, the sculpture in front of her. The ad is no doubt humorous in a disturbing way. But it is difficult to imagine how this ad helps promote the brand. What does the ad suggest about Starburst customers? How does this ad fit into a long-term strategy for Starburst? There are countless similar examples, from the Quiznos ads that have used a man suckling on a wolf, and "Spongmonkeys," creatures that looked like rats with bad teeth, to promote a restaurant, to the horrendous Just for Feet ad described in Chapter 9. These sorts of humorous ads are probably more fun to show at corporate meetings than serious campaigns, and they may help ad agencies win creativity awards, but it is unlikely that they help build long-term brand equity. Humor used appropriately can have strong positive effects, but humor used inappropriately can be disastrous, as demonstrated by Just for Feet.

What We Do Not Know: Directions for Future Research

A tremendous amount of research has been conducted related to humor in advertising. This book has reviewed hundreds of studies from different disciplines. Yet much remains to be learned. The recent trend has been away from what might be called main effects of humor, which in the early days asked whether there was a generalized humor effect. Work matured by looking

199

at product level effects and some individual level contingencies, such as gender, need for humor, and need for cognition. Most recently, the humor process itself has been explored in research looking at incongruity, surprise, and humorousness. These studies are all positive steps forward, but huge gaps exist in our understanding. On a general level, there is an opportunity for more direct theory testing with humor. In Chapter 2 we enumerated some of the theories that may explain how humor works but which have been almost void of explicit study. For example, classical conditioning studies conducted by Gorn (1982) and Shimp, Stewart, and Rose (1991) could be replicated using various types and intensities of humor. Additional tests of the distraction hypothesis called for by Nelson, Duncan, and Frontczak (1985) twenty years ago deserve testing under varied the conditions they called for. On a more basic level we suggest future research in the area of message, context, media effects, and interactions.

Message Research

The most glaring gap is in the testing of varied humor executions. For example, many recent studies have used cartoons embedded in print ads to manipulate humor. Although these studies provide a clean manipulation, we need to exhibit caution when drawing conclusions from them because they represent a fairly narrow genre of message. The Speck comparison of five humor types stands alone as the only examination of the efficacy of different humor types on perceived humor and higher order effects. The result indicates that humor effects can vary widely between humor types. As noted earlier, the use of disparagement in satire and in full comedy may have negative effects on trust and knowledge of the source while sentimental comedy (arousal and incongruity) has a strong positive impact on these source measures. Though a number of studies have counted the frequency of use of different humor styles in TV and magazines, we know very little about their impact. By the same token, beyond some recent studies that have looked at the incongruity-surprise connection, we know little about the role of the other basic humor mechanisms, arousal-safety and disparagement, in triggering a mirth effect or higher order effects in an advertising context.

Further unresolved message issues are the importance of thematic relatedness, humor dominance, message quality, and level of humor. The relationship between humor complexity and wear out has been suggested but not explored. Additionally, the suggestion that varied humor executions of the same theme (i.e., a humor campaign) can delay wear out needs more investigation. Further, most humor research has focused on individual executions and single exposures rather than humor campaigns with multiple exposures and multiple executions.

Context Research

In 1992 we called for more research on context effects as they relate specifically to humorous advertising (Weinberger and Gulas 1992). Research has been conducted on context since that call (Perry et al. 1997a; De Pelsmacker, Geuens, and Anckaert 2002). Yet much more research needs to be conducted in this important area. Questions still remain about the serious versus humorous surrounding programming, editorial or event context, and the general expectation of whether humor will be contained in an advertisement. A particularly unstudied context area concerns product placements and event sponsorships, two areas of emerging advertising spending.

The roots of product placement in entertainment films date back to the 1920s or earlier (Segrave 2004). But the use of product placement in feature films grew slowly until recently. Marketers are increasingly using the practice as they seek ways to reach consumers who are immune from zapping, zipping, and other advertising avoidance tactics. Placements are the frontlines of the merger between advertising and entertainment. Donaton (2004) has argued that the very survival of advertising is dependent on its ultimate convergence with entertainment. Although some may think Donaton has overstated the case, the convergence between advertising and entertainment is well under way and product placement is a central part of this convergence.

As the use of product placement has grown, it has attracted scholarly interest (see e.g., Gupta and Lord 1998; Gupta, Balasubramanian, and Klassen 2000; Karrh, McKee, and Pardun 2003; Russell 2002). Karrh, McKee, and Pardun (2003) found that the biggest concern among practitioners regarding the use of product placement as a promotional technique was that the product would be portrayed in a positive light, in other words, context. This is not surprising since marketers have significantly less control over how a product is shown in a placement than the absolute control they have in advertising executions. An area where marketers do, however, exhibit great control is in the selection of the film, television show, video game, or other placement venue in which to place products. Yet this issue has been overlooked to date in the marketing literature. It does not appear that anyone has studied whether there is a difference between placements in a humorous context (e.g., a humorous film) compared to placements in a dramatic context. Since the line between context and ad is intentionally blurred in product placement, it would seem likely that context effects would be stronger in product placement than in traditional advertising. An emerging issue of humor research may be the differences between product placements in a humorous context and placements in a non-humorous context.

The growth of product placement has also spawned the emergence of "situ-mercials" (Steinberg 2004). Unlike typical television spots, which are created in a context-independent manner, situ-mercials are designed with the programming context specifically in mind. For example, ads for Geico insurance that feature a jail setting and a somber tone, until the punch line is delivered, are placed in courtroom dramas and police shows (Steinberg 2004). This practice captures some of the benefits of product placement. Since the ads fit the context very closely, they appear to be almost a part of the programming and thus they may be less likely to elicit a zipping or zapping response. Correspondingly, these ads are likely to be significantly affected by context, and thus situ-mercials placed in a humorous context may perform differently from situ-mercials in a serious context or from standard humorous ads not linked to program context. This type of context-dependant advertising has not been examined to date in the humor-in-advertising literature.

Media Effects

Advertising humor research has focused on a few major media and completely neglected others. At the most basic level there is no published research about the amount and type of humor in major media such as outdoor and direct mail. At a deeper level, advertising campaigns often employ multiple media in a single campaign but we have not explored the combined effect of the same ad in magazines and TV or of a TV ad and the radio soundtrack of the same ad. These issues will continue to grow as advertisers diversify spending to more media to reach an ever more elusive consumer. Consumers are faced with an ever-growing array of media choices. These choices will at the same time make it more difficult for advertisers to reach ever more elusive consumers and ever more fragmented audiences, and open new opportunities for creative marketing communications. Creative new executions of humor are emerging all of the time. Jerry Seinfeld appears with an animated Super Man in short Internet films for American Express. Burger King hosts the subservient chicken that obeys the commands of Web site visitors. The Web is already well established as a "new" medium. Other new media possibilities for advertisers are still emerging. These include blogs, cell phone SMS (short message service), satellite radio, and media down-loaded to iPods and similar devices some of which now go beyond MP3 song files and accept photos and video clips. Shelly Lazarus, chairman and CEO of Ogilvy & Mather Worldwide, stated that "the most creative part of any presentation these days is the media part" (Steinberg 2004, B11). Yet, most of what we have learned about humor in advertising is restricted to traditional media. The extent to which new media are similar to or different from traditional forms of media with regard to humor is an issue in need of research.

Humor in Marketing Communications

The focus of this book is humor in advertising, although we have noted other forms of marketing communications. We have focused on advertising since the bulk of the research regarding humor in marketing communications is specifically directed at advertising. Additionally, despite numerous procla-mations by business pundits and others that advertising is dead, traditional media advertising remains a vital and significant component of marketing communications. That being said, it would be shortsighted to ignore the changes that are occurring in marketing communications. The growing use of the Internet, product placements, viral marketing, event marketing, and other emerging techniques has changed the nature of marketing communica-tions. Little if any scholarly research has been done regarding the use of humor in these forms of marketing communications.

On Valentine's Day 2005, a stunned woman ran off the court of a televised Orlando Magic basketball game in tears, while her boyfriend remained on his knees, after an apparent failed public marriage proposal. The event was reported on local television news in Florida and nationally on news Web sites. The following day the entire episode was revealed to be a hoax de-signed by the Orlando Magic as a "marketing ploy to spice up the NBA experience" (local6.com 2005). This is a use of disparaging humor in a mar-keting context, but it is very different from advertising. This form of market-ing, often referred to as "buzz marketing" or "stealth marketing," is one of the fastest growing forms of marketing communications (Vranica 2005a). Stealth marketing has growth to the extent that it is now the subject of a recently formed trade group, the Word of Mouth Marketing Association, which has developed a set of guidelines regarding the ethical use of buzz marketing techniques (Vranica 2005a). However, no scholarly research has examined whether the use of humor in stealth marketing is effective.

Interactions of Audience Factors

We have learned that audience factors such as involvement, need for cognition, need for levity, self-monitoring, and other factors influence humor outcomes. Similarly, demographic factors and the commonality principle may affect perception of humor. However, very little is known about how these factors interact with each other. To what extent does need for cognition influence involvement? Does need for levity overcome the commonality principle? Does male preference for aggressive humor diminish among high-self-monitoring males? Dozens of such questions can be framed. The answers to some of these questions may be important to scholars and/or advertising practitioners.

Other Interactions

Many other complex interactions among audience, media, product, and context remain to be explored. In some ways the more we learn about humor in advertising the less we know. What is clear is that humor can be a very useful tool for advertisers, but it is a tool to be used carefully.

Parting Words

This book is the result of a fifteen-year collaboration between the authors on humor in advertising. Advertising has changed a great deal in those fifteen years. During that time, the World Wide Web, e-mail, SMS, and satellite radio have emerged as new advertising media. Stadium naming rights, product placements, and event sponsorships feature in the communications strategies of many marketers as never before. And CRM software has been implemented that now allows for customer-triggered communication on a mass scale as never before possible. During these fifteen years the role of magazines has declined and the role of newspapers, which was the dominant medium in the United States for decades, has declined precipitously. Advertising will change even more in the next fifteen years. Some have even predicted the death of media advertising altogether. Whether or not this occurs, and we think it will not, what will not change is the need for marketers to connect to consumers.

In all cultures, throughout recorded history, humor has been a part of human communications. Humor has been a part of marketing communications since the emergence of commerce. It will continue to be a part of marketing communications. We have learned a great deal about how, where, and when humor works. We have attempted to report all of that in this book. There is still much we do not know. We have attempted to report that as well. As media changes, as culture changes, and as communications research progresses, we will have to revisit many of these issues again. We will see you in fifteen years . . . maybe.

Note

1. This ad, and other television ads, can be shown in streaming video on the Web. However, this is more accurately described as an alternative delivery system for an ad, rather than a separate media form in these cases.

Bibliography

Aaker, David, and Douglas Stayman. 1990. "Measuring Audience Perceptions of Commercials and Relating Them to Ad Impact," *Journal of Advertising Research* (August/September): 7–17.

Abernethy, Michael. 2003. "Male Bashing on TV," *Pop Matters,* www.popmatters.com /tv/features/030109-male-bashing.shtml. Accessed on August 5.

"Ad Meter No. 1 Hall of Fame." 2005a. *USA Today,* www.usatoday.com/money/advertising/admeter/2005–01–31-previous-winners_x.htm. Accessed on February 7.

"The Advertising Century." 2003. *Advertising Age*, www.adage.com/century/people /people028.html. Accessed on June 13.

Advertising Standards Authority. 2003. *Advertising Standards Authority Annual Report 2003.* London.

Advertising Standards Bureau. 2004. www.advertisingstandardsbureau.com.au. Accessed on August 19.

Advertising Standards Canada. 1997. *1997 Ad Complaints Report.* Toronto.

Alden, Dana L., and Wayne D. Hoyer. 1993. "An Examination of Cognitive Factors Related to Humorousness in Television Advertising," *Journal of Advertising* 22 (June): 29–37.

Alden, Dana L., Wayne D. Hoyer, and Chol Lee. 1993. "Identifying Global and Culture-Specific Dimensions of Humor in Advertising: A Multinational Analysis," *Journal of Marketing* 57 (April): 64–75.

Alden, Dana, and Drew Martin. 1995. "Global and Cultural Characteristics of Humor in Advertising: The Case of Japan," *Journal of Global Marketing* 9 (1/2): 121–42.

Alden, Dana, Ashesh Mukherjee, and Wayne D. Hoyer. 2000. "The Effects of Incongruity, Surprise and Positive Moderators on Perceived Humor in Television Advertising," *Journal of Advertising Research* 29 (2): 1–13.

Altsech, Moses B., Thomas Cline, and James Kellaris. 1999. "Can Humor Enhance the Impact of Strong Message Arguments?" Proceedings of the Society for Consumer Psychology, ed. J. Inman. San Antonio, Texas.

American Heritage Dictionary of the English Language. 1978. Boston: Houghton Mifflin.

An, Daechun. 2003. "Content Analysis of Advertising Visuals in the Magazine Advertisements: The Roaring Twenties and the Great Depression," www.scripps .ohiou.edu/wjmcr/vol06/6-3a-b.htm. Accessed on September 29, 2004.

Anand, Punam, and Brian Sternthal. 1990. "Ease of Message Processing as a Moderator of Message Effects in Advertising," *Journal of Marketing Research* 27 (August): 345–53.

Ananova. 2003. "Advert's 'Fat' Joke Ruled Funny, Not Offensive," www.ananova.com /business/story.sm_817753.html." Accessed on September 10.

Applegate, Edd, and John McDonough. 2003. "Lasker, Albert D.," in *Advertising Age Encyclopedia of Advertising,* ed. John McDonough. New York: Fitzroy Dearborn.

Archer, Belinda. 1994. "Does Humor Cross Borders?" *Campaign* (June 17): 32–34.

Austin, Mark, and Jim Aitchison. 2003. *Is Anybody Out There? The New Blueprint for Marketing Communications in the 21st Century.* Singapore: John Wiley & Sons.

Barnes, James H. Jr., and Michael J. Dotson. 1990. "An Exploratory Investigation into the Nature of Offensive Television Advertising," *Journal of Advertising* 19 (3): 61–69.

Bateson, G. 1953. "The Position of Humor in Human Communication," in *Cybernetics,* ninth conference, ed. H. von Foerster, 1–47. New York: Macy Foundation.

"Battling the Bimbo Factor." 1991. *Time* 13 (21): November 25, 70.

Bauerly, Ronald John. 1989. "An Experimental Investigation of Humor in Television: The Effects of Product Type, Program Context, and Target Humor on Selected Consumer Cognitions (Commercials)." Unpublished dissertation, Southern Illinois University.

———. 1990. "Humor in Advertising: Does the Product Class Matter?" Proceedings of the 6th Annual Conference of the Atlantic Marketing Association, ed. Rustan Kosenko and Robert Baer (6): 9–13.

BBC News. 2003. "Easyjet Breast Ad 'Not Offensive,'" http://news.bbc.co.uk/go/pr /fr/-/1/hi/uk/3108309.stm. Accessed on August 18.

Belch, George E., and Michael A. Belch. 1984. "An Investigation of the Effects of Repetition on Cognitive and Affective Reactions to Humorous and Serious Television Commercials," *Advances in Consumer Research* 11: 4–10.

Bender, Jay. 1993. "Gender Differences in the Recall of Humorous Advertising Material," unpublished doctoral dissertation, Nova University.

Berlyne, Daniel E. 1969. "Laughter, Humor, and Play," in *Handbook of Social Psychology,* ed. G. Lindzey and E. Aronson, vol. 3, 795–852. New York: Addison-Wesley.

———. 1970. "Novelty, Complexity, and Hedonic Value," *Perception and Psychophysics* 8: 279–86.

———. 1972. "Humor and Its Kin," in *Psychology of Humor,* ed. J.H. Goldstein, and P.E. McGhee, 43–60. New York: Academic Press.

Best of 2001: The Clio Gold Award Winners. 2002. Video no. BVL11750, Princeton, NJ: Films for Humanities and Sciences.

Bianco, Anthony. 2004. "The Vanishing Mass Market," *Business Week,* July 12, 61–68.

Biel, Alexander, and Carol A. Bridgwater. 1990. "Attributes of Likable Television Commercials," *Journal of Advertising Research* 30 (June/July): 38–44.

Blue Fusion. 2004. www.bfusion.com/adage/bluefusionadreport.pdf. Accessed on July 20.

Bornstein, Robert F. 1989. "Exposure and Affect: Overview and Meta-Analysis of Research, 1968–1987," *Psychological Bulletin* 106 (September): 256–88.

Bram, Jason, James Orr, and Carol Rapaport. 2002. *Measuring the Effects of the September 11 Attack on New York City.* New York: Federal Reserve Bank of New York.

Braun, Kathryn A. 1999. "A Postexperience Advertising Effects on Consumer Memory," *Journal of Consumer Research* 25 (4): 319–32.

Brooker, George. 1981. "A Comparison of the Persuasive Effects of Mild Humor and Mild Fear Appeals," *Journal of Advertising* 10 (4): 29–40.

Bulik, Beth Snyder. 2004. "DVR Players, and Options, Mushroom," *Advertising Age* (June 28): 10.

Burtt, Harold Ernest. 1938. *Psychology of Advertising*. Boston: Houghton Mifflin.

"Bus Ban on Sex Ads." 2004. *New York Daily News,* www.nydailynews.com/news /local. Accessed on January 26, 2005.

Cacioppo, John T., and Richard E. Petty. 1979. "Effects of Message Repetition and Position on Cognitive Response, Recall and Persuasion," *Journal of Personality and Social Psychology* 37 (1): 97–109.

———. 1982. "The Need for Cognition," *Journal of Personality and Social Psychology* 42: 116–31.

Cacioppo, John T., Richard E. Petty, and Chuan Feng Kao. 1984. "The Efficient Assessment of Need for Cognition," *Journal of Personality Assessment* 48 (3): 306–7.

Calder, Bobby J., Lynn W. Phillips, and Alice M. Tybout. 1981. "Designing Research for Application," *Journal of Consumer Research* 8 (September): 197–207.

Campbell, Margaret C., and Kevin Lane Keller. 2003. "Brand Familiarity and Advertising Repetition Effects," *Journal of Consumer Research* 30 (2): 292–304.

Cann, Arnie, and Lawrence G. Calhoun. 2001. "Perceived Personality Associations with Differences in Sense of Humor: Stereotypes of Hypothetical Others with High or Low Senses of Humor," *Humor* 14 (2): 117–30.

Cantor, Joanne R., and Pat Venus. 1980. "The Effect of Humor on Recall of a Radio Advertisement," *Journal of Broadcasting* 24 (1): 13–22.

Caples, John. 1974. *Tested Advertising Methods*. 4th ed. Englewood Cliffs, NJ: Prentice Hall.

Cappo, Joe. 2003. *The Future of Advertising: New Media, New Clients, New Consumers in the Post-Television Age*. Chicago: McGraw-Hill.

Caron, James E. 2002. "From Ethology to Aesthetics: Evolution as a Theoretical Paradigm for Research on Laughter, Humor and Other Comic Phenomena," *Humor* 15 (3): 245–81.

Catanescu, Codruta, and Gail Tom. 2001. "Types of Humor in Television and Magazine Advertising," *Review of Business* (Spring): 92–95.

Chan, James, Dennis Park, and Dina Shek. 1997. "The Daniel K.E. Ching Collection: A Preliminary Look at Its Trade Cards and Sheet Music," *Chinese America: History and Perspectives* (11) 148–76.

Chapman, Antony J., and Hugh C. Foot, eds. 1976. *Humour and Laughter: Theory, Research and Application*. London: John Wiley & Sons.

Chattopadhyay, Amitava, and Kunal Basu. 1990. "Prior Brand Evaluation as a Moderator of the Effects of Humor in Advertising," *Journal of Marketing Research* 27 (4): 466–76.

Chung, Hwiman, and Zinshu Zhao. 2003. "Humour Effect on Memory and Attitude: Moderating Role of Product Involvement," *International Journal of Advertising* 22 (1): 117–44.

Cline, Thomas W. 1997. "The Role of Expectancy and Relevancy in Humorous Ad Executions: An Individual Difference Perspective," unpublished doctoral dissertation, University of Cincinnati.

Cline, Thomas W., and James Kellaris. 1999. "The Joint Impact of Humor and Argument Strength in a Print Advertising Context: A Case for Weaker Arguments," *Psychology and Marketing* 16 (1): 69–86.

Cline, Thomas W., Moses B. Altsech, and James J. Kellaris. 2003. "When Does Humor Enhance or Inhibit Ad Responses?" *Journal of Advertising* 32 (3): 31–45.

CNN. 2002. "Official! World's Funniest Joke," CNN.com, Science & Space, www.cnn.com/2002/TECH/science/10/03/joke.funniest. Accessed on October 7.

Costley, Carolyn, Scott Koslow, and Graeme Galloway. 2002. "Sense of Humor and Advertising: A Funny Thing Happened on the Way to the Model," *Advances in Consumer Research* 29: 225–26.

Coulter, Keith S. 1998. "The Effects of Affective Responses to Media Context on Advertising Evaluations," *Journal of Advertising* 27 (4): 41–51.

Crane, Ben. 2004. "A Brief History of Trade Cards," www.tradecards.com/articles/history/history.html. Accessed on July 27.

Crawford, Mary. 2003. "Gender and Humor in Social Context," *Journal of Pragmatics* 35, 1413–30.

Critchley, Simon. 2002. *On Humour.* London: Routledge.

Cuneo, Alice Z. 2000. "Can an Agency Be Guilty of Malpractice?" *Advertising Age* 71, 5 (January 31): 24–25.

Davies, Ann P., and Michael J. Apter. 1980. "Humour and Its Effect on Learning in Children," in *Children's Humour,* ed. Paul McGhee and A. Chapman, 237–53. London: John Wiley & Sons.

Davies, Christie. 1982. "Ethnic Jokes, Moral Values and Social Boundaries," *British Journal of Sociology* 33 (3): 383–403.

De Pelsmacker, Patrick, and Maggie Geuens. 1998. "Reactions to Different Types of Ads in Belgium and Poland," *International Marketing Review* 15 (2): 277–90.

De Pelsmacker, Patrick, Maggie Geuens, and Pascal Anckaert. 2002. "Media Context and Advertising Effectiveness: The Role of Context Appreciation and Context/Ad Similarity," *Journal of Advertising* 21 (2): 49–61.

Dews, Shelly, et al. 1996. "Children's Understanding of the Meaning and Functions of Verbal Irony," *Child Development* 67: 3071–85.

Donaton, Scott. 2004. *Madison & Vine: Why the Entertainment and Advertising Industries Must Converge to Survive.* New York: McGraw-Hill.

Duchaj, Karen A. 1999. "Humor Appreciation: Using Semantic Scripts to Explain Gender Differences," *Women & Language* 22 (2): 52–54.

Duncan, Calvin. 1979. "Humor in Advertising: A Behavioral Perspective," *Journal of the Academy of Marketing Science* 7 (4): 285–306.

Duncan, Calvin, James E. Nelson, and Nancy T. Frontczak. 1984. "The Effect of Humor on Advertising Comprehension," *Advances in Consumer Research* 11: 432–37.

Duncan, Calvin P., and James E. Nelson. 1985. "Effects of Humor in a Radio Advertising Experiment," *Journal of Advertising* 14 (2): 33–40, 64.

EASA. 2004. "EASA: Issue Briefing–Gender Stereotyping and the Portrayal of Women and Men," www.easa-alliance.org/about_sr/en/genderstereotyping-issuebrief.html. Accessed on August 5.

Edell, Julie A., and Richard Staelin. 1983. "The Information Processing of Pictures in Print Advertising," *Journal of Consumer Research* 10: 45–61.

Fahri, Paul. 2000. "Whassup? Bud's Buzzword Borrows from Male Ritual," www.enquirer.com/editions/2000/03.23.loc_whassup_buds.html. Accessed on March 23.

Fawcett, Adrienne Ward. 1995. "The 50 Best," *Advertising Age: 50 Years of TV Advertising* (Spring): 36–39.

Feltham, Tammi S., and Stephen J. Arnold. 1994. "Program Involvement and Ad /Program Consistency as Moderators of Program Context Effects," *Journal of Consumer Psychology* 3 (1): 51–77.

filmsite.org. 2004. www.filmsite.org/30sintro3.html. Accessed on November 23.

Flaherty, Karen, Marc. G. Weinberger, and Charles S. Gulas. 2004. "The Impact of Perceived Humor, Product Type and Humor Style in Radio Advertising," *Journal of Current Issues and Research in Advertising* 26 (1): 25–36.

Foot, Hugh C., and Antony J. Chapman. 1976. "The Social Responsiveness of Young Children in Humorous Situations," in *Humour and Laughter: Theory, Research and Application,* ed. Antony J. Chapman, and Hugh C. Foot, 187–214. London: John Wiley & Sons.

Fournier, Susan. 1998. "Consumers and Their Brands: Developing Relationship Theory in Consumer Research," *Journal of Consumer Research* 24 (4): 343–74.

Freud, Sigmund. (1905) 1960. *Jokes and Their Relation to the Unconscious.* New York: Norton. (First German edition 1905.)

Friedman, Hershey H., and Linda Friedman. 1979. "Endorser Effectiveness by Product Type," *Journal of Advertising Research* 19: 63–71.

Furnham, Adrian, Barrie Gunter, and Deidre Walsh. 1998. "Effects of Programme Context on Memory of Humorous Television Commercials," *Applied Cognitive Psychology* 12: 555–67.

Gallivan, Joanne. 1991. "What is Funny to Whom, and Why?" Paper presented at the Ninth International Conference on Humour and Laughter. Brock University, St. Catharines, Ontario, Canada.

Gallois, Cynthia, and Victor J. Callan. 1985. "The Influence of Ethnocentrism and Ethnic Label on the Appreciation of Disparagement Jokes," *International Journal of Psychology* 20: 63–76.

Gamble, Jennifer. 2001. "Humor in Apes," *Humor: International Journal of Humor Research* 14 (2): 163–79.

Garfield, Bob. 1999. "The Year in Ad Review," *Advertising Age* 70, 52 (December 20): 18–19.

———. 2001. "Ads Must Be Sensitive, But Don't Try to Profit from Grief," *Advertising Age* 72 (38): 29.

———. 2003. *And Now a Few Words from Me: Advertising's Leading Critic Lays Down the Law Once and For All.* New York: McGraw-Hill.

Gelb, Betsy D., and Charles M. Pickett. 1983. "Attitude-Toward-the-Ad: Links to Humor and to Advertising Effectiveness," *Journal of Advertising* 12 (2): 34–42.

Gelb, Betsy D., and George M. Zinkhan. 1985. "The Effect of Repetition on Humor in a Radio Advertising Study," *Journal of Advertising* 14 (4): 13–20, 68.

———. 1986. "Humor and Advertising Effectiveness After Repeated Exposures to a Radio Commercial," *Journal of Advertising* 15 (2): 15–20, 34.

Geuens, Maggie, and Patrick De Pelsmacker. 1998. "Feelings Evoked by War, Erotic, Humorous or Non-Emotional Print Advertising," *Academy of Marketing Science Review* (1998) 1–19.

———. 2002. "The Role of Humor in the Persuasion of Individuals Varying in Need for Cognition," *Advances in Consumer Research* 29: 50–56.

Godkewitsch, Michael. 1976. "Physiological and Verbal Indices of Arousal in Rated Humour," in *Humour and Laughter: Theory, Research and Application,* ed. Antony J. Chapman and Hugh C. Foot, 117–38. London: John C. Wiley & Sons.

Goldberg, Marvin E., and Gerald J. Gorn. 1987. "Happy and Sad TV Programs: How They Affect Reactions to Commercials," *Journal of Consumer Research* 14 (December): 387–403.

Goldsmith, Charles. 2004. "Dubbing in Product Plugs," *Wall Street Journal,* December 6, B1+.

Goldstein, J.H., and P.E. McGhee. 1972. *The Psychology of Humor.* New York: Academic Press.

Goodrum, Charles, and Helen Dalrymple. 1990. *Advertising in America: The First Two Hundred Years.* New York: Harry N. Abrams.

Gorn, Gerald J. 1982. "The Effects of Music in Advertising on Choice Behavior: A Classical Conditioning Approach," *Journal of Marketing* 46 (Winter): 94–101.

Greenwood, Dara, and Linda M. Isbell. 2002. "Ambivalent Sexism and the Dumb Blonde: Men's and Women's Reactions to Sexist Jokes," *Psychology of Women Quarterly* 26: 341–50.

Greppi, Michele. 2003. "Nielsen: Finding Lost Boys," *Television Week* 22, 46 (November 17): 1–3.

Grisaffe, Christie, Lindsey C. Blom, and Kevin L. Burke. 2003. "The Effects of Head and Assistant Coaches' Uses of Humor on Collegiate Soccer Players Evaluation of Their Coaches," *Journal of Sports Behavior* 26 (2): 103–8.

Gruner, Charles R. 1967. "Effect of Humor on Speaker Ethos and Audience Information Gain," *Journal of Communications* 17 (3): 228–33.

———. 1970. "The Effect of Humor in Dull and Interesting Informative Speeches," *Central States Speech Journal* 21 (3): 160–66.

———. 1991. "On the Impossibility of Having a Taxonomy of Humor," paper presented at the Ninth International Conference on Humour and Laughter. Brock University, St. Catharines, Ontario, Canada.

———. 1997. *The Game of Humor.* New Brunswick, NJ: Transaction Publishers.

———. 2000. *The Game of Humor: A Comprehensive Theory of Why We Laugh.* New Brunswick, NJ: Transaction Publishers.

Gunn Report. (1999–2003) 2004. www.flaxmanwilkie.com/the_gunn_report. Accessed on June 29.

Gupta, Pola B., Siva K. Balasubramanian, and Michael Klassen. 2000. "Viewers' Evaluations of Product Placements in Movies: Public Policy Issues and Managerial Implications," *Journal of Current Issues and Research in Advertising* 22 (2): 41–52.

Gupta, Pola B., and Kenneth R. Lord. 1998. "Product Placement in Movies: The Effect of Prominence and Mode on Audience Recall," *Journal of Current Issues and Research in Advertising* 20 (1): 47–59.

Haley, Russell I., and Allan L. Baldinger. 1991. "The ARF Copy Research Validity Project," *Journal of Advertising Research* 31 (April/May): 11–31.

Hall, Bruce F. 2002. "A New Model for Measuring Advertising Effectiveness," *Journal of Advertising Research* 40 (March/April): 23–31.

Haugtvedt, Curtis P., Richard E. Petty, and John T. Cacioppo. 1992. "Need for Cognition and Advertising: Understanding the Role of Personality Variables in Consumer Behavior," *Journal of Consumer Psychology* 1 (3): 239–60.

Hehl, Franz-Josef, and Willibald Ruch. 1990. "Conservatism as a Predictor of Responses to Humor—III. The Prediction of Appreciation of Incongruity-Resolution Based Humour by Content Saturated Attitude Scales in Five Samples," *Personality and Individual Differences* 11 (5): 439–45.

212

Helgesen, Thorolf. 1994. "Advertising Awards and Advertising Agency Performance Criteria," *Journal of Advertising Research* (July/August): 43–53.

Heltzel, Paul. 2000. "Review: Online 'Translations' of Dennis Miller's Football Commentary," CNN.com, Technology/Computing, www.cnn.com/2000/TECH/computing/10/16/pda.mnf.idg/index.html. Accessed on October 16.

Herold, Don. 1963. *Humor in Advertising and How to Make It Pay.* New York: McGraw-Hill Book.

Herzog, Thomas R. 1999. "Gender Differences in Humor Appreciation Revisited," *Humor* 12 (4): 411–23.

Herzog, Thomas R., and Maegan R. Anderson. 2000. "Joke Cruelty, Emotional Responsiveness, and Joke Appreciation," *Humor* 13 (3): 333–51.

Herzog, Thomas R., and Beverly A. Bush. 1994. "The Prediction of Preference for Sick Humor," *Humor* 7 (4): 323–40.

Herzog, Thomas R., and Joseph A. Karafa. 1998. "Preferences for Sick Versus Nonsick Humor," *Humor* 11 (3): 291–312.

Herzog, Thomas R., and David A. Larwin. 1988. "The Appreciation of Humor in Captioned Cartoons," *Journal of Psychology* 122 (6): 597–607.

Hoffman, Martin. 1986. "Affect, Cognition and Motivation," in *Handbook of Motivation and Cognition: Foundations of Social Behavior,* ed. Richard M. Sorrentino and E. Tory Higgins, 244–80. New York: Guilford.

Hopkins, Claude. (1923) 1927. *Scientific Advertising and My Life in Advertising.* Chicago, 1966: Reprinted by Advertising Publications.

Howard, Theresa. 2002. "Advertisers, Viewers: It's OK To Be Funny Again," www.usatoday.com/money/advertising/adtrack/2002-12-29-year-end_x.htm. Accessed on October 26.

Janiszewski, Chris. 1993. "Preattentive Mere Exposure Effects," *Journal of Consumer Research* 20 (December): 376–92.

Jones, Edgar. 1959. *Those Were the Good Old Days.* New York: Simon and Schuster.

Jones, J.M. 1970. "Cognitive Factors in the Appreciation of Humor: A Theoretical and Experimental Analysis," unpublished doctoral dissertation, Yale University.

Juni, Samuel, and Bernard Katz. 2001. "Self-Effacing Wit as a Response to Oppression: Dynamics in Ethnic Humor," *Journal of General Psychology* 128 (2): 119–42.

Kamins, Michael A., Lawrence J. Marks, and Deborah Skinner. 1991. "Television Commercial Evaluation in the Context of Program Induced Mood: Congruency Versus Consistency Effects," *Journal of Advertising* 20 (2): 1–14.

Kanner, Bernice. 2004. *The Super Bowl of Advertising: How Commercials Won the Game.* Princeton, NJ: Bloomberg Press.

Kant, I. 1790. *Kritik der Unterkraft.* Berlin: Lagarde.

Karrh, James A., Kathy Brittain McKee, and Carol J. Pardun. 2003. "Practioners' Evolving Views on Product Placement Effectiveness," *Journal of Advertising Research* 43 (2): 138–49.

Kelly, Patrick J., and Paul J. Solomon. 1975. "Humor in Television Advertising," *Journal of Advertising* 4 (3): 31–35.

Kelly, William E. 2002. "An Investigation of Worry and Sense of Humor," *Journal of Psychology* 136 (6): 657–66.

Kennedy, Allan J. 1972. "An Experimental Study of the Effects of Humorous Message Content upon Ethos and Persuasiveness," unpublished doctoral dissertation, University of Michigan.

Kennedy, Dan. 1999. "Tastelessness Compounded by Bad Timing," http://home
.earthlink.net/~dkennedy56/phoenix_990430zits.html. Accessed on October 11.

Kennedy, John R. 1971. "How Program Environment Affects TV Commercials," *Journal of Advertising Research* 11 (1): 33–38.

Kenney, W. Howland. 1976. *Laughter in the Wilderness.* Kent, OH: Kent State University Press.

Kent, Robert J., and Chris T. Allen. 1994. "Competitive Interference Effects in Consumer Memory for Advertising: The Role of Brand Familiarity," *Journal of Marketing* 58 (3): 97–105.

Klaassen, Abbey. 1005. "IPod Threatens $20B Radio-Ad Biz," *Advertising Age* (January 24): 1+.

Koestler, Arthur. 1964. *The Act of Creation.* New York: Macmillan.

Krishnan, H. Shankar, and Dipankar Chakravarti. 1993. "Varieties of Brand Memory Induced by Advertising: Determinants, Measures, and Relationships," in *Brand Equity and Advertising: Advertising's Role in Building Strong Brands,* ed. David A. Aaker and Alexander Biehl, 213–31. Hillsdale, NJ: Lawrence Erlbaum Associates.

———. 2003. "A Process Analysis of the Effects of Humorous Advertising Executions on Brand Claims Memory," *Journal of Consumer Psychology* 13 (3): 230–45.

Kruger, Arnold. 1996. "The Nature of Humor in Human Nature: Cross-Cultural Commonalities," *Counselling Psychology* 9 (3): 235–41.

Krugman, Herbert E. 1962. "An Application of Learning Theory to TV Copy Testing," *Public Opinion Quarterly* 26: 626–34.

———. 1966. "The Measurement of Advertising Involvement," *Public Opinion Quarterly* 30 (4): 583–97.

Krugman, Herbert E., and Eugene L. Hartley. 1970. "Passive Learning from Television," *Public Opinion Quarterly* 34 (2): 184–91.

Kuhn, Thomas S. 1970. *The Structure of Scientific Revolutions.* 2nd ed. Chicago: University of Chicago Press.

La Fave, Lawrence, Jay Haddad, and William Maesen. 1976. "Superiority, Enhanced Self-Esteem, and Perceived Incongruity Humour Theory," in *Humour and Laughter Theory, Research and Application,* ed. Antony J. Chapman and Hugh C. Foot, 63–91. London: John C. Wiley & Sons.

Lammers, H. Bruce. 1991. "Moderating Influence of Self-Monitoring and Gender Responses to Humorous Advertising," *Journal of Social Psychology* 131 (1): 57–69.

Lammers, H. Bruce, Laura Liebowitz, George E. Seymour, and Judith E. Hennessey. 1983. "Humor and Cognitive Responses to Advertising Stimuli: A Trace Consolidation Approach," *Journal of Business Research* 11 (2): 173–85.

Lampman, Jane. 2004. "A 'Moral Voter' Majority? The Culture Wars Are Back," *Christian Science Monitor* 96, 241 (November 8): 4.

Larwood, Jacob, and John Camden Hotten. (1866) 1951. *English Inn Signs: Being a Revised and Modernized Version of History of Signboards.* London: Chatto and Windus.

Lawton, Christopher. 2004. "In Molson Ads, Tips to Get Girls Turns Some Off," *Wall Street Journal,* July 28, B1–B2.

Leavitt, Clark. 1970. "A Multidimensional Set of Rating Scales For Television Commercials," *Journal of Applied Psychology* 34 (5): 427–29.

Lee, Angela Y., and Brian Sternthal. 1999. "The Effects of Positive Mood on Memory," *Journal of Consumer Research* 26 (2): 115.

Lee, Yih Hwai, and Charlotte Mason. 1999. "Responses to Information Incongruency in Advertising: The Role of Expectancy, Relevancy, and Humor," *Journal of Consumer Research* 26 (2): 156–69.

Leonard, Devin, and Doris Burke. 2004. "Nightmare on Madison Avenue," *Fortune* 149 (13) June 28: 92–100.

Leventhal, Howard, and Gerald Cupchik. 1976. "A Process Model of Humor Judgement," *Journal of Communication* 26 (Summer): 190–204.

Library of Congress, Help Desk. 2002. "Radio: Bob Hope and American Variety," www.loc.gov/exhibits/bobhope/radio.html. Accessed on June 13, 2003.

Liodice, Bob. 2004. "The Road to Marketing Accountability," *ANA Marketing Musings,* http://ana.blogs.com/liodice/2004/08/index.html. Accessed on December 15.

local6.com. 2005. "Wedding Proposal at Magic Game Was Hoax," www.local6.com /sports/4199099/detail.html. Accessed on February 17.

Long, D.L., and A.C. Graesser. 1988. "Wit and Humor in Discourse Processing," *Discourse Processes* 11: 35–60.

Lowis, Michael J. 2003. "Cartoon Humor: Do Demographic Variable and Political Correctness Influence Perceived Funniness?" *Mankind Quarterly* 43 (3): 273–89.

Lull, P.E. 1940. "The Effectiveness of Humor in Persuasive Speech," *Speech Monographs* 7: 26–40.

MacArthur, Kate. 2003. "Coors Slammed for Targeting Kids," *Advertising Age* 74, 44 (November 3): 1–2.

MacInnis, Deborah J., and Bernard J. Jaworski. 1989. "Information Processing from Advertisements: Toward an Integrative Framework," *Journal of Marketing* 53 (4): 1–23.

Madden, Thomas J. 1982. "Humor in Advertising: Applications of a Hierarchy of Effects Paradigm," unpublished doctoral dissertation, University of Massachusetts.

Madden, Thomas J., and Marc G. Weinberger. 1982. "The Effects of Humor on Attention in Magazine Advertising," *Journal of Advertising* 11 (3): 8–14.

———. 1984. "Humor in Advertising: A Practitioner View," *Journal of Advertising Research* 24 (4): 23–29.

Maier, N.R.F. 1932. "A Gestalt Theory of Humour," *British Journal of Psychology* 23: 69–74.

Manchanda, Rajesh V., Darren W. Dahl, and Kristina D. Frankenberger. 2002. "Shocking Ads! Do they Work?" *Advances in Consumer Research* 29: 230–31.

Marin Institute. 2004. "Molson Redefines Deceptive Advertising," www.marinin stitute.org/take_action/alerts_madison.com. Accessed on July 29.

Markiewicz, Dorothy. 1972. "The Effects of Humor on Persuasion," unpublished doctoral dissertation, Ohio State University.

Martin, G. Neil, and Colin D. Gray. 1996. "The Effects of Audience Laughter on Men's and Women's Responses to Humor," *Journal of Social Psychology* 136 (2): 221–31.

Mathur, Mahima, and Amitava Chattopadhyay. 1991. "The Impact of Mood Generated by Television Programs on Responses to Advertising," *Psychology & Marketing* 8 (1): 59–77.

McAllister, Matthew P. 1999. "Super Bowl Advertising as Commercial Celebration," *Communication Review* 3 (4): 403–28.

McCarthy, Michael. 2003. "Miller Lite's 'Catfight' Ad Angers Some Viewers," *USA Today,* January 15, 1.

McCollum/Spielman and Co. 1982. "Focus on Funny," *Topline* 3 (3): 1–6.

McCullough, Lynette S., and Ronald Taylor, K. 1993. "Humor in American, British, and German Ads," *Industrial Marketing Management* 22: 17–28.

McDonough, John. 2003a. "Lord & Thomas," in *Advertising Age Encyclopedia of Advertising,* ed. John McDonough and Karen Egolf, 953–58. New York: Fitzroy Dearborn.

———. 2003b. "Wells, Rich, Greene, Inc." in *Advertising Age Encyclopedia of Advertising,* ed. John McDonough and Karen Egolf, 1647–50. New York: Fitzroy Dearborn.

McFadden, Margaret. 2003. "'WARNING-Do Not Risk Federal Arrest by Looking Glum!': *Ballyhoo* Magazine and the Cultural Politics of Early 1930s Humor," *Journal of American Culture* 26 (1): 124–33.

McGhee, Paul E. 1979. *Humor: Its Origin and Development.* San Francisco: W.H. Freeman.

———. 1983. "The Role of Arousal and Hemispheric Lateralization in Humor," in *Handbook of Humor Research: Basic Issues,* ed. P.E. McGhee and J. Goldstein, 13–37. New York: Springer-Verlag.

McGhee, Paul E., and Nelda S. Duffey. 1983. "The Role of Identity of the Victim in the Development of Disparagement Humor," *Journal of General Psychology* 108: 257–70.

McGhee, Paul E., and Sally A. Lloyd. 1981. "A Developmental Test of the Disposition Theory of Humor," *Child Development* 52: 925–31.

McKendrick, Neil, John Brewer, and J.H. Plumb. 1982. *The Birth of a Consumer Society and the Commercialization of Eighteenth-Century England.* Bloomington: Indiana University Press.

Meyers, Scott A., Barbara Lorene Ropong, and R. Pierre Rodgers. 1997. "Sex Differences in Humor," *Psychological Reports* 81 (1): 221–22.

Meyers-Levy, Joan, and Alice Tybout. 1989. "Schema Congruity as a Basis for Product Evaluation," *Journal of Consumer Research* 16 (June): 39–54.

Michaels, Steven L. 1997. "Cognitive and Affective Responses to Humorous Advertisements," unpublished doctoral dissertation, Wayne State University.

Michaelson, Elizabeth. 2001. "Bob Dole Owes Joy of . . . to Pepsi-Cola," *Shoot* (February 9): 10–11.

Mikkelson, Barbara, and David P. Mikkelson. 2004. "Sportka," Snopes, www.snopes.com/photos/commercials/sportka.asp. Accessed on August 19.

Mobbs, Dean, Michael D. Greicius, Eiman Abdel-Azim, Vinod Menon, and Allan L. Reiss. 2003. "Humor Modulates the Mesolimbic Reward Centers," *Neuron* 40: 1041–48.

Moorman, Marjolein, Peter C. Neijens, and Edith G. Smit. 2002. "The Effects of Magazine-Induced Psychological Responses and Thematic Congruence on Memory and Attitude Toward the Ad in a Real Life Setting," *Journal of Advertising* 21 (4): 27–40.

Moran, Carmen C., and Margaret M. Massam. 1999. "Differential Influences of Coping Humor and Humor Bias on Mood," *Behavioral Medicine* 25 (1): 36–42.

Morreall, John. 1983. *Taking Laughter Seriously.* Albany: State University of New York Press.

———. 1989. "Enjoying Incongruity," *Humor: International Journal of Humor Research* 2: 1–18.

Morrison, Deborah K. 2003. "Bernbach, William (Bill)," in *Advertising Age Encyclopedia of Advertising,* ed. John McDonough, 165–67. New York: Fitzroy Dearborn.

Muir, Hazel. 2000. "Family Fun," *New Scientist* 166 (2234): 13.

Murphy, John H., Isabella C.M. Cunningham, and Gary Wilcox. 1979. "The Impact of Program Environment on Recall of Humorous Television Commercials," *Journal of Advertising Research* 8 (2): 17–21.

Murphy, John H., Deborah K. Morrison, and Michael Zahn. 1993. "A Longitudinal Analysis of the Use of Humor in Award-Winning Radio Commercials: 1974–1988," in *The Proceedings of the 1993 Conference of the American Academy of Advertising,* ed. Esther Thorson, 118–24. Columbia: School of Journalism, University of Missouri–Columbia.

Murry, John P., Jr., John L. Lastovicka, and Surenda N. Singh. 1992. "Feeling and Liking Responses to Television Programs: An Examination of Two Explanations for Media-Context Effects," *Journal of Consumer Research* 18 (March): 441–51.

Naik, Prasad A. 1999. "Estimating the Half-life of Advertisements," *Marketing Letters* 10 (3): 351–62.

NASA. 2003. "NASA LaRC Formal Methods Humor, http:shemesh.larc.nasa/gov /fm/fm-humor.html." Accessed on September 12.

Nathanson, Paul, and Katherine K. Young. 2001. *Spreading Misandry: The Teaching of Contempt for Men in Popular Culture.* Montreal: McGill-Queen's University Press.

Nelson, James, E., Calvin P. Duncan, and Nancy T. Frontczak. 1985. "The Distraction Hypothesis and Radio Advertising," *Journal of Marketing* 49 (Winter): 60–71.

Nerhardt, Goran. 1977. "The Operationalization of Incongruity in Humor Research: A Critique and Suggestions," in *It's a Funny Thing, Humour,* ed. Antony J. Chapman and Hugh C. Foot, 47–51. Oxford: Pergamon Press.

Nevo, Ofra. 1986. "Humor Diaries of Israeli Jews and Arabs," *Journal of Social Psychology* 126 (3): 411–13.

Nevo, Ofra, Baruch Nevo, and Janie Leong Siew Yin. 2001. "Singaporean Humor: A Cross-Cultural, Cross-Gender Comparison," *Journal of General Psychology* 128 (2): 143–56.

"Nike Ads Run into Rough Patch." 2000. *Advertising Age* 71 (45): October 30, 6.

Norris, Claire E., and Andrew M. Colman. 1992. "Context Effects on Recall and Recognition of Magazine Advertisements," *Journal of Advertising* 21 (3): 37–46.

———. 1993. "Context Effects on Memory for Television Advertisements," *Social Behavior and Personality* 21 (4): 279–96.

———. 1994. "Effects of Entertainment and Enjoyment of Television Programs on Perception and Memory of Advertisements," *Social Behavior and Personality* 22 (4): 365–76.

Norris, Claire E., Andrew M. Colman, and Paulo A. Aleixo. 2003. "Selective Exposure to Television Programmes and Advertising Effectiveness," *Applied Cognitive Psychology* 17: 593–606.

Oakner, Larry. 2002. *And Now a Few Laughs from Our Sponsor.* New York: John Wiley & Sons.

Ogilvy, David. 1963. *Confessions of an Advertising Man.* London: Longman.

Ogilvy, David, and Joel Raphaelson. 1982. "Research on Advertising Techniques That Work—And Don't Work," *Harvard Business Review* 60 (4): 14–16.

Olson, David. 1985. "The Characteristics of High Trial New Product Advertising," *Journal of Advertising Research* 25 (5): 11–16.

Otnes, Cele C., and John McDonough. 2003. "DDB Worldwide, Inc.," in *Advertising Age Encyclopedia of Advertising,* ed. John McDonough, 449–55. New York: Fitzroy Dearborn.

Palmer, Camilla. 2003. "What's Cannes Worth?" *Creative Review* (July): 49–50.

Paul, Pamela. 2002. "One Nation, Under God?" *American Demographics* 24, 1 (January): 16–17.

Pechmann, Cornelia (Connie) and David W. Stewart. 1989. "The Multidimensionality of Persuasive Communications: Theoretical and Empirical Foundations," in *Cognitive and Affective Responses to Advertising,* ed. Patricia Cafferata and Alice Tybout, 35–65. Lexington, MA: Lexington Books.

Percy, Larry. 1997. *Strategies for Implementing Marketing Communication.* Lincolnwood, IL: NTC Business Books.

Perry, Stephen D. 2001. "Commercial Humor Enhancement of Program Enjoyment: Gender and Program Appeal as Mitigating Factors," *Mass Communication & Society* 4 (1): 103–16.

Perry, Stephen D., et al. 1997a. "Using Humorous Programs as a Vehicle for Humorous Commercials," *Journal of Communications* 47 (1): 20–39.

———. 1997b. "The Influence of Commercial Humor on Program Enjoyment and Evaluation," *Journalism & Mass Communication Quarterly* 74 (2): 388–99.

Petty, Richard, and John T. Cacioppo. 1981. *Attitudes and Persuasion: Classic and Contemporary Approaches.* Dubuque, IA: Wm. C. Brown.

Piccalo, Gina. 2004. "TiVo Will No Longer Skip Past Advertisers," latimes.com .www.latimes.com/business. Accessed on November 18.

Pornpitakpan, Chanthika, and Tze Ke Jason Tan. 2000. "The Influence of Incongruity on the Effectiveness of Humorous Advertisements: The Case of Singaporeans," *Journal of International Consumer Marketing* 12 (1): 27–45.

Prendergast, Gerard, Benny Ho, and Ian Phau. 2002. "A Hong Kong View of Offensive Advertising," *Journal of Marketing Communications* 8: 165–77.

Prerost, Frank J. 1975. "The Indication of Sexual and Aggressive Similarities Through Humor Appreciation," *Journal of Psychology* 91: 283–88.

———. 1995. "Sexual Desire and the Dissipation of Anger Arousal Through Humor Appreciation: Gender and Content Issues," *Social Behavior and Personality* 23 (1): 45–52.

Presbrey, Frank. 1929. *The History and Development of Advertising.* Garden City, NY: Doubleday, Doran.

Preston, Lynne. 2000. "Sexual Hunk or Rocket Scientist?" *Marketing* (January), online, www.marketing.ie_old_site.January_00/article_b.htm. Accessed August 5, 2004.

Provine, Robert R. 2000. "The Science of Laughter," *Psychology Today* 33 (6): 58–62.

Ragged Edge Online. 2004. "Nike Issues Formal Apology," www.raggededge magazine.com/extra/nikead.htm. Accessed on June 25.

Raine, George. 2003. "9.11.01: Two Years Later Special Programming the Exception this Year Most Media Treat 2nd Anniversary as Another Business Day," www.sfgate.com/chronicle/archive/2003/09/11. Accessed on November 23.

Rapp, Albert. 1951. *The Origins of Wit and Humor.* New York: E.P. Dutton.

Raskin, Victor. 1985. *Semantic Mechanisms of Humor.* Boston: D. Reidel.

rateitall. 2004. "Six Flags Dancing Man/'It's Playtime' (Six Flags Theme Parks)," www.rateitall.com. Accessed on July 22.

Reeves, Rosser. (1961) 1977. *Reality in Advertising*. New York: Alfred A. Knopf.

Rentas-Giusti, Laura. 2003. "Research Shows That Creativity in Advertising Is Crucial to Success," *Caribbean Business* (May): 18–22.

Rossiter, John R., Larry Percy, and Robert J. Donovan. 1991. "A Better Advertising Planning Grid," *Journal of Advertising Research* 31 (October/November): 11–21.

Rothbart, Mary K. 1976. "Incongruity, Problem Solving and Laughter," in *Humour and Laughter: Theory, Research and Application*, ed. Antony Chapman and Hugh C. Foots, 37–54. London: John C. Wiley & Sons.

Rothbart, Mary K., and Diana Pien. 1977. "Elephants and Marshmallows: A Theoretical Synthesis of Incongruity-Resolution and Arousal Theories of Humour," in *It's a Funny Thing, Humour,* ed. Antony J. Chapman and Hugh C. Foots, 37–40. Oxford: Pergamon Press.

Ruch, Willibald, and Franz-Josef Hehl. 1986. "Conservatism as a Predictor of Responses to Humour—II. The Location of Sense of Humour in a Comprehensive Attitude Space," *Personality and Individual Differences* 7 (6): 861–74.

Russell, Cristel Antonia. 2002. "Investigating the Effectiveness of Product Placements in Television Shows: The Role of Modality and Plot Connection Congruence on Brand Memory and Attitude," *Journal of Consumer Research* 29 (3): 306–18.

Russell, J. Thomas, and W. Ronald Lane. 1996. *Kleppner's Advertising Procedure,* 13th ed. Englewood Cliffs, NJ: Prentice Hall.

Rust, Roland T., and Richard W. Oliver. 1994. "The Death of Advertising," *Journal of Advertising* 23 (4): 71–77.

Sanders, Lisa. 2004. "Virgin Atlantic Winns Top Cannes Direct Award," www.adage.com/news.cms?newsId=40866. Accessed on June 25.

Saroglou, Vassilis. 2002. "Religion and Sense of Humor: An a Priori Incompatibility? Theoretical Considerations from a Psychological Perspective," *Humor* 15 (2): 191–214.

Schindler, Robert M., and Morris B. Holbrook. 2003. "Nostalgia for Early Experience as a Determinant of Consumer Preferences," *Psychology & Marketing* 20 (4): 275–302.

Schlinger, Mary Jane. 1979a. "Attitudinal Reactions to Advertising," in Attitude Research Under the Sun, ed. John Eighmey, 9, 171–97. Proceedings series American Marketing Association. Tarpon Springs, Florida.

———. 1979b. "A Profile of Responses to Commercials," *Journal of Advertising Research* 19 (April): 37–46.

Schopenhauer, A. 1819. *Die Welt als Wille und Vorstellung*. Leipzig: Brockhaus.

Schultz, Thomas R. 1976. "A Cognitive Development Analysis of Humour," in *Humour and Laughter: Theory, Research and Application,* ed. Antony J. Chapman and Hugh C. Foot, 11–36. London: John C. Wiley & Sons.

Scott, Cliff, David M. Klein, and Jennings Bryant. 1990. "Consumer Response to Humor in Advertising: A Series of Field Studies Using Behavioral Observation," *Journal of Consumer Research* 16 (March): 498–501.

Scott, Walter Dill. 1904. "The Psychology of Advertising," *Atlantic Monthly: A Magazine of Literature, Science, Art, and Politics* 93 (555): 29–36.

———. 1908. *The Psychology of Advertising: A Simple Exposition of the Principles of Psychology in Their Relation to Successful Advertising*. Boston: Small, Maynard.

Segrave, Kerry. 2004. *Product Placement in Hollywood Films: A History*. Jefferson, NC: McFarland.

Sewall, Murphy C., and Dan Sarel. 1986. "Characteristics of Radio Commercials and their Recall Effectiveness," *Journal of Marketing* 50 (January): 52–60.

SGB: Sporting Goods Business. 2000. "The Other Shoe Drops at Just for Feet," 33, 4 (February): 14, 10.

Shalit, Ruth. 1999. "The Ad from Hell," http://archive.salon.com/media/col/shal/1999/05/28/kenya/print.html. Accessed on June 29.

Shammi, Prathiba, and Donald T. Stuss. 1999. "Humour Appreciation: A Role of the Right Frontal Lobe," *Brain: A Journal of Neurology* 122 (4): 657–66.

———. 2003. "The Effects of Normal Aging on Humor Appreciation," *Journal of the International Neuropsychological Society* 9 (6): 855–63.

Shapiro, Michael A., and Annie Lang. 1991. "Making Television Reality: Unconscious Processes in the Construction of Social Reality," *Communication Research* 18 (5): 685–705.

Shimp, Terrence, Elnora Stewart, and Randall W. Rose. 1991. "A Program of Classical Conditioning Experiments Testing Variations in the Conditioned Stimulus and Context," *Journal of Consumer Research* 18 (1): 1–12.

"16th Annual Ad Meter." 2004. *USA Today,* www.usatoday.com/money/advertising/2004-super-bowl-ad-meter-chart.htm. Accessed on February 7.

Smith, Allen E. 2003. "Magazine Advertising," in *Advertising Age Encyclopedia of Advertising,* ed. John McDonough, 977–83. New York: Fitzroy Dearborn.

Smith, Steven. 1993. "Does Humor in Advertising Enhance Systematic Processing?" *Advances in Consumer Research* 20(1): 155–58.

Smoot, Carrie. 2003. "FedEx Corporation," in *Advertising Age Encyclopedia of Advertising,* ed. John McDonough, 571–74. New York: Fitzroy Dearborn.

Snyder, Mark, and Elizabeth Decker Tanke. 1976. "Behavior and Attitude: Some People Are More Consistent Than Others," *Journal of Personality* 44 (3): 501–17.

Soldow, Gary F., and Victor Principe. 1981. "Response to Commercials as a Function of Program Context," *Journal of Advertising Research* 21 (2): 59–65.

Speck, Paul Surgi. 1987. "On Humor and Humor in Advertising," unpublished doctoral dissertation, Texas Tech University.

———. 1991. "The Humorous Message Taxonomy: A Framework for the Study of Humorous Ads," in *Current Issues and Research in Advertising,* ed. James H. Leigh Jr. and Claude R. Martin, 1–44, vol. 13. Division of Research, Michigan Business School: University of Michigan.

Spencer, H. 1860. "The Physiology of Laughter," *Macmillan's Magazine* 1: 395–402.

Spotts, Harlan E. 2003. "Hard-Sell/Soft-Sell," in *Advertising Age Encyclopedia of Advertising,* ed. John McDonough, 716–719. New York: Fitzroy Dearborn.

Spotts, Harlan E., Marc G. Weinberger, and Amy L. Parsons. 1997. "Assessing the Use and Impact of Humor on Advertising Effectiveness: A Contingency Approach," *Journal of Advertising* 26 (3): 17–32.

Stanley, Louis T. 1957. *The Old Inns of London.* London: B.T. Batsford.

Stein, Lee Marc. 2002. "Humor in Direct Response Advertising," www.leemarcstein.com/012003.htm. Accessed on December 30, 2004.

Steinberg, Brian. 2004. "Newest TV Spinoffs: 'Situ-mercials,'" *Wall Street Journal,* March 2, 11.

Stern, Barbara. 1996. "Advertising Comedy in Electronic Drama: The Construct, Theory and Taxonomy," *European Journal of Marketing* 30 (9): 37–59.

Sternthal, Brian, and C. Samuel Craig. 1973. "Humor in Advertising," *Journal of Marketing* 37 (October): 12–18.

Stewart, David M., and David H. Furse. 1986. *Effective Television Advertising.* Lexington, MA: D.C. Heath.

Stewart, Ivy McClure, and Kate Kennedy. 2001. "Madison Avenue Man: He's Dumb, He's a Slob, He's Selling Kleenex," *Women's Quarterly* (Spring), online, www.findarticles.com/p/articles/mi_moluk/is_201_spring/ai_75453034. Accessed September 29, 2004.

Stewart-Hunter, David. 1985. "Humour in Television Advertising: The Search for the Golden Rule," *ADMAP* (May): 268–79.

Suls, Jerry M. 1977. "Cognitive and Disparagement Theories of Humor: A Theoretical and Empirical Synthesis," in *It's a Funny Thing Humour,* ed. A.J. Chapman and H.C. Foot, 41–46. Oxford: Pergamon Press.

———. 1983. "Cognitive Processes in Humor Appreciation," in *Handbook of Humor Research,* ed. Paul E. McGhee and Jeffrey H. Goldstein, 39–58, vol. 1. New York: Springer-Verlag.

"Super Bowl XXXIX 17th Annual Ad Meter." 2005b. *USA Today,* www.usatoday.com /money/advertising/admeter/2005-ad-meter-results-chart.htm. Accessed on February 7.

Sutherland, John C., and Lisa A. Middleton. 1983. "The Effect of Humor on Advertising Credibility and Recall of the Advertising Message," Paper presented at the Convention of the American Academy of Advertising, ed. D.W. Jugenheimer, 17–21. Lawrence, KS: William Allen White School of Journalism and Mass Communications, University of Kansas.

Tavassoli, Nader T., Clifford J. Shultz, and Gavan J. Fitzsimons. 1995. "Program Involvement: Are Moderate Levels Best for Ad Memory and Attitude Toward the Ad?" *Journal of Advertising Research* 35 (5): 61–72.

Taylor, Charles R., Gregg P. Bonner, and Michael Dolezal. 2002. "Advertising in Czech Republic: Czech Perceptions of Effective Advertising and Advertising Clutter," *Advances in International Marketing* (12): 137–49.

Teinowitz, Ira. 2004. "Vote for Values Smites Edgy Ads," *Advertising Age* (November 8): 1+.

"10 Who Made a Mark on Marketing." 2004a. *Advertising Age* (December 20): 6.

Tomkovick, Chuck, Rama Yelkur, and Lori Christians. 2001. "The USA's Biggest Marketing Event Keeps Getting Bigger: An In-Depth Look at Super Bowl Advertising in the 1990s," *Journal of Marketing Communications* 7: 89–108.

"Top Spots: Ad Age/IAG's Quarterly Recall Report." 2004b. *Advertising Age* (August 2): 21.

Toncar, Mark F. 2001. "The Use of Humor in Television Advertising: Revisiting the US-UK Comparison," *International Journal of Advertising* 20 (4): 521–39.

Tugend, Alina. 2002. "Maybe Not," *American Journalism Review* 24 (4): 50–53.

TV Acres. 2004. "Swedish Bikini Team," www.tvacres.com/ethnic_swedish.htm. Accessed on August 5.

Unger, Lynette S. 1995. "Observations: A Cross-Cultural Study on the Affect-Based Model of Humor in Advertising," *Journal of Advertising Research* (January–February): 66–71.

United States Department of Justice. 2004. "Former Executive Vice President of Just for Feet, Inc. Agrees to Plead Guilty," www.usdoj.gov/opa/pr/2004/February /04_crm_110.htm. Accessed on July 28, 2004.

U.S. Census Bureau. 2003. *Statistical Abstract of the United States, 2003.* Online, www.census.gov/prod/www/abs/statab.html. Accessed November 23, 2004.

"USA Today's 15th Annual Ad Meter Winners." 2003. *USA Today,* January 27, 5.

Vakratsas, Demetrios, and Tim Ambler. 1999. "How Advertising Works: What Do We Really Know?" *Journal of Marketing* 63 (1): 26–43.

VanRaaij, Fred W. 1989. "How Consumers React to Advertising," *International Journal of Advertising* 8 (3): 261–73.

Vaughn, Richard. 1980. "How Advertising Works: A Planning Model," *Journal of Advertising Research* 20 (October): 27–33.

———. 1986. "How Advertising Works: A Planning Model Revisited," *Journal of Advertising Research* 26 (1): 57–66.

Viegas, Jennifer. 2000. "Nurture Not Nature, http://abcnews.go.com/sections/science/DailyNews/twinhumor000414html. Accessed on April 14.

Viveiros, Beth Negus. 2003. "No Laughing Matter: Use of Humor in Direct Mail Marketing," *Direct Marketing and Business Intelligence,* http://directmag.com /marketingnolaughingmatterz/. Accessed on December 30, 2004.

Vogel, Bob. 2004. "Nike Apology Worse than the Offense," www.newmobility.com /nike_article.cfm. Accessed on July 27.

Vranica, Suzanne. 2005a. "Getting Buzz Marketers to Fess Up," *Wall Street Journal,* February 9, B9.

———. 2005b. "Patriotism, P. Diddy Shine in a Less-Than-Super Ad Bowl," *Wall Street Journal,* February 7, B1+.

Vranica, Suzanne, and Brian Steinberg. 2005. "Crotch Jokes Are Out as Super Bowl Ads Tap into Nostalgia," *Wall Street Journal,* February 3, B1+.

Ward, Alyson. 2004. "Red State Blue State," www.dfw.com/mld/dfw/living. Accessed on December 16.

Weaver, James, Dolf Zillmann, and Jennings Bryant. 1988. "Effects of Humorous Distortions on Children's Learning from Educational Television: Further Evidence," *Communication Education* 37 (July): 181–87.

Wegner, Duane T., Richard E. Petty, and Stephen M. Smith. 1995. "Positive Mood Can Increase or Decrease Message Scrutiny: The Hedonic Contingency View of Mood and Message Processing," *Journal of Personality and Social Psychology* 69 (July): 5–15.

Weinberger, Marc G., and Leland Campbell. 1991. "The Use and Impact of Humor in Radio Advertising," *Journal of Advertising Research* 31: 644–52.

Weinberger, Marc G., Leland Campbell, and Beth Brody. 1994. *Effective Radio Advertising.* New York: Lexington Books.

Weinberger, Marc G., and Charles S. Gulas. 1992. "The Impact of Humor in Advertising: A Review," *Journal of Advertising* 21 (December): 35–59.

Weinberger, Marc G., and Harlan Spotts. 1993. "Differences in British and American Television and Magazine Advertising: Myth or Reality?" in *European Advances in Consumer Research,* ed. W.F. Van Raaij and G.J. Bamossy, 176–181, vol. 1. Provo, UT: Association for Consumer Research.

Weinberger, Marc G., Harlan Spotts, Leland Campbell, and Amy L. Parsons. 1995. "The Use and Effect of Humor in Different Advertising Media," *Journal of Advertising Research* 35 (May/June): 44–56.

Weinberger, Marc G., and Harlan E. Spotts. 1989. "Humor in U.S. vs. U.K. TV Commercials: A Comparison," *Journal of Advertising* 18 (2): 39–44.

Weller, Leonard, Ella Amitsour, and Ruth Pazzi. 1976. "Reactions to Absurd Humor by Jews of Eastern and Western Descent," *Journal of Social Psychology* 98 (April): 159–63.

Wells, William D. 1989. "Lectures and Dramas," in *Cognitive and Affective Responses to Advertising,* ed. Patricia Cafferata and Alice Tybout, 13–20. Lexington, MA: Lexington Books.

Wells, William, Clark Leavitt, and Maureen McConville. 1971. "A Reaction Profile for TV Commercials," *Journal of Advertising Research* 11 (6): 11–17.

Whipple, Thomas W., and Alice E. Courtney. 1981. "How Men and Women Judge Humor, Advertising Guidelines for Action and Research," in *Current Issues and Research in Advertising,* ed. J.H. Leigh and C.R. Martin, 43–56. Ann Arbor, MI: Division of Research, Graduate School of Business Administration, University of Michigan.

White, Timothy. 2002. "Working in the House Wanamaker Built," *Billboard* 114 (19): May 11, 3.

Wierzbicki, Michael, and Richard David Young. 1978. "The Relation of Intelligence and Task Difficulty to Appreciation of Humor," *Journal of General Psychology* 99: 25–32.

Woltman-Elpers, Josephine L.C.M., Ashesh Mukherjee, and Wayne D. Hoyer. 2004. "Humor in Television Advertising: A Moment-to-Moment Analysis," *Journal of Consumer Research* 31 (December): 592–98.

Woltman-Elpers, Josephine L.C., Michel Wedel, and Rik G.M. Pieters. 2003. "Why Do Consumers Stop Watching TV Commercials? Two Experiments on the Influence of Moment-to-Moment Entertainment and Information Value," *Journal of Marketing Research* 40 (4): 437–53.

Wu, Bob T.W., Kenneth E. Crocker, and Martha Rogers. 1989. "Humor and Comparatives in Ads for High- and Low-Involvement Products," *Journalism Quarterly* 66 (Autumn): 653–61, 780.

Wyer, Robert S., and James E. Collins. 1992. "A Theory of Humor Elicitation," *Psychological Review* 99 (4): 663–88.

Zajonc, Robert B. 1968. "Attitudinal Effects of Mere Exposure," *Journal of Personality and Social Psychology* 9 (2): 1–27.

———. 1980. "Feeling and Thinking: Preferences Need No Inferences," *American Psychologist* 35 (2): 151–75.

Zhang, Yong. 1992. "Audience Involvement and Persuasion in Humorous Advertising," unpublished doctoral dissertation, University of Houston.

———. 1996. "Responses to Humorous Advertising: The Moderating Effect of Need for Cognition," *Journal of Advertising* 25 (Spring): 15–32.

Zhang, Yong, and George M. Zinkhan. 1991. "Humor in Television Advertising," in *Advances in Consumer Research* 18: 813–18.

Zielske, Herbert. 1959. "The Remembering and Forgetting of Advertising," *Journal of Marketing Research* 23 (January): 230–43.

Zillmann, Dolf. 1983. "Disparagement Humor," in *Handbook of Humor Research,* ed. Paul McGhee and Jeffrey Goldstein, vol. 1, 85–107. New York: Springer-Verlag.

Zillmann, Dolf, Jennings Bryant, and Joanne R. Cantor. 1974. "Brutality of Assault in Political Cartoons Affecting Humor Appreciation," *Journal of Research in Personality* 7: 334–45.

Zillmann, Dolf, and Joanne R. Cantor. 1976. "A Disposition Theory of Humor and Mirth," in *Humour and Laughter: Theory, Research and Application,* ed. Antony J. Chapman and Hugh C. Foots, 93–116. London: John C. Wiley & Sons.

Zillmann, Dolf, and Joanne R. Cantor. (1976) 1996. *A Dispositional Theory of Humor and Mirth.* New Brunswick, NJ: Transaction.

Zillmann, Dolf, et al. 1980. "Acquisition of Information from Educational Television as a Function of Differently Paced Humorous Inserts," *Journal of Educational Psychology* 72 (2): 170–80.

Zinkhan, George M., and Betsy D. Gelb. 1990. "Repetition, Social Settings, Perceived Humor, and Wearout," *Advances in Consumer Research* 17 (1): 438–41.

Ziv, Avner. 1988. "Teaching and Learning with Humor: Experiment and Replication," *Journal of Experimental Education* 57 (1): 15–32.

Zuckerman, Mortimer B. 2004. "A Closer Look at America," *U.S. News & World Report* 137 (21): December 13, 68.

Name Index

Subject Index

About the Authors

Charles S. Gulas, PhD, University of Massachusetts, is an associate professor of marketing at Wright State University in Dayton, Ohio. His research has been published in the *Journal of Advertising,* the *Journal of Current Issues and Research in Advertising,* and in other business publications. His interest in humor dates back to the 1980s, when he was the owner of a comedy club and a comedy booking agency.

Marc G. Weinberger, PhD, Arizona State University, is a professor of marketing at the University of Massachusetts–Amherst. His work includes articles in the *Journal of Marketing, Journal of Advertising,* and the *Journal of Advertising Research*. His first book, *Effective Radio Advertising,* was published in 1994. He was recently cited as one of the top thirty authors in the field of advertising.